Organizational Theory in Higher Education

Organizational Theory in Higher Education offers a fresh take on the models and lenses through which higher education can be viewed by presenting a full range of organizational theories, from traditional to current. By alternating theory and practice chapters, noted scholar Kathleen Manning vividly illustrates the operations of higher education and its administration. Manning's rich and interdisciplinary treatment enables leaders to gain a full understanding of the perspectives that operate on a college campus and ways to adopt effective practice in the context of new and continuing tensions, contexts, and challenges.

Special features include:

- A unique presentation of each organizational model that includes both a theory chapter for contextual background and a case chapter illustrating the perspective in practice.
- Coverage of eight organizational approaches, both traditional and those often excluded from the literature—organized anarchy, collegium, political, cultural, bureaucratic, new science, feminist, and spiritual.
- Consistent organizational elements across each theoretical chapter—including theoretical foundation, structure, metaphor, characteristics, and strengths and weaknesses—so that readers can better assess appropriate fit of theory to particular situations.
- Questions for Discussion and Recommended Readings assist the reader to make connections to their practice and to develop an in-depth understanding of the organizational theories.

Organizational Theory in Higher Education provides a clear understanding of how organizational models can be used to elicit the most effective practice and to navigate the complexity of higher education today. This important book is ideal for courses in higher education administration and organizational theory, and for administrators and practitioners seeking to gain insight into innovative ways to approach organizations.

Kathleen Manning is a Professor in the Higher Education and Student Affairs Program, Department of Leadership and Developmental Science, at the University of Vermont, USA.

Core Concepts in Higher Education

Series Editors: Edward P. St. John and Marybeth Gasman

Organizational Theory in Higher Education

Kathleen Manning

Routledge
Taylor & Francis Group

NEW YORK AND LONDON

First published 2013
by Routledge
711 Third Avenue, New York, NY 10017

Simultaneously published in the UK
by Routledge
2 Park Square, Milton Park, Abingdon, Oxon OX14 4RN

Routledge is an imprint of the Taylor & Francis Group, an informa business

Library of Congress Cataloging in Publication Data
Manning, Kathleen, 1954-
 Organizational theory in higher education / Kathleen Manning.
 p. cm. — (Core concepts in higher education)
 Includes bibliographical references and index.
 1. Universities and colleges—Administration. I. Title.
 LB2341.M285 2012
 378.1'01—dc23
 2012026905

ISBN: 978-0-415-87466-3 (hbk)
ISBN: 978-0-415-87467-0 (pbk)
ISBN: 978-0-203-83675-0 (ebk)

Typeset in Minion
by EvS Communication Networx, Inc.

Printed and bound in the United States of America
by Edwards Brothers, Inc.

CONTENTS

LIST OF TABLES AND FIGURES

viii • List of Tables and Figures

SERIES EDITOR'S INTRODUCTION

Kathleen Manning's *Organization Theory in Higher Education* provides an excellent new book that advances understanding of organizational frames and their uses in decision making and governance. The basic texts on organizational frames of politics, bureaucracy, and collegiality are out of date and, as a consequence, not always directly applicable to the study of higher education or social justice today. There is clear need for a good textbook for professionally-oriented masters' and doctoral programs in higher education. Manning meets these challenges with great expertise and success.

Concepts of organizational frames have been frequently applied in studies of both colleges and universities as organizations and of leadership in higher education. Yet the statements of the frames in much of the research have seemed strained because the original concepts were frequently generated from other fields, so researchers had to explain how the frames relate to the study of higher education. By starting her depiction of frames with organized anarchies, a view of organizations developed in the study of higher education, Kathleen Manning creates a set of frames of universities as organizations, which advances our collective understanding of the role of frames in research and practice.

Kathleen Manning substantially extends the types of frames considered, to include newer perspectives related to science, feminism, and spirituality, providing better additional ways of viewing social justice and injustice. This new use of frames in the study of higher education organizations represents the most important advance in this book. Manning not only updates statements of traditional frames for studying organizations, she also synthesizes new ways of viewing organizations from the literature on education and social issues. The result is a set of new perspectives on organizations and social change that enhances and complements traditional ways of understanding organizations.

Most importantly from the perspective of professional education, Manning includes case studies that demonstrate how frames can be used to stimulate dialogue in graduate classrooms about conceptions of organizations and problem solving within them. The cases demonstrate the ways the frames apply to student support services as well as other business and policy matters. In sum, this book is an excellent contribution to higher education as an academic and professional field.

Not only do I congratulate Kathleen Manning on her excellent book, I also encourage colleagues to try out innovative ways of using this new text within courses on organization, leadership, and administration in higher education and student affairs. This is a highly noteworthy book that both advances knowledge and encourages ethical professional practice.

Edward P. St. John
Algo D. Henderson Collegiate Professor
Center for the Study of Higher and Postsecondary Education
University of Michigan, Ann Arbor

PREFACE

INTRODUCTION

In 1991, Robert Birnbaum published a book about higher education organizational theory that became a mainstay for graduate students, administrators, faculty, and others wanting to understand "how colleges work." Birnbaum described four frames of organizational functioning and illustrated his text with cases reflective of the different types of institutions one finds in U.S. higher education. Much has changed in higher education since Birnbaum published *How Colleges Work*. One might speculate that the tensions and pressures that traditionally challenged higher education are even more prevalent today than when he first published his well-regarded text.

In the last 20 years, there has been no shortage of pundits expressing their opinion that higher education in the United States is in crisis. The list of complaints includes unsatisfactory graduation rates, high tuition, lack of coherence between knowledge taught and job skills needed, excessive executive salaries, inadequate faculty oversight, and content taught that is irrelevant to global needs. Despite these complaints, higher education in the United States remains a remarkable system. Among other achievements, the educational system produces scholars who make a difference in the world; it remains a place where young people come of age; it profoundly changes lives; and enables the generation of life saving research. But because of the rapid pace of change, including seismic changes occurring in countries such as China and India, new perspectives are warranted on the older theories about how colleges work. To be effective, as faculty, administrators, and staff and as an educational system, we must get out ahead of the noteworthy transformations occurring in higher education. Only with knowledge of how higher education works can we realistically explore the many options available for success.

With or without agreement about the nature of crises in higher education, colleges and universities are unique organizations. Although many, particularly members of boards of trustees attempt to borrow organizational and policy models from corporations and other sources, those of us who work in this sector of society know that these organizations have ways of operating that have much different needs from those of higher education. This book points out those differences with an eye to defining how higher education can remain relevant in today's environment.

In this text, *Organizational Theory in Higher Education*, I seek to add to the higher education literature by elucidating organizational theory directly related to higher education and theory from noneducational sources. The tried and true frames so familiar in the past are currently inadequate to the task of getting out ahead of the changes that are occurring and that show no signs of abating. In the book, I have included newer theories such as spirituality, feminist, and new science to encourage all who are involved in higher education to be innovative and forward thinking. These theories, similar to organized anarchy theory, are creative. They point to opportunities that could be taken advantage of if a shifted perspective were used to view our colleges and universities. To get out ahead, higher education requires the innovation and creativity evident in the earliest U.S. colleges and universities. While the challenges are daunting, they are also exciting. The prospect of shaping the older organizations into new forms holds tremendous promise for the next era of U.S. higher education.

AUDIENCES

Several audiences will find value in this text. Faculty who are seeking to understand the organizations in which they work can gain knowledge about their institutions by reading *Organizational Theory in Higher Education*. Because faculty play such a crucial role in college and university leadership, the fullest understanding of organizational structure and operating factors can assist them as they shape the curriculum and policy that addresses the challenges alluded to above. Graduate students who are studying higher education and related subjects must have a thorough knowledge of organizations if they are to be considered proficient intellectuals in their field. Faculty who teach higher education organization and management courses will find this book a foundation text to use in their courses. The book was written as a foundational treatment of organizational theory and higher education administration. Both masters' and doctoral students will find this a helpful introductory text. Higher education administrators and practitioners seeking to gain insight into innovative ways to approach organizations can find inspiration in this text. Through reading about the different perspectives, new ways of operating, and new decision-making needs, there can be a new focus on issues. Trustees can only effectively lead these organizations if they understand the faculty culture, historical influences, and ways of operating. State, national, and international policy makers seeking a better understanding of higher education institutions can find some answers in this text.

As a long term member of U.S. higher education, I am committed to the future success of these organizations. This book is an effort to achieve that goal. I hope you find it useful.

Kathleen Manning
Burlington, Vermont

1

INTRODUCTION AND CONTEXT SETTING

The major dilemma in organization theory has been between putting into the theory all the features of organizations we think are relevant and thereby making the theory unmanageable, or pruning the model down to a simple system, thereby making it unrealistic. (Cyert & March, 2005, p. 136)

Higher education is a complex enterprise open to a wide range of understandings and interpretations. Its complexity is expressed in the types of institutions, environmental pressures exerted, multiple and simultaneously occurring organizational structures, and numerous professional identities of its members. Those working in higher education can only make sense of this complexity by understanding and using a combination of theoretical perspectives through which to view their work. This book presents multiple perspectives on organizational theory and provides higher education administrators, faculty, staff, and students with a variety of lenses through which to view their practices.

The higher education "enterprise," in business terms, is a mature industry (Levine, 2001; Manning, 1997). Organizational theorists postulate that organizations progress through a life cycle: birth and early development, institutionalization, and maturity (Baden-Fuller & Stopford, 1994; Beatty & Ulrich, 1991; Doeringer, 1987; Kimberly, 1980). Mature organizations are slow to change. Their structure is concrete; some would say fossilized, with less room for quick modifications or novel innovations. The labor force is specialized by function with minimal flexibility within a set of self-perpetuating functions. These organizations are often complacent about the security of their market niche. "Mature organizations have a choice to stay dynamic or pass into decline. Mature organizations, with their potentially fossilized structures, must actively work to remain dynamic. This entails astute environmental analysis and an adaptable belief system" (Manning, 1997, p. 6). Given the mature state of higher education organizations, a fresh look at potential organizational perspectives can help colleges and universities rejuvenate and revitalize rather than decline and deteriorate.

TRADITIONAL TENSIONS WITHIN HIGHER EDUCATION

Higher education is a societal entity beset with challenging though interesting tensions (see Table 1.1). The rapidly changing and increasingly demanding contexts in which higher education currently exists exacerbate these tensions.

In terms of the curriculum, for example, decades-long debates have raged about whether it is better to specialize in majors and minors or integrate knowledge through core curricula and general education requirements. The highly professional nature of faculty and the department structure have limited the ability of colleges and universities to quickly adapt to market-driven curriculum changes and student needs. The efficacy of the individual versus community and vice versa is an argument that has long raged in higher education, particularly in residence halls, academic departments, and amongst members of boards of trustees. The effective mix of interdependence and independence, particularly among faculty, is an elusive goal exacerbated by the ease of communication now available through e-mail and social media. Unique practices such as tenure and long-term employment across employee groups create tension between the values of a stable structure versus the adaptability of a flexible, responsive organizational architecture. Whether higher education is a public or private good is a debate that has occupied many a student and practitioner of higher education. A final tension influencing higher education is the competitive versus cooperative tendencies plaguing all organizations. Often voiced in gender-identified language, opinions abound about whether productivity is best achieved by pitting employees in healthy competition or engaging them in cooperative initiative.

The contexts and tensions outlined here describe a higher education condition requiring significant expertise and understanding to effectively manage in today's environment. An understanding of how higher education organizations operate in the context

Table 1.1 Historical and Current Tensions in Higher Education

Specialization versus Integration
(particularly as expressed in the curriculum)

Professionalism versus Adaptability
(particularly as expressed in faculty relations)

Individualism versus Community
(particularly as expressed in student life)

Interdependence versus Independence
(particularly as expressed in academic freedom)

Flexibility versus Structure
(particularly as expressed in organizational forms)

Public versus Private Good
(particularly as expressed in public financing of higher education)

Competitive versus Collaborative
(particularly as expressed in administrative practice)

of new and continuing tensions, contexts, and challenges is essential for effective leadership. This expertise extends to the varieties of organizational perspectives available for use within colleges and universities. Without an understanding of how colleges and universities work, administrators, faculty, and higher education stakeholders remain puzzled about why their institutions remain impervious to change, difficult to manage, and resistant to innovation. Without knowledge of organizational structure, faculty are hard pressed to make policy decisions regarding curriculum and other issues; trustees struggle to determine effective institutional purposes; and administrators fight to keep up with the rapid pace of change. This expansive knowledge and expertise is particularly important as old models of competition are replaced with newer models of collaboration.

Organizational theory has a long history in sociology, education, psychology, and business, among other disciplines. To better express the complexity of organizational functioning, an interdisciplinary approach underscores the organizational perspectives discussed in this book (see Table 1.2). The interdisciplinary perspective adopted in this book enables readers to better understand colleges and universities as a means to support effective leadership and management. Whether called frames (Birnbaum, 1991), metaphors (Morgan, 2006), or models (Clark, 1986), the organizational perspectives described in this book can help administrators, faculty, stakeholders, and students better understand the challenges of a postmodern, complex, and globally connected world. Metaphors for each perspective, visually and pictorially, describe the organizational perspective as well.

As an overview for the material presented in the chapters, Table 1.3 outlines organizational elements for each organizational perspective presented. The extent of the information included in this chart merely scratches the surface of the complexity of the perspectives and the range that faculty and practitioners need to bring to the task of understanding colleges and universities.

Alternating chapters discuss theoretical perspectives and case study applications that scholars and practitioners can use to view higher education organizations. Some perspectives overlap with others, some conflict, some are complementary. All perspectives offer ways to expand the repertoire of conceptual tools available to higher education faculty, staff, administrators, students, and stakeholders. The perspectives offer a

Table 1.2 Theoretical Foundations and Metaphors for Organizational Theory

Organizational Perspective	Theoretical Foundation	Metaphor
Organized Anarchy	political philosophy	anarchy
Collegium	sociology	circle
Political	sociology	jungle
Cultural	anthropology	carnival and theater
Bureaucracy	modernist	machine
New Science	philosophy of science	hall of mirrors, hologram, woven fabric, the "world as a great thought"[1]
Feminist	feminist theory	web
Spiritual	psychology	journey

1 Cited from Margaret Wheatley (2010).

Table 1.3 Summary of Organizational Frames

Organizational Elements	Chapter 2 Organized Anarchy	Chapter 4 Collegial	Chapter 6 Political	Chapter 8 Cultural	Chapter 10 Bureaucracy	Chapter 12 New Science or Quantum	Chapter 14 Feminist	Chapter 16 Spiritual
disciplinary foundation	political philosophy	sociology	sociology	anthropology	modernity	philosophy of science	feminist theory	psychology
decision-making mode	garbage can model	participative decision making	compromise; conflict	meaning making	rational decision making	uncertainty; multiple perspectives	collaborative	cooperative and collaborative
actions based on	fluid participation	consensus; discussion	conflict, loyalties, policy	enactment	technical; standard operating procedures	inter-relationships	shared purposes	intellect and gut feeling; emotions allowed
mechanism for reality creation	multiple realities	shared constructions	defined by those in power	socially constructed	"natural"; external; ideal type from nature	multiple realities	shared meaning	individual interpretation
sources of meaning	complexity	academic disciplines	conflict	rituals, myths, sagas, language, tradition	objective rules	complexity	collaboration and relationships	mind, body, spirit
power	diffused	expert; professional	charisma; influence	symbols, history, tradition	legitimate	diffused throughout organization	egalitarian	power emerges from all participants
structure	varied	circular	flat	varied	hierarchical; pyramid	depends on the purpose	roughly circular; web	varied
metaphor	anarchy	circle	jungle	carnival and theater	machine	hall of mirrors, hologram, woven fabric, the "world as a great thought"[1]	web	journey

examples/ archetype	colleges and universities	legal process; faculty senate; professional associations	legislature; unions; private club	church; sports; fraternities	military; church	corporations (e.g., dot coms)	learning organization	corporations, colleges
leadership	constructed and symbolic	first among equals	coalitions; defined by power structures and influence	heroes and heroines; mythical; the stuff of saga	top down; legitimate authority; leadership emanates from office	no distinction between leaders and followers	collaborative; emanates from the center	rotating; transformational
communication	intermittent	protracted; oral based	covert	explicit and implicit; oral; storytelling	top down; written predominates	all sources	uni-directional; open	power shared through open communication and other networks
scope of influence	pockets	faculty	institutional	institutional	institutional	global	institutional	global
reward structure	individual	expertise in discipline; peer review	connections	tradition	merit	personal meaning	relational	compromise between personal and organizational goals
source of structure	chaos	academic disciplines	humans; city state	culture	nature	the moment	leader	whole; universe
how you perceive co-workers	fellow professionals	colleagues	adversaries	actors and cast	worker bees	depends on the context	teammate	fellow journeyers

1 Cited from Wheatley (2010)

full range of explanatory power that takes many organizational structures and ways of operating into account. The later perspectives offered in the book (e.g., new science, spiritual, feminist) are helpful as higher education institutions continue their goal to become more inclusive, entrepreneurial, virtual, and collaborative. These more inclusive approaches to higher education are necessary as older economic models are supplanted with newer approaches that require higher education degrees and increased skill levels among employees. An entrepreneurial spirit is required for higher education systems that are expanding globally, have multiple structural forms, and require a more expansive vision, one that is achievable given the virtual innovations of higher education. Collaboration will not only improve working conditions for all in higher education, but can create meaningful roles for staff, students, and others who traditionally have been excluded from the power structures within colleges and universities. Knowledge of these organizational perspectives and the complexity they depict can help us all understand why higher education is so difficult to manage, a challenge to organize, and impossible to control. This book illustrates how different organizational perspectives can provoke more richly effective leadership and practice within higher education.

The desire to include orthodox (e.g., bureaucratic, political, cultural, and collegial) and nonorthodox (e.g., organized anarchies, new science, feminist, and spiritual) perspectives drove the choice of the eight organizational approaches included in the book. A goal for this book was to include contemporary organizational perspectives (the nonorthodox perspectives) often excluded from previous texts. Traditional organizational theory, if used with an eye for control, order, and rationality, limits ideas about how organizations can be innovatively created and managed. This is particularly important because colleges and universities have always been "unique organizations, differing in major respects from industrial organizations, government bureaus, and business firms" (Baldridge, Curtis, Ecker, & Riley, 1974, p. 7). The interconnected and complex world in which colleges and universities exist demands more nuanced and imaginative approaches to organizing structures, functions, and processes. In this book, a fuller range of options are presented for integrating theory and practice, important in today's postmodern, postindustrial world. The nonorthodox theories can replace, supplement, and complement the orthodox theories. These eight are not all-inclusive (see, for example, Morgan, 2006). The voluminous range of organizational perspectives could not be presented so choices were made about the most pertinent theories to include. Resources at the end of each chapter guide readers toward additional models.

The theories discussed in *Organizational Theory in Higher Education* are presented in the order of significance to higher education institutions. While the historical and paradigmatic significance of those theories to higher education orders (see Table 1.1) could certainly be debated, certain theories are more closely related to higher education operations than others. Because the theoretical chapters outlining the different organizational perspectives were written as stand-alone pieces, readers can choose the order that best fits their purposes. The chapters can be read in chronological order, by paradigm, or for their significance to higher education. Each chapter concludes with a contemporary application of that perspective. These contemporary discussions are completed in less depth than the theories they accompany. This is the case because the text was purposely written from a foundational point of view. References at the end of the chapters refer readers to more in-depth discussions of those contemporary applications.

Table 1.4 Organizational Perspectives by Chronological, Paradigmatic, and Interest to Higher Education

By Chronological Order	By Paradigm	By Significance to Higher Education Administration
Political	*Newtonian:*	Organized Anarchy
Collegium	Bureaucratic	Collegium
Bureaucracy	Political	Political
Organized Anarchy	Collegium	Cultural
Cultural	Organized anarchy	Bureaucratic
New Science	*Post-Modern or Post-Industrial:*	New Science
Feminist	Cultural	Feminist
Spiritual	Feminist	Spiritual
	New Science	
	Spiritual	

Because higher education organizations always contain several simultaneously operating organizational perspectives shaping a complex range of activities, readers are strongly urged to understand all the perspectives as gestalt, or combinations of several ways (not *a* singular way), to understand higher education. Whether as a system or a single institution, no one perspective or model will explain *all* aspects of higher education. One lens through which to view colleges and universities is not complex enough to provide the skilled leadership necessary to confront the present and future challenges that colleges and universities will encounter. Each perspective is an opportunity to think differently about colleges and universities. In combination, all or several perspectives can expose elements of higher education invisible from one perspective. The organizational perspectives used to understand higher education institutions are, on several levels, an individual choice given the institutional context. The perspectives are expressed differently across the various departments and offices, and their prevalence ebbs and flows depending on the task at hand. This is only one of the many reasons why colleges and universities as organizations are complex and difficult to understand.

In addition to thinking holistically and creatively about the organizational perspectives, the following idioms are offered as ways to playfully consider the perspectives and theories discussed in this text:

Organized Anarchy: "Don't try to make sense of it—just trust that it works."
Collegial: "We're all equal colleagues here. Let's discuss this over coffee."
Political: "I'll scratch your back if you scratch mine."
Cultural: "We have a legacy and tradition to maintain. This is not about us but about the past and the future."
Bureaucratic: "A place for everyone and everyone in their place."
New Science: "We're so interconnected with our environment, it's hard to tell where we start and it stops."

Feminist: "Come on in, we're all in this together."
Spiritual: "If we accomplish the task but don't bring our whole selves to it, we've failed."

A discussion of the organizational perspectives as viewed within the current higher education environment can help those within and outside these institutions comprehend why they are so difficult to understand. Trustees, parents, and external stakeholders are frequently perplexed by characteristics of higher education organizations that are absent in other organizations such as corporations, political institutions, or other nonprofits. These characteristics include:

1. *Highly professional employees.* Although corporate models are often used to explain higher education, colleges and universities are more similar to hospitals than corporations. Faculty possess professional authority which places them in the role of expert, in similar fashion to medical doctors and nurses. Administrators also possess expert knowledge and high professional status as evidenced by advanced degrees and highly specific job requirements.
2. *Presence of cosmopolitans.* Organizational members (e.g., faculty) often have allegiances to entities (e.g., discipline, professional associations, alma maters) outside their place of employment. These divided and potentially scattered loyalties can result in insufficient attention to circumstances and developments at the home institution.
3. *Multiple organizational structures.* Several organizational structures occur simultaneously within colleges and universities. A bureaucracy exists alongside a collegium; political dynamics can accompany feminist perspectives. Few other organizations have the complexity resulting from these simultaneously occurring structures.
4. *Conflict over the appropriate product of higher education.* Despite the urging of many state legislatures and national pundits and critics, colleges and universities struggle to conclusively identify or measure the end product of their labors. Credits generated, retention and graduate rates, faculty–student ratios, and faculty productivity as measured by full-time equivalent measures are proxies for the true product of higher education: an educated person. Although a college degree is vigorously sought after and paid for dearly, the worth that a degree confers is difficult to definitively identify.
5. *Multiple, often-conflicting roles.* Faculty, administrators, staff, students, and external stakeholders by structure, temperament, and responsibilities play vastly different roles within higher education organizations. Sometimes at odds with one another, the delineation of these roles is becoming more pronounced with the introduction of technology, the increasingly complex fiduciary responsibilities expected of administrators and trustees, and the raised expectations of students, parents, and other stakeholders.

The traditional tensions within higher education demand that faculty, administrators, trustees, and other stakeholders get out ahead of the current changes occurring within higher education. With the ongoing and upcoming shifts in higher education functioning, both old and new ways of operating should be included in the knowledge base of all who work in higher education.

While aspects of each organizational perspective are present in every higher education institution, it is argued that the newer models provide more complex and cooperative ways to approach the issues challenging higher education. These newer approaches can be a source of innovation, collaboration, and creativity.

THEORY TO PRACTICE

The disciplinary foundation, structure, metaphor, assumptions, and other elements of each organizational perspective are integrated into the theoretical chapters of the book. Each of these chapters is followed with a case chapter, illustrating the uses of that perspective in practice. Although the cases are matched to specific organizational perspectives, each case could be analyzed using more than one perspective. The use of only one perspective per case is a heuristic, so that readers can best learn how to apply that theory to practice. In the complex world of higher education, it is important to use more than one theory and analyze each situation from a variety of viewpoints. Similar to Alfred Korzybski's saying, "A map is not the territory it represents, but if correct, it has a similar structure to the territory, which accounts for its usefulness," the organizational perspectives are not an exact depiction of life within higher education institutions. The cases are maps that can guide thinking about the specific organizational perspectives. Travel through the territory of higher education requires a complete understanding of the various organizational perspectives and comprehension of how all operate in concert within colleges and universities. As the organizational perspective theories are read and understood, readers are urged to revisit previous case chapters and use different organizational perspectives to analyze the cases. Knowledge of the organizational perspectives can reveal the complexity of higher education organizations. These complexities can be discussed in the context of the case studies.

To lead effectively, administrators, faculty, and staff must envision solutions to organizational issues that plague college campuses. To assist the reader to make connections to their practice, questions for discussion are provided at the end of each chapter. These questions, in conjunction with recommended readings and case studies, can assist the reader to develop an in depth understanding of the organizational choices available. References at the end of each theory chapter direct the reader to additional resources on organizational theories.

Questions for Discussion
- How can the organizational perspectives under consideration help college and university leaders get out ahead of the rapid change occurring in higher education?
- How do the different organizational perspectives enable or constrain innovation?
- What knowledge bases will faculty, administrators, trustees, and others involved in higher education need to develop to help these institutions thrive?
- What are the power dynamics within the different organizational perspectives?
- How is human agency enabled or constrained within the organizational perspectives?
- What aspects of an institution are best explained by a particular organizational perspective? What parts are not well explained?

Recommended Readings Related to Higher Education Organizing

Bergquist, W. H., & Pawlak, K. (2008). *Engaging the six cultures of the academy* (2nd ed.). San Francisco, CA: Jossey-Bass.

Brown, D. G. (Ed.). (2006). *University presidents as moral leaders* (Series on Higher Education). Westport, CT: American Council on Education and Praeger.

Gumport, P. J. (Ed.). (2007). *Sociology of higher education: Contributions and their contexts.* Baltimore, MD: Johns Hopkins University Press.

Tierney, W. G. (Ed.). (2006a). *Governance and the public good.* Albany, NY: State University of New York Press.

Tierney, W. G. (2006b). *Trust and the public good: Examining the cultural conditions of academic work.* New York: Peter Lang.

2

ORGANIZED ANARCHY

The American college or university is a prototypic organized anarchy. It does not know what it is doing. Its goals are either vague or in dispute. Its technology is familiar but not understood. Its major participants wander in and out of the organization. These factors do not make a university a bad organization or a disorganized one; but they do make it a problem to describe, understand, and lead. (Cohen & March, 1986, p. 3)

More than one author has used the above quote by Cohen and March to poke fun at institutions of higher education. Colorful metaphors and tongue in cheek phrases aptly describe the organizations that many have found confusing. Though playful, Cohen and March put their finger on essential elements of modern higher education institutions. These organizations are paradoxical: familiar yet hard to describe, unpredictable though at times oddly rational, rooted in the past yet optimistically gazing into the future, traditional though educating many to anticipate change.

Organized anarchy is a theory first proposed by Cohen and March (1986) in their book, *Leadership and Ambiguity*. These researchers conducted their research on college presidents in the 1970s, research that yielded a particularly helpful perspective from which to understand higher education institutions. Several authors and theorists conflate Cohen and March's ideas about organized anarchies with the organizational concept of loosely coupled systems. The latter is an organizational theory with a set of theoretical characteristics (i.e., causation, typology, effects, compensations, and organizational outcomes) different from organized anarchies. The stance advanced by Orton and Weick (1990) that "the concept of organizations as loosely coupled systems is widely used and diversely understood" (p. 203) is adopted here. Organized anarchies as structural forms may be loosely coupled but are not loosely coupled systems as defined by Weick. Readers are directed to Weick (1976, 1989) and Orton and Weick (1990) for explication of loosely coupled systems.

Organized anarchies necessitate a paradigm of understanding different from the traditional modernist approach. To fully grasp the concept of this organizational form, the foundational paradigm must address the complexity and ambiguity proposed from an organized anarchy perspective. While this organizational perspective cannot describe all characteristics of organizations in all circumstances, the organized anarchy perspective provides a unique way to view the paradoxical yet uniquely normal institutions of higher education.

POLITICAL PHILOSOPHY AS A FOUNDATION FOR ORGANIZED ANARCHIES

The idea of anarchy is perhaps one of the most misunderstood concepts in the constellation of organizational theories. A discussion of the political philosophy approach to anarchy can assist higher education faculty, administrators, faculty, and students to better understand the organizations in which they learn, live, and work.

As opposed to popular ideas about anarchy as violence, chaos, and disorder, political theorists discuss anarchy in the context of community, mutual respect, and cooperation. Emma Goldman (1910) said of anarchy:

> Anarchism ... really stands for the liberation of the human mind from the dominion of religion; the liberation of the human body from the dominion of property; the liberation from the shackles and restraint of government. Anarchism stands for a social order based on the free grouping of individuals for the purpose of producing real social wealth; an order that will guarantee to every human being free access to the earth and full enjoyment of the necessities of life. (p. 68)

Rather than the absence of order, anarchies rely on community among human beings for organization. Within anarchies, everyone is expected and urged to participate. In a twist that may seem ironic, the individualism upon which U.S. democracy is based, according to the anarchists, interferes with the human tendency to form communities. The point of anarchy is not chaos; "rather lack of community is chaos" (Walsh, 1992, p. 5). Political theory assumptions about anarchy include the following:

- Humans must form community as a way to survive.
- Individualism interferes with community formation.
- Anarchy provides freedom and places responsibility on organizational members.
- Libertarians are concerned with individual rights, anarchists with community obligations.
- Affinity groups form the basis of organizational structure in anarchies.

There are significant differences between authentic anarchy as discussed above and the organized anarchy discussed in this chapter. Yet, the ideas underscoring anarchy have utility for understanding higher education organizations, especially those that value the goals of community, mutual cooperation, and shared responsibility. Strengths and weaknesses of anarchy as an underlying philosophical perspective are outlined in Table 2.1.

METAPHOR

Of the organizational perspectives discussed in this book, organized anarchy is the most richly metaphorical. Using anarchy as a metaphor and means to view organizations,

Table 2.1 Strengths and Weaknesses of the Political Philosophy Perspective

Strengths	Weaknesses
Provides a foundation for the community activities often found on college and university campuses	May be incongruent with the individualistic values of Western cultures, particularly the United States.
Creates an expectation of individual responsibility in the context of community-oriented behaviors.	May imply violence and confusion, particularly when associated with historical forms of higher education activism.
Provides a helpful alternative to the mechanized approach of bureaucracies.	Does not provide adequate explanation for the autonomy of higher education faculty members.
May be congruent with the community of scholars value within higher education.	May not adequately account for the professional and legitimate power present in higher education organizations.

Cohen and March (1986) attached the modifier "organized" as a good-humored way to convey the paradoxical nature of higher education. While the assumptions of political philosophy are informative, the term *anarchy,* as used by Cohen and March, was defined using the popular (and largely misunderstood) view; one of chaos, disorder, and lack of control.

> In a university anarchy each individual in the university is seen as making autonomous decisions. Teachers decide if, when, and what to teach. Students decide if, when, and what to learn. Legislators and donors decide if, when and what to support. Neither coordination ... nor control ... [is] practiced. (Cohen & March, 1986, p. 33)

Organized anarchies are similar to other contemporary organizational perspectives (e.g., see later chapters on the web of inclusion, new science, and spiritual perspectives) in the way the theorists use rich metaphors to describe complex systems. Although these rich and colorful metaphors communicate dynamism and complexity, they risk overstatement and confusion. The metaphor overstates because it exaggerates higher education's irrational and sometimes absurd side at the risk of understating its well-managed, cogent aspects. This confusion is particularly at risk among external stakeholders such as legislators and parents if the modifier, "organized," is omitted or underemphasized. While it may be playful or clever to think of colleges and universities as anarchistic, the "organized" descriptor introduces and establishes balance.

STRUCTURE

An organization from the perspective of the organized anarchy

> is a collection of choices looking for problems, issues and feelings looking for decision situations in which they might be aired, solutions looking for issues to which they might be the answer, and decision makers looking for work. (Cohen & March, 1986, p. 81)

Departing from the assumptions of rationally based organizational approaches, organized anarchies adopt a nonorthodox approach to theorizing. Simplicity, determinism, linear causality, and objectivity are supplanted by complexity, indeterminism, mutual causality, and perspective taking (Clark, 1985). This paradigm shift results in newer, postmodern approaches that better match reality as lived in organizations. There is some order (many argue, through a loosely coupled structure) in organized anarchies: "organizational processes are not always ordered as conventionally assumed [but that does] not mean that the processes should exhibit no order" (Olsen, 2001, p. 192). Referring to change, a central feature of organized anarchies, March (1981) speculated that "change takes place because most of the time most people in an organization do about what they are supposed to do; that is they are intelligently attentive to their environments and their jobs" (p. 564).

ASSUMPTIONS

The organized anarchy perspective assumes multiple realities. Faculty experience the organization from their various disciplinary points of view, administrators from their different understandings, students from yet others. The situation is further complicated by the presence of internal (e.g., boards of trustees) and external (e.g., state legislators) stakeholders. No one person, regardless of power or position, fully understands the many realities and perceptions present in the organization, a situation that introduces uncertainty into the organizational structure. Though tempered by culture, history, and tradition that shape beliefs in particular directions and away from others (Manning, 2001), the presence of multiple realities within organized anarchies is undeniable.

MAJOR CONCEPTS, CHARACTERISTICS, AND TERMS

Three properties define organized anarchies: problematic goals, unclear technology, and fluid participation (Cohen & March, 1986).

Problematic Goals

The fact that higher education institutions have unclear, contested, and often ambiguous goals makes these organizations profoundly different from other organizational forms. Corporations, hospitals, schools, and nonprofit organizations normally have a clearly focused purpose guiding their work. They may, for example, raise money to eradicate cancer, treat the sick, or assist refugee resettlement into the local community. A cancer association may raise money to eradicate cancer but also produce events that entertain while they raise those funds. A hospital may add to the professional workforce and city tax base while healing the sick. The refugee resettlement program may introduce diversity into a community while assisting people fleeing their homeland. Subgoals are part and parcel of any organization. While subgoals can exist within any organization, the full constellation of higher education organizational goals rivals the goals and purposes present within non-higher education organizational types. The difference with higher education is the number of ambiguous goals, the conflicting nature among the primary goals, and the vehemence with which institutional members may object to goals that remain foundational to the college or university's purposes. Universities, for example, focus on teaching, research, and service as their three-part primary purpose. Despite the longstanding presence of these goals, heated arguments rage over whether or not teaching and research are mutually exclusive; how central service should be to faculty life; and whether teaching assistants, adjunct professors, or full-time faculty should bear primary responsibility for the teaching mission.

Conflict about the appropriate goals for a higher education institution occurs via internal and external stakeholder involvement. A municipal council or city mayor may view serving the community as the major purpose of a college or university. While a substantial number of university members may agree with this priority, others may see themselves serving a worldwide disciplinary or professional community, far beyond the scope of the local community. Conflict and complexity regarding the unclear, ambiguous, and conflicting goals or purposes is expressed most vividly with board of trustee members. This stakeholder group often struggles to understand the voracity with which members of colleges and universities cling to their individual goals; for example, research that is important to a discipline but less relevant to the institution. Faculty and researchers may remain committed to goals that board of trustee members view as unrelated to institutional business.

Baldridge, Curtis, Ecker, and Riley (1978) claimed that the unclear and contested goal structures of higher education institutions means that nearly anything can be justified and almost anything could be attacked as illegitimate. Some may find it hard to imagine how any organization could survive with its basic purposes so unclearly defined and executed. Birnbaum (1991) argued that this characteristic of higher education is a strength not a weakness. He contended that several institutional purposes could be achieved simultaneously because multiple, even conflicting, goals exist within the same institution. These organizations are more adaptable because they distribute their efforts in several rather than one area allowing numerous societal purposes to be achieved at the same time. Perhaps the presence of multiple goals is in part responsible for the fact that colleges and universities are among the oldest existing organizational structures in the world. Colleges and universities have, in many ways, maintained the structure conceived in medieval times. Though notable innovations such as academic departments, elective courses, and electronic technology have been introduced, the underlying structure of faculty–student interaction, faculty governance, knowledge generation, and administration–faculty relationships remains medieval.

Unclear Technology

A second characteristic of organized anarchies is their use of unclear technology. This concept refers to the fact that "although the organization manages to survive and even produce, its own processes are not understood by its members" (Cohen, March, & Olsen, 1972, p. 1). As client-serving institutions (Baldridge et al., 1978), technologies must be employed to meet the needs of various participants. Students learn differently; community members have diverse needs; and research requires a variety of methodologies and approaches. As professionals, faculty and administrators use approaches, which may, to the uninitiated or unfamiliar, seem strange, incomplete, or ill advised. A fundamental purpose of higher education, teaching, is at best an inexact science. Some teaching methods work well with some students but not others. Certain faculty successfully execute teaching methods that elude other professors or instructors. In the end, any measurement of what an educated person looks like is open to debate and disagreement. Higher education does not have the luxury of clear technologies. The unclear technologies of higher education, particularly with its primary tasks of teaching and learning, have been the source of significant public criticism (U.S. Department of Education, 2006). When organizations cannot clearly prove that they have achieved their foremost mission, public trust, benefactor funding, and community support are difficult to maintain and cultivate.

Fluid Participation

The third primary characteristic of organized anarchies is fluid participation; the idea that the involvement of organizational members "varies from one time to another" (Cohen, March, & Olsen, 1972, p. 1). Students occupy the institution for a limited period of time (e.g., 4 to 6 years for full-time students, longer for part-time participants). Some faculty spend an entire professional career at a single institution while others advance their careers within multiple institutions. College presidents, the chief executive officers of these institutions, also exercise fluid participation. The average tenure for college presidents was 8 years in 2006, the last year for which data are available (American Council on Education, 2007).

Fluid participation extends beyond institutional members' duration within an institution. The committee and meeting structures of colleges and universities are predicated on the reality of fluid participation. Faculty who were highly involved at one stage of a decision-making process are often uninvolved in later stages. Seen as a secondary or tertiary responsibility after teaching and research, administrative service is relegated by faculty to a lesser role. Meetings are missed, sabbaticals interfere, and professional judgment regarding the importance of attendance intervenes in a system that tolerates, or perhaps promotes, fluid participation.

The characteristic of fluid participation introduces dynamism, unpredictability, and complexity into higher education organizational structures. Participants carry less knowledge about the history and culture of the organization when movement into and out of the organization is the norm. Rather than being possessed by individuals, history, tradition, and stability must be carried by the organizational structure, among other institutional mechanisms. Unfortunately, the structure does not have the capacity to carry institutional memory in the same ways or to the same degree to which participants do. While the structure has some concrete aspects, it is always malleable; always subject to change and interpretation. With fluid participation, mistakes are remade, history repeated, and decisions forgotten or overturned.

Higher education institutions have traditionally been places where multiple voices are given expression. Whether the faculty through self-governance structures, students through representation on committees, or administrators through formal processes, higher education differs from corporations in the way that participants' voices are given substantial freedom of expression. This circumstance means that communication comes from many sources and directions. Depending on where you are located in the organization (e.g., the provost's office, a dean's office), it may feel as if communication, feedback, and opinion are coming from everywhere. The omnidirection of communication in organized anarchies introduces complexity into colleges or universities. One can never predict or assess where communication will come from, what form it will take, and which aspects of that communication will be judged most valuable. In organized anarchies, it can be difficult to separate personal disputes from informed, professional judgment. Each voice is given an opportunity to be heard, sometimes with excellent results regarding consensus building and informed decision making and at other times with disastrous results of damaging rumors and skewed expectations of leadership capabilities.

In organized anarchies, one can never expect that communication will be complete. The fluid participation in organized anarchies often results in missed and intermittent communication. Organizational complexity and the demands of a professional's responsibilities will always interfere with that person's ability to effectively communicate. Due to uncertainty, unintended consequences, and unanticipated circumstances, one can never fully communicate all aspects of a decision or circumstance because the full range of those circumstances can never be known. In a postmodern context, reality is not objective, stagnant, or static. Even if one could communicate the aspects of the transitory reality in that moment in time, that reality changes in the next moment. In this way, communication is always incomplete and dynamic. The best one can hope for is to collect and communicate an adequate amount of pertinent information to make an informed, effective decision. Tolerance for ambiguity and nimbleness in response are more appropriate goals than attempts to obtain and communicate comprehensive information. Administrators who understand the dynamics of organized anarchies should always be prepared for an accusation of inadequate and incomplete communication. By its very nature, the fluid participation and unclear technology of higher education make this situation a reality.

Because communication in an organized anarchy is intermittent, omnidirectional, and incomplete, expectations about what can and cannot be accomplished are likewise affected. This situation has, ironically, been exacerbated with the advent of electronic communication through e-mail and the World Wide Web. The presence of readily available information increases the number of stakeholders, introduces complexity into already multifaceted decision-making processes, and raises expectations about the availability of widespread communication.

Client-Serving, Professionally Populated, and Environmental Vulnerability

In addition to the three characteristics of problematic goals, unclear technology, and fluid participation introduced by Cohen and March (1986), Baldridge et al. (1978) had proposed several additional characteristics to the organized anarchy approach. Organized anarchies serve clients who demand input into the decision-making process; they are peopled with professionals who demand a large measure of control over the institution's decision processes; and they are highly vulnerable to their environments (Baldridge et al., 1978, p. 25).

Client-Serving

The client-serving nature of higher education institutions introduces complications into the structure in ways that are absent from other types of institution. When stakeholder groups differ about whether students should be considered clients, customers, or learners, the sheer number of opinions and ways of operating introduce confusion. Stakeholders often have conflicting ideas about who the clients are, how they are to be served, and what they are to be served. This circumstance makes it difficult to determine the basic nature of the higher education client.

Professionalized Organizations

The problematic nature of the client served by higher education institutions interacts with the high professionalism present, particularly among faculty. In contrast to bureaucratic structures that rely on positional authority, expert authority is a significant dynamic within higher education institutions. The positional authority of administrators (e.g., presidents, provosts, department chairs) competes poorly with the professional or expert authority of faculty. Administrators lack the authority to convince faculty to accept certain definitions (e.g., students as customers), the best technology (e.g., distance learning) to be used, or the best way (e.g., bureaucratic expediency) to do a particular task. Each professional has firm beliefs, informed by professional practice and experience, about the best approach to be taken. Professionally informed opinions about organizational life and its technologies abound: how decisions should be made, how teaching is undertaken, what courses should be taught, and how relationships with colleagues should progress. This firm belief in the veracity of professional opinion often extends to decisions made and policies set by college and university administrators. Regardless of the extent to which a faculty member may or may not be informed about those decisions and policies, that person may hold tenaciously to a professionally defined right to exercise an opinion. This includes the right to exercise a vote of no confidence if the person believes that institutional leaders are making or have made ill-conceived decisions. Opposition based on professional opinion also occurs if a faculty member believes that the traditional purposes of the institution or higher education are being compromised.

The expression of professionally informed, but potentially conflicting opinion is another source of complexity and anarchy in higher education organizations. Administrators, legislators, students, or other higher education stakeholders should not view the exercise of these voices as interference or misinformation. For example, faculties, particularly those with a long-term commitment to the institution, have significant institutional history and memory. Their opinions are informed by past experience within the context of the institution. Their long-range view, though sometimes debatably anachronistic, represents a knowledgeable historical view. These points of view can often be more richly informed than administrators with less institutional history. Both views are necessary for effective management in higher education. Faculty voice and prolonged deliberation on decisions can slow or stop an overly ambitious administrator from making decisions that ultimately have a negative impact on the organization (Birnbaum, 1991). In this way, the dynamic tension between faculty and administrators introduces structure and organization to the anarchistic nature of organized anarchies.

Environmental Vulnerability

The last characteristic of organized anarchies proposed by Baldridge et al. (1978) to the original three proposed by Cohen and March (1986) is environmental vulnerability. Organizations exist in systems that are exposed to and are affected by the external environment. "Organizations are remarkably adaptive, enduring institutions, responding to volatile environments routinely and easily, though not always optimally" (March, 1981, p. 564). Higher education, because of its strong dependence on tuition dollars, the national and international economies, reputational measures of quality, and fluidity of the client group served, is particularly affected by environmental change. Students are a transient population in the way they attend multiple institutions, sometimes simultaneously. They frequently postpone or interrupt their college attendance or enroll in college in a variety of ways (e.g., full-time, part-time, online). The 24-hours-a-day, 7-days-a-week circumstance of many higher education institutions operations exposes these institutions to variations in utilities, food, and maintenance costs. As such, environmental factors exact a heavier toll on higher education than organizations operating on a 9-to-5 basis. The emergence of new competition, increased virtual education, and internationalization of higher education combined with the repercussions of the global financial crises, government-mandated requirements, and market-driven pressures have intensified the impact of the external environment on higher education organizations (Newman, Couturier, & Scurry, 2004). Because these institutions are nonprofit and tuition dependent with relatively few sources of income, changes in the environment can have a harsh and rapid impact. Higher education institutions have minimal to no safety cushion with which to ease the impact of these environmental influences. This vulnerability introduces complexity and anarchy into the organizational structure.

STRENGTHS AND WEAKNESSES OF ORGANIZED ANARCHIES

The organized anarchy perspective, similar to all organizational perspectives summarized in this book, possesses strengths and weaknesses (see Table 2.2). Similar to any organizational theory, this approach cannot be implemented without attention to these features.

To provide direction on ways to manage and administer organized anarchies, Cohen and March (1986) presented several helpful rules.

- "Spend time" (p. 207). Because time and energy are scarce resources within organizations, those who can dedicate time to decision and policy making will have influence.
- "Persist" (p. 208). Decisions are made over time and through multiple attempts. Because higher education organizations are constantly changing, a defeated idea one day may find champions the next.
- "Exchange status for substance" (p. 208). Cohen and March warned of the dangers of presidents becoming embroiled in their own importance. They recommend concentrating on substance to avoid the pitfalls of this self-importance trap.
- "Facilitate opposition participation" (p. 209). By drawing in people from outside the customary circles, different voices can be heard, assorted ideas shared, and a

Table 2.2   Strengths and Weaknesses of the Organized Anarchy Perspective

Strengths	Weaknesses
The professionalized nature of higher education institutions means that there is a system of checks and balances regarding institutional power and authority.	The organized anarchy perspective is descriptively rich but practically incomplete.
Organized anarchies are more democratic because the multiple, even conflicting goals, creates more opportunities for disparate points of view to be expressed.	The rationale and recommendations for practice concerning organized anarchies fly in the face of accepted bureaucratic and rational management procedures.
Higher education organizations, which are organized anarchies, better prepare students for a complex, post-modern world.	Because ambiguity is central to organized anarchies, administrators, faculty, and students with little tolerance for uncertainty may struggle in an organization functioning in this manner.
There are more opportunities for critical thinking and multicultural perspective taking in organized anarchies.	The organized anarchy perspective cannot adequately explain all parts of a college or university.

more democratic process achieved. Although the goal of coopting others can be an outcome of facilitating opposition, that is not the purpose here. One can hope that all sides of the debate can be informed by increased contact and communication.

- "Overload the system" (p. 210). If many programs and ideas are proposed, some of them must, through persistence, be enacted. "Someone with the habit of producing many proposals, without absolute commitment to any one, may lose any one of them ... but cannot be stopped on everything" (Cohen & March, 1986, p. 210).
- "Manage unobtrusively" (p. 212). Higher education organizations are difficult to manage. If one forces solutions or aggressively directs the organization in particular directions, failure is likely. Cohen and March (1986) suggest that leaders are more successful when they "let the system go where it wants to go with only the minor interventions that make it go where it should" (pp. 212–213). An aspect of this approach is to make small adjustments in a range of places rather than a concerted and large effort in one place. The chances of success, through these multiple means, are increased.

Leaders, including college and university presidents, believe in their capability to effect organizational change. The organized anarchy perspective, while paying homage to the facility of leadership, explains why and how organizations operate even in the presence of weak leadership. The fact that higher education institutions have a life of their own despite the efforts of presidents and other organizational leaders may be disconcerting for those seeking to control and manage these institutions.

NEXT STEPS: BRINGING THE ORGANIZED ANARCHY PERSPECTIVE INTO CURRENT USE

The organized anarchy perspective was proposed in the 1970s and is used as a metaphor to this day. Subsequent conceptualizations add currency to the theory, particularly theorizing on institutionalization theory.

Institutionalization Theory

Institutionalization theory has an updated application to the organized anarchy perspective. Basic elements informing institutionalization theory are that (a) institutional contexts influence organizations including beliefs about appropriate conduct; (b) organizations with unclear technologies and difficult to assess outputs such as colleges and universities are particularly affected by institutional pressures; (c) to obtain social approval, legitimacy, and ultimately survival, organizations become isomorphic or congruent with their institutional context, (d) conformity to institutional pressures, especially when it conflicts with beliefs about efficiency, may be ceremonial; and (e) institutional practices are widely understood, accepted, and taken for granted and are, as such, resistant to change (Greenwood, Oliver, Sahlin, & Suddaby, 2008, p. 6).

Institutions from the institutionalization theory perspective are "supraorganizational patterns of activity rooted in material practices and symbolic systems by which individuals and organizations produce and reproduce their material lives and render their experiences meaningful" (Thornton & Ocasio, 2008, p. 101). Institutions (e.g., the state, family, international political orders, democracy, capitalism) are larger entities than the organizations they shape. These institutions are the archetype for organizational structure, action, and practice. Through human cultural action, they convey the rules, assumptions, and classifications upon which organizational structure is built. Commitment to and interaction with these institutional social structures and beliefs create stability and integration. The smaller organizations are "institutionalized" when interaction, adaptation, and ways of operating coalesce into structures modeled after the all-encompassing institutional structures that exist in the environment. Through institutionalization, organizations take on particular character, reach certain competence or, unfortunately, adopt practices that interfere with their ability to perform. According to Selznick (1996), leadership must monitor the costs and benefits of institutionalization within organizations including organizational structure, institutional norms and ideologies, and myths and rituals.

People in organizations respond to their understanding of the rules: rules about identity, structure, and decision making. These rules are the institutional logic upon which action, decision, and basic aspects of organizational function as based. Although human action within organizations is theoretically unfettered and open to the imagination, organizational actors rarely perform in entirely new and inventive ways. Instead, they fashion their actions on the existing examples of what behavior is acceptable, what has been used in the past, and the tried and true approaches to success.

> Actors behave in accordance with their interpretation of rules and practices that are socially constructed, publicly known, anticipated and accepted. A polity (and society) is a community of rule followers with distinctive sociocultural ties, cultural connections, intersubjective understandings based on shared codes of meaning and ways of reasoning, and senses of belonging. Identities and rules are constitutive as well as regulative and are molded by social interaction and experience. (Olsen, 2001, p. 193)

In one sense, institutional structures (e.g., language, rule of law, bureaucracy) enable choice and action upon which choices are made. Correspondingly, societal and institutional values, mores, and ways of operating constrain or limit the full range of choices. Because institutional structure simultaneously enables and constrains action (Giddens, 1979, 1984), institutionalization theorists are often optimistic about the potential for humans to transform their organizations. Human agency, imagination, and existing structural forms are resources available for that transformation.

> While institutions constrain action they also provide sources of agency and change. The contradictions inherent in the differentiated set of institutional logics provide individuals, groups, and organizations with cultural resources for transforming individual identities, organizations, and society. (Thornton & Ocasio, 2008, p. 101)

Institutionalization theorists reason that in addition to the ways that specific organizations adopt the forms provided from the supraorganizational institutions (DiMaggio & Powell, 1991), institutions subsequently integrate those organizations with each other through rules and patterns of identity and meaning (Olsen, 2001; Thornton & Ocasio, 2008). Rather than a neatly arranged structure, institutionalization theorists view organizations as a grouping of coalitions, a federal structure of sorts. With permeable boundaries, these coalitions, loosely organized and inherently flexible, interact with their environments in ways that engender complexity. The client-serving nature of organized anarchies corresponds with the coalition structure described in the institutionalization approach. Serving clients can result in coalitions of supporters and allies; the clients themselves can coalesce into coalitions to further advocate for their objectives. Higher education institutions are a good example of this process of organizational and institutional shaping. Colleges and universities are part of systems (i.e., institutions). States, as institutions, provide the history, requisite forms, and ways of operating across a public, state-supported system of higher education. Those state systems also shape and are shaped by the larger U.S. system of higher education that has distinct characteristics (e.g., funding tendencies, vocational emphasis or lack thereof, the meaning of a college degree in the larger society). In this way, the institution of higher education, writ large, becomes a pattern and is subsequently patterned by the state systems and individual colleges and universities.

Human Action and Rationality

Institutionalization theorists, using tenets that are similar to those of organized anarchies, reject the assumption that people are rational actors. A shift in focus exists in this organizational approach from the modernist logic of rationality to that of identity. Actors exercise agency based on the appropriateness of action about who they believe themselves and the organization to be (Olsen, 2001). This approach enables higher education faculty, stakeholders, and practitioners to better understand why some practices in organizations seem "right" albeit irrational. Rationality is not assumed to be an explanation for organizational structure or action (Thornton & Ocasio, 2008). When organizational processes are not ordered as conventionally assumed, it does not mean that those processes are without logic (Olsen, 2001). The logic may be identity-based, cultural, or formed by habit rather than by rationality.

In their rejection of the modernist assumptions about efficiency and rationality, institutionalization theories overlap with organized anarchy ideas. Eschewing assumptions about rationality, efficiency, and discipline, new institutionalization theorists see benefit in the openness and flexibility of organized anarchies. Rational choice models are supplanted with garbage can models of decision making. Tidy structures and adept functioning are replaced with messy, multiple, often conflicting goals. Rationality is neither sought nor desired to sort out the mismatched goals. Higher education institutions lack rational explanations but embody legitimacy, are effective though inefficient, and stand the test of time despite their awkwardness.

According to institutionalization theory, institutions impose order through the shared meaning and logics assumed about, for example, what colleges and universities are supposed to look like and do. The rules, meanings, and assumptions become self-reproducing within the social order that then applies pressure on individual colleges and universities. With unclear technology as a definitional hallmark of organized anarchies, this uncertainty about effective and efficient ways of operating exposes higher education institutions to forceful pressures from these rules. These organizations with their extensive networks of internal and external stakeholders are particularly prone to the institutional contexts and subsequent logics about structure, identity, and action. Colleges and universities must conform to these pressures or risk significant resistance, even closure. If a college does not obey the institutional rules about what it is to look like, students may not recognize it as an institution of higher learning, trustees may urge administrators to take a more conforming course of action, and external funding sources may distrust the organization as a fitting place in which to invest.

CONCLUSIONS

When administrators, faculty, and students use the organized anarchy perspective to understand organizations, there is a shift in traditional expectations about communication, decision making, and participation. In contrast to a traditional top-driven approach, all members of the institution come to understand the role they play. Intermittent communication means that influence can be exerted from a number of sources. Fluid participation means that pressure, power, and influence can be exerted at any point of the decision- or policy-making process. The reality of multiple goals means that the institution can adopt a new direction without fundamentally changing the college or university's mission and purpose. The newly adopted purpose may have been lingering as a subgoal for years, waiting for the right environmental context. Rather than weakness, the flexibility of organized anarchies can provide strength to higher education institutions.

Higher education's pace, including the degree of change and need for response, has increased significantly in the past 20 years. Despite the fact that higher education institutions have been chronically and historically underresourced and staffed, the imperative to do more with less is now amplified. The survival and health of higher education institutions and systems depend on rapid and flexible responses to internal and external changes. This pace has a significant negative impact on higher education participants' ability to communicate fully, adequately collect information, and satisfactorily vet decisions. The increased pace and increased environmental and organizational complexity has made the organized anarchy perspective more relevant today than ever.

Effective administration requires that administrators and faculty operate from the viewpoint of several organizational perspectives. The organized anarchy perspective provides a helpful approach to managing higher education institutions in ways that are more congruent with and accommodating to their unique structures and approaches. Unique to higher education and other client-serving organizations, the organized anarchy perspective provides a way to think about colleges and universities that can result in the achievement of a wide variety of institutional goals and societal purposes.

Questions for Discussion

- How might multiple goals and purposes increase the effectiveness of higher education institutions?
- How does the unclear technology of higher education institutions leave these organizations open to public criticism?
- How does the presence of multiple professional communities increase the complexity of a college or university's organizational structure and operating procedures?
- What institutional structures, assumptions, and expectations are ordained on higher education organizations?
- What aspects of organized anarchies make higher education more adaptable or less adaptable?

- How can the organized anarchy perspective help faculty, stakeholders, and practitioners make sense of the traditional tensions in higher education?

Recommended Readings Related to Organized Anarchies and Institutionalization

Bastedo, M. N. (2009). Convergent institutional logics in public higher education: State policymaking and governing board activism. *The Review of Higher Education, 32*(2), 209–234.

Cohen, M. D., & Sproull, L .S. (Eds.). (1996). *Organizational learning.* Thousand Oaks, CA: Sage.

Daft, R. L. (2007). *Organization theory and design* (10th ed.). Mason, OH: Cengage Learning.

March, J. G. (1981). Footnotes to organizational change. *Administrative Science Quarterly, 26*(4), 563–577.

March, J. G. (1994). *A primer on decision making: How decisions happen.* New York: Free Press.

March, J. G., & Shapira, Z. (2007). Behavioral decision theory and organizational decision theory. In G. R. Ungson & D. N. Braunstein (Eds.), *Decision making: An interdisciplinary inquiry* (pp. 293–345). Boston, MA: Kent.

Mintzberg, H., & Westly, F. (2010). Decision making: It's not what you think. In P. C. Nutt & D. C. Wilson (Eds.), *Handbook of decision making* (pp. 73–82). Hoboken, NJ: Wiley.

Peterson, M. W. (2007). The study of colleges and universities as organizations. In P. J. Gumport (Ed.), *Sociology of higher education: Contributions and their contexts* (pp. 147–184). Baltimore, MD: Johns Hopkins University Press.

Sporn, B. (2006). Governance and administration: Organizational and structural trends. *International Handbook of Higher Education, 18*(1), 141–157.

Tierney, W. G. (2001). Why committees don't work: Creating a structure for change. *Academe, 87*(3), 25–29.

Thornton, P. H. (2004). *Markets from culture: Institutional logics and organizational decisions in higher education publishing.* Stanford, CA: Stanford University Press.

3

CASE

Missions, Garbage Cans, and Decision Making

Every higher education institution has a mission, vision, and set of goals. Colleges and universities have historically been asked to fulfill a herculean task for society. They are to transmit, preserve, and create knowledge through teaching and research while simultaneously enacting social change. Colleges and universities provide an analytical view on societal issues, whether through well-practiced and historically justified student activism or via the public intellectual and social critic roles exercised by faculty. Their libraries house the most significant knowledge known to human beings. The intellectual riches contained on college campuses are nearly unimaginable. Traditional college students come of age on college campuses; nontraditional students gain an education to change careers and get a second chance at life.

The responsibilities and societal tasks as described above dictate that colleges and universities are among the most complex institutions in society. This is as true for U.S. institutions as it is for universities across the globe. The case outlined below describes the complexity of higher education decision making through the processes of strategic planning. As discussed in chapter 2, universities can be viewed as organized anarchies (Cohen, March, & Olsen, 1972). The competing demands, high expectations for performance, and individual and group preferences that exist within a strategic planning process create an apt circumstance to discuss organized anarchies and the garbage can model of decision making.

DECISION MAKING IN ORGANIZED ANARCHIES

Cohen and March (1986) described decision making as a fundamental activity of organized anarchies. Using the metaphor of a garbage can, a model meant to "encourage colleagues to play with the basic ideas" (Olsen, 2001, p. 192), decision making in these organizations is an opportunity to make choices.

> The garbage can process is one in which problems, solutions, and participants move from one choice opportunity to another in such a way that the nature of

the choice, the time it takes, and the problems it solves all depend on a relatively complicated intermeshing of elements. These include the mix of choices available at any one time, the mix of problems that have access to the organization, the mix of solutions looking for problems, and the outside demands on the decision makers. (Cohen, March, & Olsen, 1972, p. 16)

Choices are constrained by the time, energy, and resources available, as well as by the circumstances of the decision and choice situations. Originally conceived as a way to describe university governance (Olsen, 2001), Cohen, March, and Olsen (1972) outlined the garbage can model of decision making as one of many ways that participants choose options within organizations. Through their research, these theorists concluded that the decisions made and choice opportunities available were less rationally obvious and more detached from the organizational structure than previously imagined.

During decision making, organizational members attend "to the strategic effects of timing (in the introduction of choices and problems), the time pattern of available energy, and the impact of organizational structure" (Cohen & March, 1986, p. 81). The model acknowledges the contextual nature of organizational life as well as the ways that timing and coincidence drive choices. Decisions are more about the ways that problems, solutions, choice opportunities, and decision makers come together at any point in time than they are about a rationally and objectively determined "right" answer to a particular problem (Olsen, 2001). When one considers the temporal and coincidental nature of events, circumstances, and people leading to a decision, higher education administrators can better understand the complex nature of decision making.

The knotty politics of participation in strategic planning and other decision-based activities are more comprehensible when one abandons the idea of an objective and rational "right" choice. Decision making is more than "simply" a matter of rationally defining the problem, determining alternative solutions, choosing among the options, and implementing the decision. Whereas the rational decision models defined choice as a decontextualized "given," an aspect of organizational life where a "correct" response can be identified, the garbage can model of decision making acknowledges the role of participants and other circumstances integral to the context of the choices available and decisions made. In fact, in this model four independent streams influence the decision made: problems, solutions, participants, and choice opportunities (Cohen & March, 1986; Cohen, March, & Olsen, 1972; Olsen, 2001).

In addition to the mix of the four streams, the specific choices made also depend on what other "garbage" is present at the time of the decision. If decisions could be "placed" in garbage cans, then:

> The mix of garbage in a single can depends partly on the labels attached to the alternative cans; but it also depends on what garbage is being produced at the moment, on the mix of cans available, and on the speed with which garbage is collected and removed from the scene. (Cohen & March, 1986, p. 81)

A decision and its attendant choices cannot be taken out of context from the other "garbage" surrounding it. Figure 3.1 illustrates a case in which the independent streams of problems, solutions, participants, and choice opportunities influence strategic change at an institution.

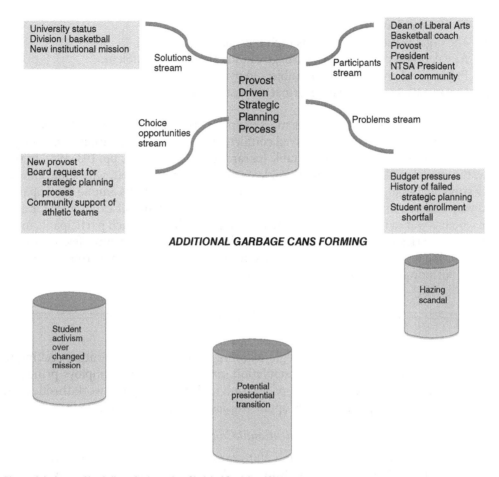

Figure 3.1 Center City College Garbage Can Model of Decision-Making

Types of Decisions in the Garbage Can Model

Decisions using the garbage can model are made by oversight, flight, and resolution. In oversight, choices become available when a problem at hand is "solved" by becoming attached to a choice at hand. In flight, unsuccessful choices become attached to a problem until a more attractive choice presents itself. The problem then "leaves the choice" and a more fruitful decision is possible. In this decision-making mode, decisions are not made so much as they are avoided. The final decision approach within the garbage can model is by resolution. Using this approach, problems are resolved when time is allocated to the selection or identification of choices leads to a solution (Cohen & March, 1986). Because problems can be independent from solutions in the garbage can model, these elements of organizational life are often elusive, may combine in unexpected ways, or may result in surprisingly original answers to persistent difficulties. A solution, rather than a rational choice discovered through deliberation, could be "'an answer actively looking for a question'" (Olsen, 2001, p. 193).

Cohen, March, and Olsen (1972), with their innovative model, elaborated on five decision-making properties that partially explain why making choices is often so difficult to accomplish.

1. Most issues have low salience for most people;
2. The organizational system has high inertia;
3. Any decision can become a garbage can for almost any problem;
4. Processes of choice are easily subject to overload; and
5. Organizations have weak information bases (Cohen & March, 1986).

Because issues have low salience for most people, participation in decision making "is not always stable ... there is unresolved conflict, and ... authority relations are ambiguous or shifting, not organized into stable hierarchies" (Olsen, 2001, pp. 193–194). In this way, the model explains why some problems persist year after year, why some choices look good but fail to solve the problem, why choice is so contentious among participants, and why decision making is so difficult. Olsen described a familiar experience for anyone who has worked in higher education organizations during which participants move "through a series of meetings on nominally disparate topics, reaching few decisions, while talking repeatedly with many of the same people about the same problems" (2001, p. 192). No amount of rationality can explain this phenomenon.

═══════════════════ CASE ═══════════════════

The following case describes a strategic planning process at an institution seeking to change its traditional mission and population served. The provost employs principles learned from the garbage can model of decision making to help her work through the complexities of participation, choice opportunities, problems, and solutions.

Institutional Context

Center City College (a pseudonym) is a 200-year-old institution with strong ties to the local community. A mainstay of both its neighborhood and surrounding city, Center City has a long history of serving first-generation college students. A primary way the institution serves the community is through NCAA Division II sports. The women and men's basketball teams are particularly popular, with sold-out season ticket sales each semester. The stands are filled with students and local community members who know the rituals involved in cheering the home team on to victory.

Influenced by the upper reputational drift of many colleges and universities, administrators at Center City College recently decided to pursue university status, increase admissions standards, and enhance the academic reputation of the institution. Included in the plans was an effort to upgrade men's basketball and women's soccer to Division I and dedicate additional money to women's field hockey and men's baseball. The subsequent athletic and academic reputations were predicted to increase the quality of students attracted to the institution.

Questions to Consider

- What pressures are externally exerted on higher education institutions to increase their reputation through university status?
- How is the overall mission of U.S. higher education fulfilled through the specialized niches of institutional types?

- How are athletics and academic reputations linked?
- How is athletics used as a recruiting tool?

List of Characters

Dr. Frank Lincoln: Dr. Lincoln has served as the College's president for 4 years. He came to Center City from a large research-extensive university in the South. His past institution embarked on a strategy of increasing student enrollment by growing athletics at the institution. Although Center City's profile and market for students is vastly different, Dr. Lincoln sees potential for using this same strategy at Center City. With the experience of 4 years to build an administrative team, Lincoln believes that now is the time to change the profile of Center City, an institution that he believes has the potential to be great. Unbeknownst to his staff, particularly the provost, President Lincoln is being courted by his old institution to assume the presidency. Although he had planned to stay at Center City for at least 7 years, the opportunity to go "back home" is extremely tempting.

Dr. Julie Kimball: Dr. Kimball, appointed the provost at Center City 6 months earlier, had moved up through the ranks of academic administrators at the institution. Currently in her honeymoon period, Dr. Kimball recognizes that action could be taken now and would meet less resistance than if it were taken later.

Dr. Kimball was in agreement with President Lincoln that Center City had the potential for greatness. Her role in the institutional transformation was to use the trustee-mandated strategic planning process to outline a new vision for the institution. As a faculty member and associate provost at the institution, Kimball was a veteran of three failed strategic planning processes. She was confident that the consultant she recently employed could assist them with their efforts to gain university status, convert two athletic teams to Division I, and increase the quality of students admitted to the institution.

Dr. Ann Royce: Dr. Royce, a history faculty member at Center City, was a veteran of new administrators and their plans. An alumna of Center City, she was dedicated to its mission to serve underrepresented populations and first-generation college students. An activist by nature, Dr. Royce had been active in the movement 10 years earlier to establish a faculty union. Although she was still active in union activities, she felt that her voice could be best heard through work as a dean. She had lobbied for and been appointed to the position of Dean of the School of Liberal Arts.

At a recent deans' council meeting, Dr. Royce and the other deans had been apprised of President Lincoln's and Provost Kimball's plans concerning the college. She, along with several other deans, was adamantly opposed to these efforts. She was determined to use her political and social capital to make sure that Center City College remained true to its original mission.

Coach Tom Daly: Coach Daly was proud of his work with the Division II men's basketball team over the past 12 years. He was thrilled when the president apprised him of his desire to seek Division I status for the team. This achievement would help Daly with his aspirations to coach a Division I team at a Big Ten institution. Coach Daly had been contacted recently by a parent of one of his players about a possible hazing incident.

Although Coach Daly took hazing seriously, he knew that a scandal at this point would jeopardize the team's chances of going to Division I. He spoke to the players, was assured that nothing had happened, and assumed that was the end of the incident.

Joe Mazel: A nontraditional, first-generation student who had grown up in the neighborhood around Center City, Joe had a special connection to the institution. For 5 years, he had taken remedial and noncredit classes in preparation for his admission to the college. He saw the institution and his eventual degree as his second chance at life. He felt so strongly about the institution's mission that he ran for and was elected president of the Non-Traditional Student Association (NTSA). An extremely active group on campus, the NTSA had gotten wind of the mission changes desired by the provost and president. They were determined to take action to prevent these changes.

Questions to Consider
- How does the increasingly short tenure for higher education presidents impact leadership within colleges and universities?
- What are some of the factors that affect the shortened tenure of college presidents?
- What is the relationship between the president and provost regarding decision making and strategic planning?
- Who is responsible for determining the mission of an institution?

A Change in Mission

Provost Kimball was excited and optimistic about today's meeting of the Strategic Planning Committee. An advocate of inclusive processes, Kimball had invited Ann Royce and Joe Mazel to be on the committee. Although both had voiced their opposition to the proposed changed mission, Kimball believed that the strategic plan would be supported only if all perspectives were expressed during the process. President Lincoln was joining today's meeting to charge the group with their task. Lincoln and Kimball were in agreement about the need for the institution to become a university and change its mission to attract a more qualified group of admitted students. But, for today's meeting, they agreed that the newly formed committee would be more responsive to a draft statement about the specific changes proposed.

The lively discussion among committee members stopped as Kimball and Lincoln entered the conference room. The first order of business was introductions followed by the president's charge (see below). Although Kimball remained optimistic about the group's ability to complete the charge, she sensed resistance in the room. She had invited Joe Mazel, president of the NTSA, and Dr. Royce, Dean of the School of Liberal Arts, onto the committee after reading an article by March (1981). The quote, "some organizations attempt to coopt difficult people (e.g., rebels), on the assumption that cooptation leads to controlled change, since opponents are socialized and provided with modest success" (p. 567), appealed to her and she heeded March's advice. Kimball was hoping that involvement on the committee could harness their ideas and give them ownership of the strategic change process. Her worst fears, however, were realized when both introduced themselves by stating their long-term commitment to the present mission of the institution and opposition to any change. Both cited their backgrounds as first-generation college students who had benefitted from institutions like Center City. Kimball knew that the shift in mission was going to be hard won.

Text of the President's Charge to the Strategic Planning Committee

The Board of Trustees tasked me to undertake a strategic planning process that refocuses and clarifies the mission of Center City College. It is their hope that this plan will guide our efforts in the upcoming years. I have directed Provost Kimball to assemble and subsequently chair a representative committee of college faculty, students, and staff to complete this responsibility. Within 6 months, the committee will present a strategic plan to my office. Upon review of this plan and vetting by the College's governance groups, I will determine the next steps regarding presentation of a plan to the Board of Trustees. This process will involve extensive discussions within the committee and among the governance groups about available options and potential directions for the College's future. The College is at the cusp of tremendous change and opportunity. We appreciate your service and dedication and trust you will map out a bright future.

Questions to Consider

- If a participants stream is one of the factors in the garbage can model, what are ways that participation can be managed? Should it be managed?
- Who gets "a seat at the table"? What implications does this have for the participants and solution streams?
- What messages in President Lincoln's charge helped build momentum for his desired changes? What messages worked against his desired changes?
- What are the garbage cans forming around the decision?

Following the reading of the charge, the President left the committee meeting and Provost Kimball opened the floor to questions about the task before them. The first question was from an Education faculty member who had been at the institution for 3 years. "Does this mean that we are going to change the mission of the institution?" Not being one to avoid a question, Provost Kimball replied, "That's one option on the table. The world of higher education is changing and we have to change with it in order to remain competitive. As you all know, the budget has been extremely tight over the last few years and we have to retain our enrollment to have the income stream necessary to run the institution."

Theory to Practice

Provost Kimball had recently read an article by March (1981) that helped her put theory behind her assumptions and practices regarding change. In five footnotes March discussed change in complex organizations such as Center City:

Footnote 1: Organizations are continually changing, routinely, easily, and responsively, but change within them cannot ordinarily be arbitrarily controlled. Organizations rarely do exactly what they are told to do.

Footnote 2: Changes in organizations depend on a few stable processes. Theories of change emphasize either the stability of the processes or the changes they produce, but a serious understanding of organizations requires attention to both.

Footnote 3: Theories of change in organizations are primarily different ways of describing theories of action in organizations, not different theories. Most changes in organizations reflect simple responses to demographic, economic, social, and political forces.

Footnote 4: Although organizational response to environmental events is broadly adaptive and mostly routine, the response takes place in a confusing world. As a result, prosaic processes sometimes have surprising outcomes.

Footnote 5: Adaptation to a changing environment involves an interplay of rationality and foolishness. Organizational foolishness is not maintained as a conscious strategy, but is embedded in such familiar organizational anomalies as slack, managerial incentives, symbolic action, ambiguity, and loose coupling. (March, 1981, p. 563)

Keeping March's footnotes in mind, Kimball asked the committee to identify several stable processes in the organization. The processes identified included

- The presence of several high quality academic programs (e.g., physical therapy, psychology, accounting, electrical engineering) with historically robust enrollments.
- The support of the local community for academic and nonacademic programs.
- A faculty and staff where the average tenure at the college was 13 and 15 years respectively.
- The presence of a president whose tenure was longer than the national average.

During the course of the identification of stable processes, Joe Mazel noted that a stable though unsettling process was the existence of a Board of Trustees whose ambitions for the institution were out of step with the college's traditional mission to serve underrepresented populations. Because she wanted to be inclusive, Provost Kimball added this process to the list and encouraged the identification of both negative and positive stable processes.

Questions to Consider
- How can stable though negative institutional processes act as catalysts for change?
- How does stability simultaneously enable and constrain change?
- What managerial tools exist that executive administrators can use to effect change?
- What are the limits of change within a college or university?

Following the identification of stable processes, Kimball asked the committee members to identify demographic, economic, social, and political forces requiring change on the part of the institution. Several of the forces identified included:

- Shifting demographics of students away from the East Coast states from which the College traditionally drew students. The Director of Admissions, a member of the committee, was particularly helpful in identifying this trend.
- The decreased enrollment of men was identified as a trend that would particularly impact engineering, math, and sciences programs.
- The shift from higher education being viewed as a public good to a private good. As a public institution, Center City could not expect to obtain the funding from the state government that it had in past years.

- The election of a governor, expected to serve two terms, who had voiced his opposition to state funding for out-of-state students.

The processes and forces identified would serve as internal and external environmental scans upon which they could build their change processes.

Questions to Consider

- What are the consequences of decreased institutional slack in the face of budget constraints?
- How do loose and intermittent connections between and among academic units affect organizational change efforts?
- How does ambiguity affect decision making?
- How can negative trends be turned into positive opportunities?

Semester-Long Committee Meetings

After several meetings of the Strategic Planning Committee, it became clear that the committee was not working. Dr. Royce rejected every suggestion made, regardless of how benign or innovative. Kimball decided that she must make the difficult decision to ask Royce to leave the committee. She was hoping that a change in the participants stream would yield different results regarding strategic change. Although Royce was furious about being asked to leave the committee, she looked at the change in participation as a way to use her influence as a dean to resist the mission change. She understood that involvement on the committee meant some level of agreement with the president and provost's plans.

In addition to changing the participants, Kimball decided, based on the ideas expressed in the garbage can model of decision making, to also change the solutions stream. If she introduced a new person with new ideas, new and different solutions would present themselves. With Royce, the only solution was to keep the historic mission of the institution. Kimball was interested in expanding, not contracting, the options.

Questions to Consider

- How does changing the mix of participants after the dynamic of a committee?
- What solutions may be attached to a different dean or community member than Royce?
- What are some of the ramifications of the provost asking a dean to resign from a committee?
- Could adjustments in the other streams be made in lieu of changing the participants stream?

Strategic Choices

After several additional months of meetings, it was clear to Kimball that the mission of the college was not going to change. Mazel, on the committee, and Royce, off the committee, had built a formidable constituency and resisted any changes in the profile of students admitted to the college. Even the director of admissions, a member of the committee, admitted that increasing the admissions criteria would be a difficult task in today's recruiting climate. The strategic planning committee was in favor of the change to Division I status for men's basketball and women's soccer. They agreed that this change would benefit the local community and attract more local students. Kimball was discouraged that the mix of participants had limited vision about the potential of the institution and a new profile of student to be recruited. She felt that she could imagine solutions and choices that were not within the purview of the committee members. The provost decided that she would bide her time and introduce the mission change in subsequent stages of the strategic planning process. Perhaps an appeal to the chair of the Board through the president could effect the change she desired.

New Garbage Cans Form

As Kimball worked with the Strategic Planning Committee, two new developments occurred that threatened to further disrupt the process. Tom Daly, the athletic coach, had confided in the president that a hazing incident had occurred at the start of the basketball season. Daly assured the president that he had explained the laws against hazing and had undertaken hazing awareness sessions with his players, but hazing occurred all the same. This particular incident occurred off campus and was out of his control. When the Strategic Planning Committee heard about the hazing, the support for pursuing Division I status eroded. Committee members felt that hazing would become more prevalent if the change in divisions was achieved. The switch to Division I for the basketball team was off the table.

As if matters could not get worse, President Lincoln announced that he was a finalist for the presidency at his old institution. He was apologetic about breaking his pledge to Provost Kimball to remain at City Central for the first 3 years of her tenure as provost but explained that this was an opportunity he could not pass up. Kimball was amazed to realize how true the garbage can model of decision making was to the situation she faced.

Questions to Consider

- How does the presence of additional "garbage cans" influence the strategic planning process?
- How might a provost disentangle strategic planning from the additional garbage cans forming?
- How are choices enabled and constrained by the presence of additional garbage cans?
- What decisions would you make if you were the provost?

DISCUSSION

Flexibility results when one abandons the idea that organizations have narrowly defined and singular goals. Flexibility, however, comes at a cost. Comfort and the feeling that organizational processes make sense are often lost in the process of more fully understanding the complexity of organizational life. The garbage can model of decision making may help administrators better understand the complexities of organizational functioning but this understanding may leave them longing for the confident feeling that progress on measurable goals is possible. A fuller understanding of the roles of organizational players may be gained but certainty and stability are lost. In the end, the important resource of human energy and effort may be saved and reinvested into the most productive areas of decision making and goal setting.

4

COLLEGIUM

The "Ideal of a University" was a village with its priests. the "Idea of a Modern University" was a town—a one-industry town—with its intellectual oligarchy. "The idea of a Multiuniversity" is a city of infinite variety. (Kerr, 2001, p. 31)

INTRODUCTION

Nowhere is the simultaneous existence of several organizational perspectives within a single institution more apparent than at the intersection of faculty and administration. Faculty adhere predominantly to a collegial model while administrators typically operate as a bureaucracy with aspects of the political and organized anarchy perspectives often obvious. This chapter discusses the collegial perspective, the original model of higher education organizations. Although collegial behavior may exist among administrators such as student affairs professionals, the collegium is most often associated with the faculty. Higher education organizations cannot be understood without knowledge of collegiums, faculty, and their unique culture.

The collegium traces its origins to medieval universities such as Bologna, Oxford, Cambridge, and Paris. The faculty tradition started in early universities where teaching guilds or student nations were organized in 12th-century Europe (Rosser, 2003).

> The guilds or nations were voluntary associations of scholars and students who shared a common ethnic or regional identity and a common vernacular language. In the Southern European tradition of Bologna, Italy, universities were formed as students' *collegia* (Haskins, 1984). The student collegia were associations of foreign apprentice-scholars or guilds of students who wanted instruction.... In ... the Northern European tradition of Paris, France, guilds of faculty members came together and formed a university or institution. Renowned faculty members from specialized disciplines began to attract large numbers of students. (Rosser, 2003, p. 4)

Table 4.1 Coexisting Bureaucratic and Collegial Aspects of Higher Education

Organizational Element	Collegium	Bureaucracy
Structure	Fluid	Rigid and stable
Authority	Expert, decentralized, emanates from the discipline and expertise	Legitimate, centralized, emanates from the position
Goals	Ambiguous, changing, and contested	Unified
Relationships	Autonomous	Inter-related to others
Purpose	Teaching, research, and service	Achieve organizational goals and maintain standards of performance
Institutional purposes	Primary	Secondary
Context	Aligned or seek alignment with national and international communities	Aligned or seek alignment with local communities
Coupling with other departments	Independent	Loose and inter-dependent
Change	Change adverse	Use change as a way to achieve institutional goals
Long range	Tenured	Non-tenured
Measures of effectiveness	Measurable product for teaching, research, and service difficult to achieve	Demand measurable product

(Adapted from Alpert, 1985 and Birnbaum, 1991)

Several characteristics of current academic life that evolved from the medieval guild structure and persist today include peer review, faculty control of the curriculum, and academic freedom. The longevity of the collegial structure of higher education institutions means that colleges and universities have one of the longest lasting organizational structures in the world.

Multiple organizational perspectives often occur simultaneously within the same college or university. Although several combinations are possible, the most common is the collegium and bureaucracy (see Table 4.1). This unique feature of higher education institutions accounts for the complexity of the organizational structures in colleges and universities and the multiple ways of operating within the same institution.

SOCIOLOGY AS A FOUNDATION FOR THE COLLEGIAL PERSPECTIVE

Sociology provides a useful lens through which to view faculty guilds and their evolved structure, the collegium (Childers, 1981). In sociology, the group, society, and community are the units of analysis and interest. This group emphasis is expressed in the collegium through emphasis on peer review, professorial authority, self-governance, and the community of scholars. In a larger sense, societal institutions (e.g., governments) and

Table 4.2 Strengths and Weaknesses of the Sociological Theoretical Perspective

Strengths	Weaknesses
Conveys insights about community building.	Over-emphasizes the importance of group characteristics.
Builds understanding about roles and responsibilities within a society.	May exclude societal members who hold different values than the dominant worldview.
Provides vigorous grounding for the purpose of higher education institutions with a society.	Introduces controversy as competing expectations and demands on higher education as a system are revealed.
Contains a powerful analysis for how cohort characteristics inform group and individual behavior.	May privilege group characteristics over individual ones.
The formidable community within collegiums provides history (i.e., saga) about the institution's identity, values, and standards.	Strong collegiums are resistant to influence by the external environment, potentially leading to isolation and missed cues.

goals (e.g., equality) are central to the mission and purposes of higher education institutions. The assumptions from the sociological perspective that relate to higher education organizations include:

- Social movements have historically been closely linked to higher education through activism, access initiatives, and social change.
- Human rights movements have a profound impact on the mission and purposes of higher education.
- Analysis of higher education from a sociological perspective speaks to social mobility, human rights, equity, and justice.
- Higher education is closely related to socialization, societal transformation, class mobility, social change, and collective advancement. (Clark, 2007; Meyer, Ramirez, Frank, & Schofer, 2007)

As with any theoretical foundation, there are strengths and weaknesses to this foundational perspective (see Table 4.2).

METAPHOR

Whether describing chairs drawn in a circle during class discussion, the shape of a table for contract negotiations, or the configuration of an organizational structure with "first among equals" leadership, the circle conveys collegiality, cooperation, and equality. The metaphor of a circle most aptly describes the spirit of collaboration at the heart of the collegial perspective. In addition to conveying equality and collegiality, the circle metaphor further expresses the structural configuration of collegiums. The structure is non-hierarchical to depict peer rather than authority relationships as the valued means of interaction and association. This flat structure with its absence of levels exists in marked contrast to the bureaucratic hierarchy in which administrators work.

STRUCTURE

Collegiums have a flat, circular structure and are above all characterized by their lack of hierarchical structure. With the elements (e.g., leadership, information flow, power) arranged in a flat structure lacking the levels and differentiated authority of hierarchy, this model may confound those who are unfamiliar with it. Members (primarily faculty) of collegiums lack close supervision; they are autonomous and independent; and they function in a structure that has variable power independent, to a large extent, from position. The dependence on expert power and absence of positional authority can be particularly disconcerting to trustees and administrators without experience as faculty. With department and program first-among-equal leaders who have variable and diffuse power and authority, one may be hard pressed to determine who is in charge.

FACULTY CULTURE

Burton Clark (1963) described the values, attitudes, and behavior of American higher education faculty members as a culture. He viewed faculty culture as a formidable force that significantly shapes higher education. Faculty culture can complement and clash with administrative culture due to dissimilar underlying assumptions. Where administrators (even those who began their academic careers as faculty) value efficiency, decisiveness, and expedience, faculty prefer thorough explication of a topic, consideration of long-term implications, and adherence to tradition.

The strength of faculty culture is shaped by, among other characteristics, institutional size, type (e.g., public, private; single sex, coed), and academic discipline. Like most cultural forms, faculty culture is difficult to understand by those outside its ranks.

> The cultures of academic men [sic], like other subcultures, are often subtle and complex. Faculty cultures have many segments, and only a few aspects can be caught in any one net, no matter how fine the webbing of the net nor how large its size. Among its many parts, a faculty sub-culture may include political values, economic attitudes, a definition of the status of academic[s] ... in society ... orientations toward work, the faculties' definitions of crucial tasks, [and] their work identities. (Clark, 1963, p. 40)

Disciplinary Orientation

Although collegium structures are flat, a hierarchy of disciplines is built into faculty culture. "Certain fields have been defined historically as areas of pure, disinterested study (the liberal arts), while other fields are defined as areas of application of the ideas generated in the 'basic disciplines'" (Clark, 1963, p. 42). A vestige of past prejudice against so-called women's disciplines, fields with practical application from other disciplines, academic majors represent the approximate ranking of this order. Some disciplines (e.g., physics, philosophy) are viewed as theoretically "pure," while others (e.g., education, nursing, business administration) are "applied." These distinctions remain in attitudes toward the liberal arts versus professional disciplines: "The distinction between the pure and the applied often bitterly divides a faculty" (Clark, 1963, p. 42).

The hierarchy of the disciplines dates back to the original seven liberal arts, divided into a *trivium* of grammar, logic, and rhetoric and *quadrivium* of arithmetic, geometry, astronomy, and music (Brubacher, 1990, p. 78). These original, highly respected academic subjects have evolved into different configurations, but the principle of greater and lesser valued disciplines remains. This early rank ordering of disciplines currently defines salary differences among faculty, the earning power of different majors, and value of scientific and theoretical developments. Lest one think that Clark's pure versus applied schema describes an outmoded concept, a glance at salary differences between arts and sciences and education faculty may illustrate the persistence of this tradition.

Loyalty to the College: Cosmopolitans and Locals

Academic specialization and loyalty to one's discipline is another key characteristic of faculty culture (Clark, 1963). Clark, working from earlier ideas about latent roles in organizations outlined by sociologist Alvin Gouldner (1957, 1958), discussed two types of faculty, cosmopolitans and locals, as a way to describe the discipline versus institutional loyalty of faculty.

Cosmopolitans

Faculty who are cosmopolitans shape their professional identity in the context of their national or international disciplinary communities. They are more loyal to their discipline (e.g., biology, political science) than to the institution that employs them. According to Clark's conception, cosmopolitans often lack the time or interest to be involved in campus administrative and political activities. These faculty focus their professional energies outside the institution through national and international allegiances and activities, particularly research. Clark (1963) described cosmopolitans as

> low on loyalty to the college, highly committed to specialized skills, and oriented to an outer reference group. What counts for the Cosmopolitan is the work and opinion of a professional or disciplinary peers, who ordinarily are in other places; when the better professional opportunity appears … [the cosmopolitan] is gone … an itinerant expert. (p. 41)

Cosmopolitans are often researchers, frequently well known and lauded in national and international settings but perhaps unknown on their home campuses. Their teaching duties are often minimal because they are "bought out" of classes through research grants. Their interest lies in research and scholarship more than in teaching and service (Clark, 1963). Energies regarding service are directed toward their disciplinary professional associations and organizations.

Locals

Faculty who are less involved in their discipline's professional communities, more involved on campus, and focused internally are called locals. Locals are first and foremost loyal to their institution. They are "low on commitment to specialized skills, and [use] a group within the college as a point of reference" (Clark, 1963, p. 41). They serve on institutional committees, are involved in administrative matters, and keep their focus on students and institutional politics. Their closest colleagues are on the immediate campus. Locals put more emphasis on teaching and service than research (Clark, 1963).

Institutional type is the most significant determinant of whether a faculty member is a local or cosmopolitan. Large research universities are less inclined to hire locals;

community colleges are less interested in the activities of a cosmopolitan. In addition to institutional type as a determinant of institutional versus disciplinary involvement, the characteristics of faculty can be viewed along a continuum. Regardless of whether they see themselves more as locals or cosmopolitans, faculty are fiercely loyal to their academic disciplines. The focus of their life's work, expertise, research reputation, and professional identity are intimately tied to the discipline to which they committed at a young age. The focus of their lives is as a local or cosmopolitan. This tight connection to their discipline creates one of the most difficult aspects of higher education administration and organizational management. Tenure and disciplinary allegiance tie faculty to an academic department. They neither want nor are qualified to teach subjects in a different department. A history professor would be hard pressed to teach English. An engineering professor can rarely teach philosophy. This close identification with their discipline results in an inflexible structure in which faculty may be permanently assigned (i.e., tenured) to departments though they teach insufficient numbers of students to meet course enrollment targets. Academic administrators are left with the task of balancing major institutional resources, faculty time, expertise, and effort, within an inflexible structure.

Current View of Cosmopolitans and Locals

Today, faculty members are not easily separated into locals and cosmopolitans (Martin, Manning, & Ramaley, 2001). The advent of the Internet and immediate communication through e-mail, listservs, and webpages has significantly changed the cosmopolitan–local dynamic. Given the global reach afforded by technology, the on-campus pressures to generate research dollars, and the relationship between campus decision making and academic life, few, if any faculty, are true locals. The information explosion and immediate, easy access to knowledge are pushing academic majors and disciplines to change rapidly. All faculty members, whether cosmopolitan or local, must remain up-to-date regarding their disciplines through engagement with national and international communities of colleagues. The internationalization and globalization of higher education means that even faculty inclined to stay close to home have contact with students, faculty, and administrators in other institutions and countries. E-mail and technologies such as social networking blur the local–cosmopolitan continuum; all can now adopt the habits of a cosmopolitan. Similarly, those inclined to be cosmopolitans, particularly at senior faculty ranks, are taking on the concerns of locals. Financial pressures, threats to tenure and academic freedom, and the encroachment of academic capitalism (e.g., corporate-style practices) require resilient faculty involvement in campus decision making, strategic planning, and policy setting (Rhoades & Slaughter, 2004; Tierney, 2006). Senior faculty, who are traditionally rewarded for their research productivity, are increasingly involved in local campus governance and politics as a means to articulate the importance of the faculty role and values of academic culture (Clark, 1980).

MAJOR CONCEPTS, CHARACTERISTICS, AND PRINCIPLES

Similar to other organizational perspectives, collegiums have unique characteristics including faculty rank and expert power; circular communication patterns; leadership as first among equals; faculty socialization; and academic freedom, tenure, peer review, and self-governance.

Faculty Rank and Expert Power

There are many titles for the various faculty positions (e.g., adjunct, clinical, research), but there are only three possible ranks: assistant, associate, and full professor. (The emeritus/a rank is assigned only upon retirement.) Faculty responsibilities (i.e., teaching, research, and service) within these ranks are nearly indistinguishable. The work of professors across the ranks is similar as they conduct research, teach, and serve on institutional committees. This flat hierarchy contrasts sharply with bureaucratic structures where those at higher levels (e.g., vice presidents) rarely interact with lower level administrators (e.g., residence directors). In the absence of a role and power structure based on position within a hierarchy, prestige among faculty in higher education institutions is based on disciplinary expertise. For example, junior faculty colleagues (e.g., assistant professors) with robust reputations and active research dollar generation may wield more power than senior faculty (e.g., associate or full professors) with weak or nonexistent professional and research reputations.

Because power in collegiums depends on expert and professional knowledge, the organizational characteristics of this perspective can be difficult to ascertain or predict. Because expertise and professional knowledge are valued, faculty exercise their power in several ways. They are adamant about control of the curriculum. They believe that decision making in curricular and academic matters rests on a tradition of expert authority, authority that only faculty possess. Expert power among faculty is the source of faculty authority to challenge executives (e.g., presidents) with votes of no confidence.

While power and authority are contextual for all organizational perspectives, this is particularly the case for collegiums. A faculty member's power in a particular circumstance may fail to carry over to a different setting. For example, power amassed from work on a curriculum review committee may not hold sway during a student discipline hearing. Faculty who feel their power is secure may find their efforts thwarted in a situation where their expertise is neither wanted nor respected. This variable power dynamic creates an ever-changing situation for administrators and faculty. It is extremely difficult to predict or shape the outcome of a committee's deliberation, faculty senate vote, or policy review due to the dynamic and complex power structure within higher education institutions. This power dynamic is at the heart of observations of organizational theorists who stress that the political perspective provides significant explanatory power for higher education organizations (Baldridge et al., 1978).

Circular Communication and Consensus Decision Making

Similar to power and authority structures, communication patterns in collegiums are also flat and variable. Communication proceeds in a circular manner as topics are dissected and analyzed to a greater extent than in organizational perspectives with efficiency as a core operating assumption. A seemingly inconsequential topic can gain substantial symbolic momentum during a faculty senate meeting as faculty use their discipline-honed skills of analysis and critique. Informal communication plays an important role as personal contacts, long-standing collegial relationships, and history affect communication patterns.

Nowhere is the circular and protracted pattern of communication in collegiums more evident than during decision making. Faculty decision making involves "participation, consensus, professional expertise and competency" (Childers, 1981, p. 26). Decisions predominantly occur through democratic (e.g., majority vote) processes. These time consuming practices, often frustrating for people who are not faculty, entail lengthy and protracted discussion that may or may not result in an outcome. Communication can flow in various directions without a discernible central focus or stopping point. The purpose of the thorough discussion is for each individual to share an interpretation of the issue with the goal of swaying others to a particular way of thinking. This process often results in interesting combinations and collaborations for a more informed, relevant decision. At other times, it results in the metaphorical horse created by a committee—a camel. In the majority of circumstances, a loose consensus results (Clark, 1963). The extended and circular communication style of collegiums is further complicated by the fluid participation of faculty (Cohen & March, 1986). Meeting attendance is neither mandatory nor, for many, central to their work at the institution. This means that the faculty present for a final vote may be different from those attending preliminary meetings and discussions. Fundamental questions may be rehashed as new participants are updated. While many, particularly administrators, may find the decision-making process in collegiums tortuous, Birnbaum (1991) argues that this method is effective over time. The time-consuming nature of decision making by faculty can prevent overly ambitious (and potentially transient) presidents and provosts from making decisions that have short-term positive effects but disastrous long-term consequences.

The value placed on consensus is a stark point of difference between collegiums and other organizational perspectives. Top-down style is vilified in collegiums. Presidents are well advised to consult with faculty or their elected representatives in faculty governance on major decisions. This is particularly important regarding curriculum decisions (Birnbaum, 1992). Faculty believe that sound decision making requires the exercise of their professional knowledge, their knowledge of institutional traditions, and opinions about what is best for the institution.

Leadership as First Among Equals

Each organizational perspective summarized in this book has a particular style of leadership that is used and valued in that approach. In collegiums, leadership as first among equals is the preferred style. "The basic idea of the collegial leader is less to command than to listen, less to lead then to gather expert judgments, less to manage than to facilitate, less to order than to persuade and negotiate" (Baldridge et al., 1978, p. 45). Leaders who take a first among equals role gain respect through attending, building consensus, and creating compromise. While their power comes from the professional expertise they wield in the academic arena, their success as a leader is based on proficient knowledge of faculty culture and processes. Emanating from the values embodied in collegiality, leaders in collegiums know they are performing a service to their professional community. Leadership selection (from department chairs to faculty senate presidents) is generally accomplished through faculty vote or designation. Though it does happen in some types of institutions and in certain circumstances, administrative selection is to be avoided for faculty appointments. In fact, the designee's colleagues may view with suspicion leaders who have been appointed by executive administrators.

Faculty Socialization

An important aspect of faculty culture is the socialization of new members. Clark (1963) claimed that faculty are socialized through

Table 4.3   Factors Related to New Faculty Socialization

Low occupational satisfaction.

Worries about succeeding.

Lack of familiarity with institutional operation including governance and informal structures.

Isolation.

Ambiguous measures of success.

Competition among department colleagues.

Department politics.

Imposter syndrome.

Absence of junior colleagues.

Lack of time to adjust to a new community.

Concern about tenure.

recruitment, in which the college recruits for the points of view seen as appropriate for its character; *interpersonal socialization* [emphasis in original], in which the demands, pressures, and rewards of the job induce the man [sic] to assume a point of view. (p. 46)

Whitt (1993a) stated that new faculty members learn norms, values, acceptable standards of behavior, and other pertinent organization practices during socialization. Faculty socialization begins in the doctoral program, prior to any commitment to the employing institution. This early disciplinary socialization explains the attachment to the academic discipline (cosmopolitans) over the institution (locals).

In addition to becoming oriented to the academic department, new faculty members must become socialized to the institution. They are exposed to their colleagues' and students' expectations, the idiosyncrasies of academic and administrative structure and process, and the history and tradition of the newly acquired institution (Whitt, 1993a). This socialization to the faculty role is fraught with stress and uncertainty. Because the cultural assumptions of both the faculty and institutional culture are implied for the insiders, conversation about values and norms rarely occurs; the norms are rarely written down. Whitt (1993a) (see Table 4.3) presents a list of new faculty experiences that can result in culture shock, disappointment, and disillusionment if the new member is not adequately guided through the socialization period.

Regardless of the difficult adjustment and socialization issues that accompany the faculty role, there are significant benefits to faculty life for individuals and institutions. Faculty independence allows them to pursue research agendas without interference. The collegial culture allows for collaboration on research, teaching, and service. The professional expertise of faculty enhances the institution's reputation through service, consultations, membership on community boards, and other opportunities within the region and community.

Academic Freedom

In the *1940 Statement of Principles on Academic Freedom and Tenure*, the definitive statement on academic freedom, the American Association of University Professors (AAUP) asserts:

1. Teachers are entitled to full freedom in research and in the publication of the results, subject to the adequate performance of their other academic duties; but research for pecuniary return should be based upon an understanding with the authorities of the institution.
2. Teachers are entitled to freedom in the classroom in discussing their subject, but they should be careful not to introduce into their teaching controversial matter which has no relation to their subject. (AAUP, 1990, p. 3)

Academic freedom, and its sister concept, tenure, are highly misunderstood. Students, parents, administrators, and, unfortunately, some faculty, believe that the practice of academic freedom means "anything goes" in teaching or research. In fact, as stated above, academic freedom relates to professional expertise within one's discipline. The principle does not give the faculty member latitude to introduce any topic, particularly untested or patently false concepts, into the learning environment. By protecting academic freedom, though imperfectly, tenure in the form of employment for life creates a "protected space" for intellectual pursuits in teaching and research (Kolodny, 2008).

Academic freedom is a tradition established in German research universities. Tenure track professors, graduate teaching assistants, contract and adjunct professors, with degrees of application, possess academic freedom or *Lehrfreiheit*, the "right of the university professor to freedom of inquiry and to freedom of teaching, the right to study and to report on his [sic] findings in an atmosphere of consent" (Rudolph, 1990, p. 412). Students also possess academic freedom or *Lerhrfreiheit*, the "absence of administrative coercion which freed the ... student to roam from university to university, to take what course he chose, live where he [sic] would, and to be free from all those restrictions ... hostile to an atmosphere of dedicated study and research" (Rudolph, 1990, p. 412). Academic freedom as expressed through these two concepts is essential to higher education's community of scholars and marketplace of ideas (Goodman, 1962).

In 1957, the U.S. Supreme Court reinforced the right to academic freedom as expressed by the AAUP. They supported the idea that academic freedom, as an aspect of higher education was essential to a healthy society.

> The essentiality of freedom in the community of American universities is almost self-evident.... To impose any straitjacket upon the intellectual leaders in our colleges and universities would imperil the future of our nation.... Teachers and students must always remain free to inquire, to study and to evaluate, to gain new maturity and understanding; otherwise, our civilization will stagnate and die. (*Sweeney v. New Hampshire*, 1957: 250 as cited in Tierney, 1998, p. 41)

Tenure

Often characterized as job security, tenure is, in actuality, intimately connected to academic freedom. Tenure, which guarantees faculty employment for life within certain conditions, shields faculty from reprisal so they can research and teach without restriction (DeGeorge, 2003; Tierney, 1998). One cannot understand academic freedom without comprehending tenure, its sister concept. Both tenure and academic freedom, embattled features of academic life, are central features of faculty culture and collegiums.

> If a faculty member lacks the freedom to teach unpopular or controversial subjects out of fear of losing her or his position, then the free exchange of ideas is

compromised. Faculty members without tenure will hardly risk pursuing cutting edge or potentially controversial research and publication (if they even have time for research), and they will avoid raising controversial or contentious subjects with their students. Tenure was designed, in large part, to protect academic freedom in research and teaching. (Kolodny, 2008, p. 5 of 7)

The protection tenure affords academic freedom has not always existed in higher education. One can easily identify examples of faculty who were fired or threatened with sanctions and reprisals for a variety of perceived transgressions: disagreeing with administrators, teaching unpopular or controversial subjects, conducting research at odds with the values of the institution, or tangling with trustees. Higher education history is peppered with cases of faculty members being fired due to an unpopular stance on institutional, national, or international matters. The AAUP, establishing tenure as a means to assure academic freedom, published the *Statement of Principles of Academic Freedom and Tenure* in 1940 (AAUP, 1990), a document that remains the pivotal statement on these matters. Seen on a continuum from being an immutable aspect of faculty life to being a relic of a bygone era, tenure generates strong feelings among many people who are associated with higher education. "Legislators do not understand its necessity. Public critics attack tenure for its ability to populate the academy with 'radicals'" (Tierney, 1998, p. 38). The litany of complaints (see Table 4.4) against this long-standing and well-established system is extensive (Chaitt, 2002; Leiser, 1994; Tierney, 1998).

From an organizational perspective, tenure is an expensive practice that limits management options within higher education institutions. The practice reduces budget flexibility and organizational responsiveness; it "rigidifies" positions (Tierney, 1998) by limiting the ability of deans, department chairs, and other administrators to change programs, initiate experimental programs, and move faculty across departments. When a faculty member receives tenure, the decision, unless the faculty member chooses to leave the institution, is an institutional commitment for the length of the faculty member's career. Every tenure decision is a multimillion dollar commitment. This is particularly relevant in light of the 1994 ruling eliminating a mandatory retirement age for faculty. Boards of trustees, state legislatures, parents, students, and other higher education stakeholders determinedly test the continuation of this practice.

Dismissal of a Tenured Faculty Member

Most people within and outside of higher education believe that a tenured faculty member cannot be dismissed. In fact, a joint AAUP and American Association of Colleges statement in the 1973 Commission on Academic Tenure outlines the reasons why a

Table 4.4 Complaints and Criticisms of Tenure

Lack of accountability among tenured faculty.

Enables "deadwood" (i.e., unproductive faculty) to retain their positions.

Allows research to take precedence over teaching.

Can lead to an abuse of faculty power, including unethical conduct toward students.

Limits structural flexibility regarding reassignment of faculty lines out of departments with low enrollment majors.

Prevents the hiring of new faculty in departments that are "tenured in."

tenured faculty member can be released due to "adequate cause." The reasons must include

> (a) demonstrated incompetence or dishonesty in teaching or research, (b) substantial and manifest neglect of duty, and (c) personal conduct which substantially impairs the individual's fulfillment of his institutional responsibilities. (AAC & AAUP as cited in Saltzman, 2008, p. 59)

Tenure can be revoked due to financial exigency, moral turpitude, or incompetence. An institution, through action of the Board of Trustees, must formally declare financial exigency, the institutional equivalent of bankruptcy. The declaration of financial exigency is a last resort for many institutions teetering on the brink of closure. It is an uncommon step that results in serious institutional consequences (e.g., drop in enrollment, loss of faculty and staff). Moral turpitude is defined as the

> kind of behavior which goes beyond simply warranting discharge and is so utterly blameworthy as to make it inappropriate to require the offering of a year's teaching or pay. The standard is not that the moral sensibilities of persons in the particular community have been affronted. The standard is behavior that would evoke condemnation by the academic community generally. (AAUP, 1990, p. 7)

Over the years, the limits of moral turpitude have been stretched. This criterion for the revocation of tenure is an extremely difficult test to meet. Many assume that the incompetence criterion for revoking tenure entails ineffective classroom teaching, advising, and research. Lack of skill in the classroom is a difficult measure to enact, particularly if it is to result in the radical action of revoking tenure. Today, incompetence has taken on a different hue with mental illness or other maladies being the test for revoking tenure. Teaching ineffectiveness is generally not grounds for removal. An example of a policy regarding this reason for revoking tenure is available from Michigan State University:

> Faculty members may be found to be incompetent if ... their performance is judged to be substantially below their relevant unit's(s') standards and criteria for acceptable faculty performance.... Dismissal of faculty members for incompetence is an extreme remedy, and other avenues, including the disciplinary procedures ... should be carefully considered as possible alternatives to correct unacceptable performance. Colleagues in departments and schools play a primary role in determining if individuals are competent to serve as faculty members.... Units (and especially the department chair) have primary responsibility to identify those rare cases where faculty members belonging to their unit are no longer competent to perform their duties at an acceptable level. (Michigan State University, 2010, p. 43)

Tenured faculty can be fired if their department or program is eliminated, although the AAUP recommends that every effort be made to relocate faculty members to another suitable department or program. Firing a tenured professor need not be the only recourse for a higher education institution regarding an underperforming faculty member. The AAUP has several possible sanctions that it recommends including a reprimand (e.g., a letter in the employee's personnel file), suspension without pay, demotion, or revocation of the faculty member's tenure.

A significant challenge to tenure and the traditional responsibilities as filled by full-time, tenured or tenure-track professors is the shift toward hiring part-time and adjunct faculty (Kezar, Lester, & Anderson, 2006). In 1975, part-time faculty composed 30.2% of the total faculty ranks. In 2007, this group of faculty composed 50.3% of the faculty across all institutional types. During the same time period, full-time tenured and tenure track faculty decreased in inverse proportion: 1975, 56.8% and 2007, 31.2% (AAUP, 2007). When fewer faculty members on any campus enjoy the protections of tenure, then academic freedom is imperiled (Kolodny, 2008). In addition to the threat to academic freedom, the prevalence of adjunct (or part-time) faculty creates a situation where fewer faculty are available to fulfill institutional service requirements (e.g., committee work; governance; reappointment, tenure, and promotion review). Adjunct faculty members are contracted to teach, not advise or meet with students outside the classroom. Adjunct faculty, who are called the "indentured servants" of academia (Duncan, 1999), carry heavier teaching loads and are often forced to cobble together several positions to earn a living. The limited faculty time available to students diminishes mentoring and advisement. The decreased hiring of tenured and tenure track faculty and increased reliance on part-time faculty members places full-time and tenured faculty, adjuncts, and students all at a disadvantage.

While the day-to-day autonomy of faculty may lead some to think that these employees are rarely evaluated or supervised, a closer look at the reappointment, promotion, and tenure processes belies this impression. The rigorous review, reappointment, and tenure processes are meant to assure peers and academic administrators that the tenure commitment is warranted, although it is admittedly "front loaded" at the beginning of a faculty member's career. In fact, many probationary faculty do not proceed to the tenure review. Instead, they change careers, are hired at a different faculty rank (e.g., from assistant professor on tenure track to nontenure track lecturer or adjunct), or leave higher education completely.

External review of tenure and promotion dossiers, editorial board appraisal of manuscripts, conference paper evaluation, and expert assessment of grant proposals are part and parcel of faculty life. Whether performed on campus as part of curricular change processes or off campus through journal review processes, peer review permeates faculty culture. This aspect of faculty culture is based on assumptions about disciplinary expertise, including the belief that faculty can only be effectively evaluated by the same or similar discipline peers. Anyone outside this collegial circle (including administrators, students, and trustees) is considered unqualified to pass judgment on the work performed in the context of the discipline. The outsider is unfamiliar with the knowledge bases, theoretical perspectives, disciplinary practices, and ethical considerations of the discipline. In addition to peer review, expert authority, and knowledge underscores another aspect of faculty culture, self-governance.

Self-Governance

Collegiums afford faculty the opportunity to determine policy, review programs, and provide input on institutional matters. These essential institutional activities occur in the context of faculty governance organizations (e.g., faculty senates). Through a variety of possible structural configurations (e.g., town meeting format, representative approach), faculty deliberate and make decisions on curricular affairs, long range planning, and budget considerations, among other institutional matters.

Whether advisory or determinative (Eckel, 2000), faculty cooperate with the administration (and often student and staff organizations) through their governance system to form a system of shared governance "composed of structures and processes, through which faculty, administrators, and other campus constituents make collective institutional decisions" (Eckel, 2000, p. 16). Tradition and desire for participative decision making dictate that faculty be consulted on major decisions undertaken by the administration (Birnbaum, 1992). In addition to the shared decision and policy making that occurs via faculty governance groups, these senates and related organizations enable faculty to exert jurisdiction over the curriculum. Faculty use peer review through the governance system to (a) approve, in the case of new majors, (b) review, in the case of program evaluation, and (c) discontinue academic programs. A variety of administrative and policy decisions may come before a faculty governance group, but it is the curricular deliberations that garner the most attention. Faculty hold fast to their duty to control the curriculum; a responsibility represented in the often heard expression, "the faculty own the curriculum."

STRENGTHS AND WEAKNESSES OF COLLEGIUMS

The collegial perspective contains strengths and weaknesses (see Table 4.5) that add to the complexity and intricacies of higher education institutions.

NEXT STEPS: BRINGING THE THEORY INTO CURRENT USE

The image of colleges and universities invoked in the media is often bucolic, a pastoral environment where faculty contemplate the life of the mind, write impressive tomes, and discourse with students and colleagues. All who work in today's higher education environment know that those images of campus life are far different from the reality. This section offers academic capitalism, as discussed by Rhoades and Slaughter (2004), and

Table 4.5 Strengths and Weaknesses of Collegiums

Strengths	Weaknesses
Provides a structure that enables faculty autonomy while creating disciplinary communities.	The emphasis on academic excellence and disciplinary accolades can breed competition among like-discipline peers.
Facilitates participative decision-making at an institution-wide level.	May result in a division between cosmopolitans who emphasize their research agenda, national and international disciplinary colleagues, and locals who emphasize institution-based activities.
Creates a range of degrees for faculty involvement in institutional planning, decision making, and policy making.	Can lead to disengagement of faculty in institutional affairs.
Allows for an array of academic excellence, both locally at the institution level and globally at the discipline level.	The value placed on extensive discussion and protracted decision making often conflicts with bureaucratic expediency.

the advocacy culture as posited by Bergquist and Pawlak (2008) as updated approaches to the collegial model.

Academic Capitalism

Academic capitalism, the antithesis of the collegial model, is the inclusion of corporate practices (e.g., outsourcing, hiring contingent faculty, corporate style executive compensation, erosion of employee benefits) into higher education.

> Corporate models for operating colleges and universities value short-term profits over long-term investment in education, and they regard students not only as products but also as customers. Professors are commodities to be exploited and traded, and academic administrators are managers whose decisions make shared governance and due process inefficient and unnecessary. (Andrews, 2006, p. 1)

Justified by administrators as ways to cut costs, maximize revenues, and manage tuition increases, many faculty, particularly through activism led by the AAUP, see this trend as an erosion of the principles upon which higher education was founded, particularly education as a public good and higher education as a site for the development of critical and democratic citizens (Aronowitz, 2000; Aronowitz & Giroux, 2000; Bok, 2003). Although academic capitalism is not an organizational theory or perspective in the same vein as those outlined in this text, the critique offered by the approach is an important development closely related to the values and assumptions long held in the collegium perspective. The damaged values include many principles of the collegial perspective: shared governance, faculty control of the curriculum, and consensus style decision making.

Academic capitalism is objectionable because it erodes the belief that higher education and education in general is a public good. As higher education institutions adopt the practices of the corporate world and reject the practices of nonprofits, arguments for higher education as a private good, one that should be paid for solely by the individuals, are strengthened. Given the high cost of higher education and historical struggles to include members from underrepresented groups, the corporate practices of academic capitalism represent a significant threat to academic integrity and access to higher education (Pasque, 2007).

Academic capitalism practices include corporate style salaries of presidents; the adoption of corporate language and mentalities; outsourcing, oftentimes to companies that lack sustainability, fair labor practices, livable wages, and social justice practices; expansion of higher education into income generating auxiliary services (e.g., shopping centers) with weak links to the educational mission; and high visibility athletics as an admissions recruitment tool. As these practices are embraced, universities adopt the goals of capitalism (e.g., profits) rather than those of education (e.g., holistic growth, intellectual engagement). But the most significant threat regarding academic capitalism has been the shift in philosophy regarding decreasing public funding of colleges and universities.

Recent changes in faculty hiring practices strengthen academic capitalism and weaken higher education values. Adjunct, contingent, and nontenure track faculty are increasingly being hired, eroding long held principles of academic freedom, academic excellence, and faculty autonomy. Tenured and tenure-track faculty now represent less than half of all faculty members on colleges campuses. While these faculty colleagues bring significant expertise to higher education, the provision of short-term contracts in exchange for their services; their necessary lack of involvement in student advising, faculty governance, and other campus service-oriented activities; and inadequate pay for their labor threatens the collegial foundations of higher education.

In addition to the corporate revenue generating practices and industry-style approaches, a significant threat to traditional collegial values concerns intellectual property rights. Academic capitalism in the new economy is not just a matter of institutions seeking to commercialize and capitalize on the intellectual products of individual faculty, it also involves bringing new actors (less autonomous adjunct faculty and professional staff) into the process by which instruction is developed and delivered (Rhoades & Slaughter, 2004). The curriculum, long the purview of the faculty, is increasingly "managed" by professionals outside the faculty. Whether through distance and online learning approaches, centers for teaching and learning staffed by nonfaculty professionals, or syllabi developed for piecemeal delivery, faculty work is increasingly homogenized and standardized. Intellectual products are being packaged with the goal of creating marketable and revenue-generating products. Through this process, the intellectual property rights and professional standing of faculty are eroding.

If one contrasts the values of the collegium with those of academic capitalism, a clash of cultures is obvious. The collegium values the life of the mind, academic capitalism values the generation of capital. Where the collegium emphasizes the acquisition of social and cultural capital, academic capitalism stresses the acquisition of wealth. Academia has a long history of skilled, intelligent people rejecting the goals of capitalism for altruistic goals and a different way of life. Academic capitalism thwarts those goals.

Advocacy Culture

Advocacy culture, as conceived by Berquist and Pawlak (2008), is a significant means to combat academic capitalism. This type of higher education culture is one of the six proposed by Berquist and Pawlak as a means to understand the unique environments of colleges and universities. The other five cultures are collegial, managerial, developmental, virtual, and tangible. Bergquist and Pawlak (2008) define advocacy culture as

> A culture that finds meaning primarily in the establishment of equitable and egalitarian policies and procedures for the distribution of resources and benefits in the institution; that values confrontation and fair bargaining among constituencies, primarily management and faculty or staff, who have vested interests that are inherently in opposition; that holds assumptions about the ultimate role of power and the frequent need for outside mediation in a viable academic institution; and that conceives of the institution's enterprise as either the undesirable promulgation of existing (often repressive) social attitudes and structures or the establishment of new and more liberating social attitudes and structures. (p. 111)

Advocacy culture is best represented in the faculty and staff unions. In advocacy culture, the traditional union issues of salary and other personnel issues are accompanied by concerns about curriculum, teaching-learning, tenure, and part-time faculty issues, among others (Berquist & Pawlak, 2008). Academic capitalism threatens the long-standing practices of academic freedom, peer review, self-governance, and curriculum excellence. Although the 1980 Supreme Court decision in *National Labor Relations Board v. Yeshiva University* (444 US 672) dampened the union organizing efforts at private universities, with or without unions, faculty employ the traditions of the advocacy culture to advocate for causes and resist managerial attempts for increased control of the curriculum and other faculty matters. Faculty unions, academic senates, and academic freedom provide room for advocacy and engagement. Proponents of the advocacy culture seek equitable and egalitarian policies and procedures as a goal of advocacy actions. They use collective bargaining as a means to obtain and retain employee considerations, sometimes in opposition to administrative interests. Power struggles typify relations between faculty and administrators with appeals to outside mediation (e.g., labor relations boards) used when necessary. Institutional change is a goal of negotiations and other actions, often through committees or involvement in strategic and institutional planning.

Although associated with faculty unions and collective bargaining, advocacy culture has a longer history than union formation. Academic freedom, the defense of the free exchange of ideas, and the presence of communities of scholars has long endowed faculty with the propensity to advocate. Collective action through student unions and faculty advocacy is a major means to combat the changes, which threaten the long-standing values of higher education. Collaboration with students is a strategy to achieve mutual goals, and faculty frequently march with student activists or support their causes.

CONCLUSIONS

The collegial perspective provides a culturally and tradition-rich approach to higher education organizations. New faculty, students, internal administrators, and external stakeholders cannot hope to understand colleges and universities without being familiar with the values and practices of the collegial perspective. Faculty self-governance, peer review, control of the curriculum, and tenure are aspects of the collegial perspective that are contested terrain in higher education. The introduction of academic capitalism has decreased faculty voice and influence. As multimillion dollar higher education operations grow in complexity and orientation to the student market, the areas where faculty can realistically exert influence decrease.

Questions for Discussion

- How might traditional ideas about academic freedom be incorporated into the current trend toward contingent (e.g., part-time, contract based, adjunct) faculty?
- How does the faculty role change with the blurring of the local–cosmopolitan continuum?
- What might faculty culture look like with fewer tenured faculty among the ranks?
- What changes in faculty governance need to occur to keep pace with the current challenges within higher education?
- How does the collegial model of first among equals correspond with newer leadership models that encourage collaboration, networked relationships, and shared decision making?

Recommended Readings for the Collegial Perspective

Altbach, P. G., Berdahl, R. O., & Gumport, P. J. (Eds.). (2011). *American higher education in the twenty-first century* (3rd ed.). Baltimore, MD: Johns Hopkins University Press.

American Association of University Professors. (1970). *Statement of principles on academic freedom and tenure with 1970 interpretive comments*. Washington, DC: Author. Retrieved from http://www.aaup.org/statements/Redbook/1940stat.htm

American Association of University Professors. (1999). Recommended institutional regulations on academic freedom and tenure. Washington, D.C.: Author. (Original work published 1957) Retrieved from http://www.aaup.org/statements/Redbook/Rbrir.htm

American Association of University Professors. (1999). *Post-tenure review: An AAUP response*. Washington, DC: Author. Retrieved from http://www.aaup.org/statements/Redbook/rbpostn.htm

Armacher, R. C., & Meiners, R. E. (2004). *Faculty towers: Tenure and the structure of higher education*. Oakland, CA: The Independent Institute.

Brown, M. C., Lane, J. E., & Zamani-Gallaher, E. M. (2010). *Organization and governance in higher education* (6th ed.). Boston, MA: Pearson Custom.

Chait, R. (Ed.). (2002). *The questions of tenure*. Cambridge, MA: Harvard University Press.

Clark, B. R. (2008). *On higher education: Selected writings, 1956–2006*. Baltimore, MD: Johns Hopkins University Press.

Hearn, J. C. (2007). Sociological studies of academic departments. In P. J. Gumport (Ed.), *Sociology of higher education: Contributions and their contexts* (pp. 222–265). Baltimore, MD: Johns Hopkins University Press.

Miller, M. T., & Caplow, J. (Eds.). (2003). *Policy and university faculty governance*. Greenwich, CT: Information Age.

Rhoades, G. (2007). The study of the academic profession. In P. J. Gumport (Ed.), *Sociology of higher education: Contributions and their contexts* (pp. 113–146). Baltimore, MD: Johns Hopkins University Press.

Rice, E. (1996). *Making a place for the new American scholar*. Washington, DC: American Association for Higher Education.

Van Note Chism, N., Baldwin, R. G., & Chang, D. A. (Eds.). (2010). *Faculty and faculty issues in universities and colleges* (3rd ed.). Boston, MA: Pearson Custom.

5

CASE

Collegiality and Disciplinary Loyalty in Reappointment, Promotion, and Tenure

Collegiality, peer review, and faculty socialization underscore the processes by which tenure is awarded in higher education. During these fundamental processes of higher education, aspects of faculty culture are readily apparent. The reappointment, promotion, and tenure process is often a time of anxiety for junior faculty, which can reveal the priorities upon which reappointment, tenure, and promotion are based. This chapter applies the concepts shared in chapter 4 to a case of reappointment and tenure in a regional university formerly focused on teacher training.

Each college of a university employs different standards, timelines, and procedures for its reappointment, tenure, and promotion processes. While the specific ways that tenure is awarded vary from institution to institution, the details of an institution's faculty collective bargaining agreements for unionized faculty and institutional faculty handbooks for nonunionized faculty detail the specific processes for any one institution. Differences in the types of materials considered for tenure often differ for schools, colleges, and departments within the same institution. Some types of higher education institutions downplay research in the name of a teaching mission; others accept scholarship in addition to original data-driven research; service may be more important at certain stages of a faculty member's career. Generalizations about reappointment, tenure, and promotion are hard to make but one aspect remains similar across institution type: tenure is a vital issue for faculty. Peer review, a noteworthy aspect of faculty culture, is part and parcel of the tenure process.

When a faculty member is hired "on tenure track" that person is considered "probationary for tenure" (American Association of University Professors, 1968). In the instance provided in the case presented in this chapter, tenure-track faculty members have 5 years (see Figure 5.1) to prepare their tenure and promotion dossier. These faculty usually carry the title of "assistant professor," which changes to "associate professor" if tenure is accompanied by a promotion in rank. The traditional ranks in a college or university are assistant professor (can be tenured or nontenured), associate professor, and full professor. There are a wide variety of additional faculty titles (e.g., research assistant, associate, or full professor; clinical professor; adjunct professor; lecturer; assistant professor without tenure) but, for this discussion, the three traditional ranks for tenure-track professors will be discussed.

TIMELINES AND PREPARATION FOR REAPPOINTMENT AND TENURE

During the probationary period, a junior faculty member will experience reviews for "reappointment." In the example illustrated in Figure 5.1, a faculty member will be hired in year 1 and have 12 to 15 months to submit refereed journal articles, apply for grants, establish a service record, and prepare a dossier for reappointment. In the example outlined in Figure 5.1, the reappointment dossier, a curtailed version of the tenure profile, is submitted in the second year of service. Reappointment papers are reviewed at the department and college/school with the standard of review being "promise" of future achievements in teaching, research, and scholarship. A positive review for reappointment results in several multiple year contract renewals, feedback about the progress being made, and, for the candidate, experience with the review process. Questions asked at both the department and college/school dean level include,

- Has the candidate established a research agenda?
- What progress has the candidate made toward publication?
- What is the quality of the publications?
- Is teaching of sufficient quality?
- What advice can be given to support the faculty member's progress toward tenure?

The probationary faculty member in the case presented here "goes up for tenure" in the fifth year after multiple year contracts and two reappointments. The reappointment and tenure review processes follow similar procedures with an external review process and several additional layers of review added for tenure decisions. The nature of the assessment shifts between reappointment and tenure. For the tenure review, committee members and deans are no longer using the standard of "future promise" in their assessment. Rather, the tenure candidate must present evidence of achievement and quality in the teaching, research, and service.

Peer Review

Prior to engaging in the reappointment, tenure, and promotion processes, faculty members are subjected to various kinds of peer review. Manuscripts for publication are submitted to journals that depend on peer review as a way to decide whether the piece warrants publication. Research grant applications, conference program proposals, and papers for presentation go through a similar peer review process. Colleagues, particularly department chairs, are invited into tenure-track professors' classrooms to assess

1st year	2nd year	3rd year	4th year	5th year	Sabbatical or Job Search
2-year contract upon hire		reappointment 2-year contract		reappointment 2-year contract; tenure review in 5th year	

Figure 5.1 Tenure Probationary Period Example

the quality of teaching and to provide feedback to junior professors. When going up for reappointment or tenure (see the example in Figure 5.2), peers assess the dossier of the tenure candidate and offer their professional judgment on the worthiness of the faculty member's teaching, research, and service.

In addition to the peer review processes of tenure that are internal to the institution, tenure entails an external peer review. Several tenured reviewers, often with full professor rank depending on the candidate's institutional type, are solicited to read samples of the tenure candidate's work and render a judgment. This key step in the process occurs only for tenure decisions and promotion to full professor. Faculty members are selected who are "at arm's length" to the candidate. Former professors, members of the candidate's dissertation committee, personal friends, and research colleagues, among others, are not eligible to serve as external reviewers.

Research and scholarship are the only basis for the external review. The external review is deemed effective if the reviewer is familiar with the candidate's work because the research and scholarship has had an impact on the field. Journal articles and other publications are reviewed to judge their quality. External reviewers do not assess professional work, in other words teaching and service that is internal to the institution. The resulting letters from external reviewers are "redacted" (e.g., any identifying information is removed) and placed in the candidate's tenure dossier. Redaction occurs so the review can be "blind," though not double blind. Reviewers know the identity of

Department Review
Papers are reviewed by department members and votes tendered.

Department Chair Review
The Department Chair writes a commentary summarizing the department faculty members' feedback and votes, which is included in the dossier.

College/School Review Committee
A representative committee of tenured faculty from across the college/school reviews the papers and advises the Dean.

Dean Review
The Dean writes a commentary, which is included in the candidate's papers. The vote from the College/School Review Committee is recorded.

Reappointment reviews stop here

University-Wide Review Committee
A representative committee from various institutional schools and colleges reviews the papers and makes a recommendation to the Provost.

Provost Review
The Provost (or a designee) reviews all tenure papers and makes a determination about the receipt of tenure based on the feedback from the previous levels of review.

Figure 5.2 Hierarchy of Tenure Review (example, for illustration purposes only)

the tenure or promotion candidate but the candidate does not know the identity of the external reviewers.

Some institutions invite the faculty tenure or promotion candidate to suggest a list of names from which the department chair draws external reviewers. Other institutions depend on the department chair's knowledge of the discipline to identify external reviewers. In both cases of tenure and promotion, the department chair manages the external review process. Its success depends on the administrative acumen of the department chair, familiarity with the candidate's discipline, and evenhandedness regarding the process. A department chair with a desire to thwart a candidate's tenure or promotion could manipulate the external review process and attempt to shape the outcome.

The Reappointment and Tenure Review Process

The reappointment and tenure process proceeds through a hierarchical process during which the faculty member's papers are reviewed up a ladder of committees and academic administrators. The number of steps in the process is determined by the size of the institution, its academic and administrative structures, and the specific review processes at the college or University.

The First Level of Review: The Department

The first level of review is by the faculty member's department colleagues. Faculty in the department read the reappointment or tenure papers and render a decision, which is reported to the department chair. Questions posed at this level include:

- Does the candidate have a well-defined and cohesive research agenda?
- Is the candidate's work cutting edge or in keeping with the expectations of the discipline?
- Was the quality of the journals in which the candidate's work is published in keeping with the expectations of the college/school and institution?
- Do the student teaching evaluations reflect the quality of teaching expected in the department and college/school?
- Is the faculty member involved in service at the department, college/school, or university levels?
- What is the involvement of the candidate in the national or international service work within the respective discipline?

The department chair summarizes the vote of the department and writes an evaluation based on department faculty members' feedback and his or her individual assessment of the candidate's progress.

To many candidates—although sometimes fraught with difficulty and political pitfalls—this stage of the process is the most important. Because peer review is central to the reappointment, tenure, and promotion process, those colleagues most familiar with the faculty member's work and discipline are, it is argued, the most qualified to make the assessment. But, familiarity can also breed contempt. Political battles, professional jealousy, and generational differences are among the issues that can emerge at this point in the process. Probationary or junior faculty are advised to get to know senior faculty who will be voting on their reappointment and tenure. Through the 5 to 6 years of probation, junior faculty are advised to tread lightly, avoid strong opinions, and play a political game with the end result of a positive tenure decision by colleagues.

In addition to possible difficult relations among colleagues, the department chair and faculty candidate relationship can be problematic. The department chair is simultaneously the candidate's mentor and assessor. This person has the task of both encouraging the candidate's career and success through the reappointment and tenure processes while balancing the goal of maintaining institutional quality within the department, college or school, and institution. If relations are strained between the chair and probationary faculty member, this balance can be a difficult one to achieve. Questions asked during the department chair review might include:

- Has the candidate met the tenure requirements as conveyed in institutional policies?
- Has the faculty candidate made a significant contribution to the academic program, institution, and discipline?
- Do the external review assessments indicate that the candidate's research and scholarship are in keeping with the ideals of the discipline?
- As indicated by the external reviewers, is the candidate's research known within his or her discipline?

The Second Level of Review: The College Faculty Evaluation Committee

A college/school committee follows the department and dean's evaluation. The committee is composed of tenured faculty who represent different departments within the college or school. Questions asked at this level are similar to those posed at the department level. At each step of the process, the candidate's record is assessed against the criteria set by the institution. Budget considerations, personality conflicts, and differences in disciplinary perspectives are not to be considered in reappointment, promotion, and tenure decisions. Instead, the candidate's record and quality of work produced is the deciding factor.

Often advisory to the dean, these committees represent some of the best aspects of peer review. Large numbers of dossiers are often reviewed, depending on the number of candidates for reappointment, promotion, and tenure. Committee members know that theirs is a once-in-a-lifetime multimillion dollar decision and they take their work seriously. Once a faculty member is tenured, they are, unless they change institutions, colleagues for life. Candidates denied tenure may see their academic careers conclude with the negative review. Positive and negative decisions have serious, long-term consequences.

The Third Level of Review: Dean's Review

Following the college/school committee review, the dean of the college or school makes an assessment. Similarly deemed one of the most important reviews, the dean is familiar with the faculty member's work and academic field. The endorsement or lack of the same at this level has a ripple effect felt throughout the remaining steps in the process. If the review is for reappointment, in some review instances, the hierarchical process often concludes here and does not advance to the institution-wide committee for deliberation and decision. Often faculty who are leaders in their field, such as deans, have a responsibility to shape the quality of their faculty. Questions asked at this stage might include:

- Is the candidate's record meritorious enough to warrant tenure?
- If there are weaknesses in the record, can those be justified in the letter that accompanies the dossier through the remaining steps of the process?
- Does the candidate match the quality of faculty sought in the dean's vision of the college or school?
- Did the candidate receive sufficient support at the department and college or school committee levels to warrant a positive review?
- Does the candidate's record indicate a continuing record of success?

The Fourth Level of Review: Institutional Committee Review

In the case of a tenure or promotion decision, the dean's review is followed by an assessment by an institution-wide committee, usually of the faculty senate or other governing group. This committee contains representatives from the colleges and schools within the institution. Notable at this point in the process, colleagues with less familiarity with the candidate's discipline deliberate on the papers. While institution-wide assessments of quality certainly occur at this level, prior reviews at the department and dean level are crucial to the work at this stage. Without those prior reviews, faculty from disciplines other than the candidate's would be at a loss to judge the quality of a discipline unfamiliar to them. Questions asked at the institutional level may include:

- Does the quality of the candidate's research meet the institutional expectations as set by the faculty?
- How did the candidate's department colleagues assess the dossier? Did they deem it as appropriate within their respective disciplines?
- How does the candidate's quality of work compare with others within the college/school and the institution as a whole?

At the conclusion of the institution-wide committee's deliberation, a vote of the committee is taken and the decision is forwarded to the chief academic officer.

The Fifth Level of Review: Provost Review

The provost or designee accomplishes the final step in the review process. All dossiers for promotion and tenure are reviewed at this level. A daunting task, this is as important a step in the process as all the others. The provost of a college or university sets the tone for academic excellence in an institution. Contrary to popular belief, the provost review is rarely a rubber stamp but is a genuine review of the candidate's papers and the procedures followed to date. Although provosts often delegate the thorough reading of the papers to an associate provost or similarly ranked administrator, the ultimate decision about whether or not to award tenure or promotion rests with the provost. The results of the provost's decision are forwarded to the Board of Trustees (and sometimes the president). Although reversals of decisions can occur at these levels, they are rare and point to political disputes or feelings of no confidence on the part of those reversing the decision.

Summary

The reappointment, promotion, and tenure processes can be a watershed experience in an academic's career. These are moments when one can take stock of a career path; when progress can be assessed and midcourse corrections made. Extensive feedback about the candidate's work is an opportunity to acutely understand the impact (or lack of impact) the faculty member is making on a field. While annual evaluations and subsequent promotions take place, tenure may be the most substantial level of review experienced in a lifetime as an academic.

While the institution is making a commitment to the faculty member, that person is making a long-term, in many cases, lifelong commitment to the college or university. While faculty are certainly free to change jobs and institutions, having tenure often means that the majority of a faculty member's career takes place at one institution. Faculty members with tenure are often reluctant to move to a different institution without a guarantee that their tenured status will continue. One may be inclined to move to an institution with a better reputation and standard of quality, but tenure at these institutions is not always guaranteed. Senior faculty with their academic successes and the rigors of the reappointment, promotion, and tenure processes behind them are often loath to move to an untenured position. While some faculty have given up the privileges of tenure in lieu of alternative arrangements (e.g., short or long range contracts, a position in an institution without the option of tenure), most remain at the institution in which their tenure was granted. As such, tenure can be a "golden handcuff."

THE CASE

Institutional Context

Baker University is a regional institution established in 1954. Founded as a teacher's college, the university has evolved over the years to provide a broad mission. Located 150 miles from the state's flagship institution, Baker has always existed in its shadow. Students denied admission at the flagship but who desire an in-state public education tend to enroll at Baker. The faculty at Baker University fall into the category of "graying." With its aging faculty, Baker has a reputation for a traditional approach to the curriculum. Cutting edge ideas and new theories are for the flagship institution, not Baker. The faculty acknowledge that scholarship and research are important but many received tenure before the institutional values shifted away from teaching and toward research. Few have made the shift with the institution, and instead devote their energies to their students rather than an agenda with research and scholarship at the center.

The executive leadership at Baker has ambitious plans for the institution and readily awaits the retirement of many traditional faculty. They anticipate that the arrival of new faculty will bring novel ideas, theories, and connections to national and international academic colleagues. To achieve this institutional transformation, the provost has pushed his deans to recruit cutting edge scholars, particularly faculty of color and women. Research dollars have been designated to help this effort. While the executive level is committed to institutional transformation from a regional to a world-class institution, financial difficulties continually derail the process. Admissions requirements have been adjusted downward to fill incoming classes of first year students. An ambitious building project including an addition to the gymnasium has been put on hold. Programs and services have been cut. It is widely believed that staff layoffs in the upcoming year are the only solution to the looming fiscal crisis.

List of Characters

Darlene McPhail: Dr. McPhail is a junior faculty member (i.e., assistant professor) in the educational foundations department of the College of Education. Having received her PhD a year prior to being hired at Baker University, Dr. McPhail specializes in critical race theory. Because her scholarship is on the cutting edge of theoretical developments in her field, Dr. McPhail was highly sought after as a candidate for assistant professor positions. She is an up and coming African American scholar with several publications in refereed journals prior to her appointment at Baker University. While she feels substantial support from the department chair and dean since her arrival, Dr. McPhail works in a department that is heavily "tenured in." The colleague closest in age to Dr. McPhail is 20 years her senior and most were tenured 30 years ago. She is the only faculty member with her theoretical expertise, which is a new area for the college.

John Sachs: Dr. Sachs has been the Dean of the College of Education for 3 years. He committed to work at Baker University because he believed in the president's mandate to bring the College of Education in line with contemporary theoretical developments in education. Despite his initial enthusiasm and determination to makeover the College, his 3 years have been fraught with controversy. Because this is Sachs's first position as dean, senior faculty view him as lacking the political acumen to navigate the university environment. His former roles as assistant dean and associate provost provided him with extensive experience in building academic programs and improving curriculum but minimal experience with faculty development, particularly mentoring faculty through the reappointment, promotion, and tenure processes.

Robin Willis: Dr. Willis has served as a department chair for 20 years. As an experienced chair, he has seen no less than 10 junior faculty through the tenure process and three colleagues to full professor promotions. No junior faculty member under his mentorship has failed to achieve tenure. His record is so strong that he gives presentations at American Association of University Professor (AAUP) conferences on tenure, academic freedom, and mentoring junior faculty.

Marge Martin: Dr. Martin is the chairwoman of the Faculty Evaluation Committee of the College of Education. A full professor with nearly 30 years experience at Baker, Dr. Martin is a well-known researcher and scholar in her field. She is an avid supporter of new faculty and believes that senior faculty should do everything in their power to help junior faculty succeed through the reappointment, promotion, and tenure process. Dr. Martin possesses a substantial amount of political capital within the College of Education and the university.

Background for the Case

The case of tenure-track professor, Dr. Darlene McPhail, is typical in the way that it proceeds in a hierarchal manner, contains potential political pitfalls, encompasses conflicting values regarding disciplinary values, and engages several types of peer review.

Professor McPhail's Perspective

Darlene McPhail had aspired to be a university faculty member since high school. At that time, she toyed with the idea of becoming a high school teacher but it was during college that she fell in love with theory and research. She knew that she would someday become a university professor who was well known and respected in her field. An ethnic studies major in college, Dr. McPhail developed a love of critical race theory, an interest that continued throughout her master's and doctoral degree programs in educational foundations. Her major advisor, Gloria Miller, a leading scholar in the area, involved Dr. McPhail in a number of research projects. As a result, Dr. McPhail arrived at Baker University with two published articles and a third in review. For each of these articles, she was the fourth author, following three tenured faculty members.

Year 1

Dr. McPhail eagerly anticipated starting her tenure-track position at Baker University. She was the only junior faculty member in her department, the only person of color, and the only person who teaches critical race theory. Out of the 13 faculty members in her department, only one was familiar with the subject matter, and his knowledge was rudimentary. Dr. McPhail's first year as a professor was hectic. With four new course preparations (as a new professor, she was given one course release), she struggled to get classes prepared and assignments read. She was unable to make any further progress on her research agenda focusing on critical race theory but was confident that the summer would be productive.

Year 2—First Reappointment

Dr. McPhail spent a good amount of time preparing for her first reappointment. She administered and compiled her teaching evaluations, made progress over the summer on two journal articles, and kept good records about her service. Most importantly, she continued her research with her dissertation advisor but not to the degree she would have liked. The distance and adjustment in the advisor/advisee relationship dictated changed circumstances. Although Dr. McPhail did not meet her goal of three published articles in her first 2 years as an assistant professor, she did publish one and the second manuscript was in draft form. Her first article was well received and honored as "Research Article of the Year" by the major professional association in her field.

As she prepared her papers for reappointment, Dr. McPhail was advised to follow the format for tenure dossiers. She closely documented her progress in the areas of teaching, research, and service and felt good about her first 2 years. Her teaching, as evidenced in student evaluations, was excellent. They appreciated her up-to-date engagement techniques and challenging theoretical material. Students reported that her classes were life changing and regularly commented how nice it was to have someone of her caliber at the institution.

For service and in the interest of time, Dr. McPhail only served on one committee. Her dissertation advisor had warned her that service was neither rewarded nor the best use of her time as she pursued tenure. Her committee involvement, therefore, consisted of the Faculty Senate Nominations Committee. This group met once a semester and involved minimal time commitment and negligible political risk. She was pleased to have found a committee that allowed her the time for her research and teaching responsibilities. Given her preparation for the faculty role through her doctoral degree, McPhail was shocked by the results of her first reappointment.

Questions to Consider

- Who decides whether a faculty member is reappointed?
- How do the reappointment and tenure processes differ?
- How can colleague familiarity with the subject matter assist a candidate for reappointment or tenure? How can familiarity disadvantage the candidate?
- What characteristics of faculty culture are evidenced in this case?

Department Chair Willis's Perspective

Chairman Willis is worried. Using his knowledge as a seasoned department chair, he had advised the dean against hiring Darlene McPhail. Because Baker is a regional university in the midst of a budget crisis, the department could not afford to hire a professor with such concentrated expertise and focused research agenda. The department, he had argued, needed generalists; people who could teach across a wide range of areas. Behind closed doors with the Dean, Willis argued that although McPhail's papers were well-written and contained evidence of teaching excellence, she was not fitting in well with her fellow colleagues, did not take her service commitments seriously, and only taught courses within a narrow range of expertise. Her publication record showed some strength but she made the mistake of counting her two prehire publications as progress. She had not heeded his instructions, issued during their meeting to discuss the dossier preparation that only articles since her appointment as an assistant professor could be listed on the dossier.

Department members were split on their vote for reappointment. Chairman Willis's department was a traditional educational foundations department, which covered required classes in history of education, psychological perspectives on education, and philosophy of education. They were cautious and did not allow just anyone teach the educational foundation classes because the faculty member needed a rich background in liberal arts to meet the needs of the department. Dr. McPhail lacked this background and, instead, brought strength in an area that was not valued by the department: critical race theory. In the reappointment vote, half the department felt that Dr. McPhail was making sufficient progress toward tenure and half did not.

Chairwoman Marge Martin's Perspective

Dr. Martin was angry. She believed that Darlene McPhail had more than met the requirements for reappointment. No matter how hard she argued in the Faculty Evaluation Committee meeting, the faculty with traditional faculty views about the primacy of quantitative research, the importance of a broad liberal arts background, and limited awareness of contemporary theories argued back that Dr. McPhail had not made sufficient progress toward tenure. While they saw value in her teaching, this area was not a top priority for the eventual tenure vote; research was the lynchpin. She needed to conduct research; in their minds, what was needed was hard, quantitative analysis of pressing issues in education. While they believed that equity and justice was important, Dr. McPhail's theoretical explorations of critical race theory was not, in their minds, going to change the condition of children, youth, and families in the school systems. Dr. Martin argued that the journal article published in her first year as a professor had won accolades and awards for its theoretical depth and connection to the field. Those arguments were not persuasive.

Questions to Consider

- Of the three categories of teaching, research, and service, which takes precedence in reappointment, tenure, and promotion decisions?
- How did the faculty culture values of peer review, collegiality, and loyalty to one's discipline influence this case?
- What is the role of the department chair in mentoring a junior faculty member through the reappointment, promotion, and tenure processes?
- What political and professional conflicts could potentially arise between the department chair and the faculty candidate?

Year 4—Second Reappointment

Dr. McPhail, having prevailed in her first reappointment vote by a slim margin, was determined to present herself in the best possible light for her second reappointment. She had published two articles with a third in press. This brought her total number of refereed journal articles to five; two published prior to her faculty appointment and three published in her first 4 years as a professor. She knew that many of her department colleagues had not published any articles in the last 10 years so she felt that her progress was above average for the department. Dr. McPhail was not as confident as she would have liked to be about her research agenda. She had failed to obtain any of the eight grants she had applied for. She continued to write about critical race theory despite the urgings of her department chair to broaden her research agenda. Because she received such positive responses from her professional colleagues outside the college, she was reluctant to take his advice.

Dr. McPhail's teaching remained strong and she had a strong following of students who signed up for all her classes, which reached maximum enrollment each semester. McPhail felt that her strong teaching was a double-edged sword. As a former teacher's college, Baker University placed a high priority on teaching excellence. But the time and effort that she put into her teaching kept her from pursuing her research agenda to the degree required for excellence in that area. On the advice of her department chair, Dr. McPhail increased her service. She accepted an invitation from the president's office to join the President's Commission on Lesbian, Gay, Bisexual, and Transgender Issues. Her term on the Senate Nomination Committee had expired so she became involved in the College of Education's Diversity Committee. Despite this increase in service, she followed her plan, based on the advice of her doctoral advisor and mentor, to avoid extending herself with too much service. This was particularly the case because, as the only African American professor in the College of Education, she carried a heavy load of formal and informal advisees, particularly students of color.

Questions to Consider:

- Is Dr. McPhail a "local" or "cosmopolitan" according to Burton Clark's definition?
- What are some of the unique circumstances regarding service and advising for faculty of color?
- What are some of the challenges of balancing teaching, research, and service? How does this balance change across the lifetime of a faculty member's career?
- What is the role of peer review in McPhail's reappointment process?

Dean Sachs's Perspective

Dean Sachs knew of the political battle in the Educational Foundations Department, but trusted that they could work it out. He had his own battles to fight and had little time to resolve disciplinary differences within the departments. The university had passed down a rescission of $1 million to the colleges and schools. This translated into a $250,000 cut for his college. In each of the 3 years of his tenure as dean, he had seen six figure cuts. They were cut to the bone and Sachs could not imagine finding another quarter of a million dollars. Willis and McPhail were going to have to find their own way out of their mess.

Chair Willis's Perspective

Willis was through advocating for Darlene McPhail's success. Despite strong evidence of his success in mentoring junior faculty, she refused to take his advice. She had not broadened her research agenda beyond the critical race theory work and she insisted on joining college and university committees that were, in his mind, tangential to the department's and college's work at the university. He would wait and see what the results of the second reappointment were but he was already thinking through the discussion during which he discouraged Dr. McPhail from pursuing tenure.

Questions to Consider

- What generational and theoretical differences between Willis and McPhail have led to differences in priorities and perspectives?
- What balance must Willis strike between the success of the junior professor and what he sees as the good of the department?
- How does the context of the university influence the emphasis placed on teaching, research, and service?
- If you were Darlene McPhail, what decisions might you make about a research agenda before tenure?

Year 5—Tenure Review

It had been a difficult summer for Darlene McPhail. Shortly before the end of last spring semester, her department chair had a very formal conversation with her. He advised her not to go up for tenure in her fifth year. He presented the evidence of the split department and college Faculty Evaluation Committee votes as indication that her tenure bid would not be successful. She consulted with Marge Martin who no longer chaired the College of Education Faculty Evaluation Committee but had been a strong advocate for Dr. McPhail's success behind the scenes. Marge encouraged her to go up despite the chair's advice but warned her that it would be a tough fight.

Questions to Consider

- What are three options related to faculty rank and academic employment that Dr. McPhail's could potentially pursue?
- If Dr. McPhail were to switch from tenure track to nontenure track, what are some ramifications?
- What legal, union-related, or institutional recourses might Dr. McPhail have?

- What long-term consequences exist for taking legal action, filing a grievance, or pursuing other routes?

Option 1: Cut Her Losses

Despite Marge Martin's encouragement, Darlene McPhail chose not to go up for tenure. She knew the statistics for women of color and tenure and chose not to fight a battle she did not believe she could win. Instead, she depended on her strong reputation as an up and coming scholar in her field and the strong support of her doctoral advisor to pursue other opportunities. After a few months of job-hunting, she was successful at finding an assistant professor, tenure-track position at a large research university. Her new institution specifically set out to recruit a critical race theorist and assured her that she would not face the disciplinary issues she experienced at Baker University. She left at the end of her fifth year at Baker to pursue her new position.

Option 2: File a Grievance

Dr. McPhail never felt comfortable with Willis as chair. He seemed to have his own agenda about what her research should entail and how she should pursue her professional goals. Instead of working closely with Willis, she took advantage of the Faculty Mentoring Program that existed at her university to get independent advice on the reappointment, tenure, and promotion process. Her mentor is a member of the College of Arts and Sciences who is very involved in the faculty union. After numerous conversations with her university mentor and a lawyer, Dr. McPhail filed a grievance. Since grievances can only be based on procedural irregularities, she was struggling to find a rationale for her case.

Option 3: Pursue Tenure without the Support of the Department Chair

Dr. McPhail was confident about her record of teaching, research, and service. She believed that she was on the right track as identified by the president and provost of Baker. Although the department vote might be split or negative, Dr. McPhail felt, after conversations with colleagues outside the College of Education, that she would prevail at the university levels of the review. She went into the tenure process with 10 juried journal articles and three book chapters. Most were coauthored but several were single authored. She had set down roots in the Baker community and was willing to take a chance on tenure. Dr. McPhail believed in the process and the new mission of the institution.

Questions to Consider:

- What are the roles and responsibilities of the Dean in the tenure process?
- How might department dynamics play a part in reappointment, promotion, and tenure?
- How does the racial identity of a faculty candidate influence the reappointment, promotion, and tenure decisions?
- How do budget considerations influence reappointment, tenure, and promotion decisions?

DISCUSSION

Reappointment and tenure may be one of the richest opportunities for the nuances of collegiality, disciplinary loyalty, and faculty culture to be expressed. While most reappointment, promotion, and tenure processes proceed without the difficulties and priority conflicts illustrated in this case, it is not unusual for political and personal clashes to be played out among faculty. The AAUP has a rich collection of guidelines on tenure, self-governance, and collegiality that can inform faculty and administrators on helpful ways to shape reappointment, promotion, and tenure procedures. Solid procedures assuring fairness and equitable procedures can help assure that reappointment, promotion, and tenure procedures are not overly defined by those challenges.

Reappointment, Promotion, and Tenure Resources

American Association of University Professors. (1968). *Statement on faculty workload with interpretive comments*. Washington, DC: Author.

American Association of University Professors. (1990). *Statement of principles on academic freedom and tenure with 1970 interpretive comments*. Washington, DC: Author.

American Association of University Professors. (2009). *Conversion of appointments to the tenure track*. Washington, DC: Author.

Chait, R. P. (Ed.) (2002). *The questions of tenure*. Cambridge, MA: Harvard University Press.

Plater, W. M. (2008, July–August). The twenty-first-century professoriate: We need a new vision if we want to create a positive future for the faculty. *Academe*.

Stanley, C. A. (2006). Coloring the academic landscape: Faculty of color breaking the silence in predominantly white colleges and universities. *American Educational Research Journal, 43*(4), 701–736.

Tierney, W. (1998). Tenure is dead. Long live tenure. In W. Tierney (Ed.), *The responsive university: Restructuring for high performance* (pp. 38–61). Baltimore, MD: Johns Hopkins University Press.

6

POLITICAL

This place is more like a political jungle, alive and screaming, than a rigid, quiet bureaucracy. (Baldridge, 1971b, p. 9)

INTRODUCTION

Regardless of any cultural beliefs about the rationality or serenity of college campuses, higher education history including the social unrest of the 1960s, intense public scrutiny of the 1990s, and economic crisis of the early 21st century shapes these organizations as contested political ground composed of stakeholders, power elites, conflicting priorities, and strategic maneuvering.

The birth of the political perspective in higher education is unmistakably identified with the writings of J. Victor Baldridge from the early 1970s. Baldridge observed that the widely accepted perspectives of bureaucracy and collegiums did not adequately explain university administration or faculty life (1971c): "we see neither the rigid, formal aspects of bureaucracy nor the calm, consensus-directed elements of an academic collegium" (pp. 19–20). The lack of fit in the bureaucratic and collegial perspectives was particularly evident regarding organizational change. Higher education organizational theorists suggested that the political perspective might better explain higher education organizations than other choices available (Baldridge et al., 1978). Although considered a taboo subject, Baldridge opened a realistic discussion of the political nature of higher education including the strengths this perspective brings to an analysis of higher education institutions.

SOCIOLOGY AS A FOUNDATION FOR THE POLITICAL PERSPECTIVE

In any organization, relationships are key to understanding behavior, structure, and interactions. At its basic level, the political perspective is about relationships because this perspective accounts for interactions, connections, and exchanges among people,

67

Table 6.1   Strengths and Weaknesses of the Sociological Theoretical Foundation

Strengths	Weaknesses
Assists administrators and faculty to understand a systems approach to organizations.	Over-explains group behavior while it under-explains individual behavior.
Explains interconnections among different campus groups and constituencies.	Inadequately accounts for organizational structure.
Provides a potent analysis of power.	Views power struggles as a central component of organizational life.
Draws connections among coalitions, interest groups, and power elites.	Places an emphasis on competition at the expense of adequate analysis of cooperation.

organizational levels, and institutional capital. Viewing an organization as an interacting set of relationships embraces the view of leadership advanced by Rost (1993): "*Leadership is an influence relationship among leaders and followers who intend real changes that reflect their mutual purposes*" (p. 102; emphasis in original). In this chapter, the sociological theoretical perspective is used to consider the interacting relationships within higher education institutions. As with any theoretical perspective, the sociological one brings strengths and weaknesses to bear on its use as a point of analysis (see Table 6.1).

METAPHOR

Though apt in many ways, the jungle metaphor, commonly used to describe political organizations, overemphasizes the negative and underemphasizes the positive aspects of the political perspective. If the negative side of political organizations—the power plays, gamesmanship, and deal making—is the primary consideration, political organizations are seen as competitive, treacherous, and suitable only for the most fit. The positive side of the political perspective—the richness of constituent involvement, potential for goal achievement, and possibility of change through policy making—go unremarked when institutions are pictured as environments teaming with danger and unpredictability. Without a view that embraces both the positive and negative aspects of politics in organizations, the negative features of the perspective (e.g., rivalry, backstabbing, and competing goals) overpower the positive features (e.g., attention cues, relationship building, and goal clarification).

Knowledge about colleges and universities as political organizations assists administrators, faculty, and students to achieve their goals in an environment containing conflict, interest groups, and divergent points of view. The ideas presented in this chapter can help administrators, faculty, and students recognize when they already are or are becoming embroiled in a political situation, particularly one they would rather avoid. "The political metaphor encourages us to recognize how and why the organizational actor is a political actor and to understand the political significance of the patterns of meaning" (Morgan, 2006, p. 205). With knowledge about the political perspective, institutional members can choose to participate, take action to cope with the situation, or stay out of the way.

STRUCTURE

Using relationships among individuals as an organizing principle, Morgan (2006) stated, "the political metaphor encourages us to see organizations as loose networks of people with divergent interests who gather together for the sake of expediency" (p. 161). The dynamics and relationships among people are areas where the political perspective is most explanatory and insightful. Coalitions form and dissolve, depending on the issue, task, or conflict; bedfellows are exchanged, subject to the goal; and conflict ebbs and flows with the passage of time and experience.

CHARACTERISTICS OF THE POLITICAL PERSPECTIVE

The political perspective has several characteristics that make this perspective unique among possible higher education organizational choices. These features include conflict as normal, interest groups and coalitions, inactivity prevails, fluid participation, and attention cues. Particularly applicable during times of intense change, a constant situation for higher education institutions, the political perspective enables insights into policymaking, change, and strategy.

Conflict as Normal

From the political perspective, conflict is natural and to be expected in organizations such as higher education institutions that are dynamic and complex (Baldridge, 1971b). Whether explicit or implicit, conflict is always present in organizations. Conflict identifies allies, empowers underrepresented groups, and motivates organizational members. "Conflict may be personal, interpersonal, or between rival groups or coalitions. It may be built into organizational structures, roles, attitudes, and stereotypes or arise over a scarcity of resources" (Morgan, 2006, p. 163). In contrast to perspectives that view conflict as dysfunctional (Childers, 1981), conflict from a political perspective exposes institutional priorities, focuses commitment to the goals, and connects people to goal achievement.

Morgan (2006) borrowed from Thomas (1976, 1977) to discuss five styles of conflict management: collaborating, compromising, accommodating, avoiding, and competing. *Collaborators* seek win-win situations and use this style when learning, integration, and relationship building is necessary to meet a goal. Negotiation is at the heart of collaboration and involves exchanges of favors, services, or future commitment. *Compromise* is an often-used style and involves give and take. Organizational members *accommodate* when they submit or comply. This approach may alleviate the conflict in the short term, but does not prevent it from arising later. Higher education administrators and faculty use *avoidance* when they wait out or ignore conflicts. Attention can be deflected to other priorities in the institution. Over time, the conflict may fade or it may become a lingering and tolerated aspect of organizational life. This approach is useful when the conflict is trivial and one must pick one's battles. *Competing*, because it creates win-lose situations, is to be avoided completely or perhaps used judiciously in higher education settings. This approach has its usefulness during emergencies or circumstances when immediate action is needed but there are always adverse consequences with this approach to managing conflict. Because "conflict arises whenever interests collide" (Morgan, 2006, p. 163), a discussion of interest groups can aid one's understanding of conflict.

Interest Groups and Coalitions

A major characteristic of higher education organizations and systems is the presence of stakeholders. Whether directly associated with the institution (e.g., faculty, alumni, parents) or not (e.g., neighbors, employers, state legislators, government officials), many have an interest in the actions and decisions of colleges and universities. Whether demanding lower tuition, increased teaching of employable skills for corporations, or provision of services to local communities, stakeholders lobby to exert their influence on higher education institutions.

> These groups articulate their interests in many different ways, bringing pressure to bear on the decision-making process from any number of angles, and using power and force whenever it is available and necessary. Once articulated, power and influence go through a complex process until policies are shaped, reshaped, and forged from the competing claims of multiple groups. (Baldridge, 1971a, p. 8)

While coalitions enable those with limited power to increase their influence, these groups can also form among those who already have sufficient positional or institutional power. Closely related to the concept of interest groups, these groups are called power elites. Powerful organizational players can combine and increase their power base by joining forces. When interest groups form among those at the top of the hierarchy (e.g., presidential cabinet members) or those with power (e.g., senior faculty), they become power elites.

While a power elite such as the president's staff is responsible for a wide range of major decisions (Baldridge, 1971b), no one group makes *all* the decisions *all* the time. Instead, several fluid and ever-changing groups determine the direction of college or university life. In higher education, the presence of faculty with professional expertise, student affairs professionals with a strong influence on student life, and trustees with fiduciary and planning responsibilities means that several power elites operate simultaneously. Faculty control the curriculum, the president and vice presidents make key budget decisions, and trustees approve or disapprove the strategic direction of the institution.

Inactivity Prevails

Although the decision-making ability of interest groups and power elites is constrained, disinterest by the majority of organizational members means that the majority of decisions are left to interest groups and power elites. The sentiment, "for most people most of the time ... they allow administrators to run the show" (Baldridge et al., 1978, p. 35), may be more true today than when this statement was first written. Academic and administrative activities have increased significantly with the advent of technology, raised expectations by parents and students, and accountability by state and federal governments. This applies to committee work, governance leadership, and service activities. Whether by preference or circumstance, many members prefer not to be involved, lack the interest to serve on campus-wide groups, are without the power to influence, or do not have access to the decision making processes impacting the organization as a whole. This detached stance is a particular preference of faculty (Baldridge et al., 1978) who see their primary roles as teaching, research, and service. From their point of view, management, decision making, and policy determination are the purviews of administrators. This inactive stance changes when and if the decisions made have a direct impact on or negatively affect faculty activities. In that case, the norms of inactivity shift to the collegial expectation of consultation and discussion.

Fluid Participation

Fluid participation is closely related to the political organization characteristic that inactivity prevails. The political perspective assumes that organizational participants will "move in and out of the decision-making process" (Baldridge et al., 1978, p. 35). Unlike bureaucratic processes that assume fixed job responsibilities and procedures, decision making from a political perspective occurs in fits and starts. If expectations are not met, previously uninvolved actors may suddenly become politically active. Seen from a political perspective, it is not unusual for organizational members to expect their opinion on an issue to be considered; even on an issue previously and thoroughly vetted. Higher education's democratic practices and the tradition of consultation built into faculty culture build expectations concerning access to decision making, the "right" to exercise voice, and a prerogative to intervene at any stage of the process. With fluid participation as an expectation, administrators, faculty leaders, and others must plan for an iterative and prolonged decision-making process. Newer technologies both help and exacerbate fluid participation. Anyone can build websites, send widely distributed e-mails, and write blogs that aid communication. These dynamic and accessible communications enhance democratic processes while simultaneously making the organization more politically sensitive.

Attention Cues

While the shift from inactivity to activism by faculty and students, in particular, often feels seismic, attention cues often foretell when institutional members are moving out of their inactive stance. Discussions about a vote of no confidence in the president, department chair rumblings of dissatisfaction about a dean's behavior, or student protests about campus social justice efforts, there are always advance cues to which politically astute administrators can attend. "Powerful political forces … cause a given issue to emerge from the limbo of on-going problems and certain 'attention cues' force the political community to consider the problem" (Baldridge, 1971c, pp. 190–191). While it may be difficult to accurately predict who will attend to specific goals and when they will do so, administrators are well advised to attend to the early cues that portend political challenges.

Access to information, expectations about consultation about decisions, and ability to exercise voice are examples of privilege held by selected organizational members.

> Privilege increases the odds of having things your own way, of being able to set the agenda in a social situation and determine the rules and standards and how they're applied. Privilege grants the cultural authority to make judgments about others and to have those judgments stick. It allows people to define reality and to have prevailing definitions of reality fit their experience. Privilege means being able to decide who gets taken seriously, who receives attention, who is accountable to whom and for what. (Johnson, 2008, p. 117)

Faculty possess privilege accrued from the double advantage of academic freedom and expert power. Executive leaders possess privilege emanating from their access to information and experience with institutional roles that led them to the positions they hold. Their privilege also arises from the deference dictated by cultural mores given to those occupying upper level positions. Regardless of the dynamic of the privilege, there is no doubt that this force operates in political situations. The political perspective offers insights on why exercising privilege is common, frequently unwise, and often undemocratic.

PROCESSES IN POLITICAL ORGANIZATIONS

Political acumen and expertise by any institutional player requires an understanding of how political organizations work. Knowledge of how power and authority interact and are expressed is particularly essential for faculty and administrators who seek to be politically astute.

Power

Power is a context-specific, relationship-oriented resource used to achieve goals and realize relationships. Power from a political perspective is dynamic, transient, and volatile. Power has been a topic of considerable speculation and discussion over the millennia, giving rise to a thought-provoking collection of quotes (see Table 6.2). If higher education is to be a force for societal transformation, power must be understood and taken into consideration as a means to achieve that goal.

Although personal style and specific situations dictate which kind of power is to be used, understanding the different forms can provide insight about the potential for organizational decisions and processes. Morgan (2006) sketched out various ways power can be expressed in organizations. Adapted for higher education organizations, expressions of power as enacted through various campus offices are outlined in Table 6.3.

Control of scarce resources is a form and source of power (Morgan, 2006). The exercise of this power is particularly effective when the resource, for example, money, is limited. But money is not the only resource and source of power. Positions, administrators' time, and space are resources available for maneuvering and acquiring power. An important resource, particularly in higher education, is knowledge. Although controlling knowledge to gain power is a less potent mechanism with the increased access to

Table 6.2 Memorable Sayings about Power

"The most common way people give up their power is by thinking they don't have any."
Alice Walker

"Knowledge is power. Information is liberating." Kofi Annan

"Power corrupts and absolute power corrupts absolutely." Lord Acton

The *"prince who bases his [sic] power entirely on ... words, finding himself completely without other preparations, comes to ruin."* Niccolo Machiavelli

"A good indignation brings out all one's powers." Ralph Waldo Emerson

"A friend in power is a friend lost." Henry Adams

Table 6.3 Power within Organizations

Autocracy "We'll do it this way."	Traditional presidents' model
Bureaucracy "We're supposed to do it this way."	Financial aid office
Technocracy "It's best to do it this way."	Registrar's office
Codetermination "Let's decide how to do it together."	Career services
Representative democracy "How do your constituents want to do it?"	Faculty senate and faculty unions
Direct democracy "How shall we do it?"	Women's Faculty Caucus

Adapted from Morgan (2006, p. 156)

information available through the Internet, gatekeepers can still gain power by controlling, shaping, or spinning information.

In the volatile climate in which higher education exists, the ability to cope with uncertainty is an important source of power. Postmodern theoretical perspectives such as critical theory, feminism, and critical race theory identify the inevitable uncertainty that exists within and outside higher education institutions. When administrators see uncertainty as opportunity rather than threat, power can increase as that person remains effective in situations where others are not. Institutional and individual reputation and the concomitant increase in power flow if situations fraught with hazards are transformed into new or renewed programs and innovative approaches.

Interpersonal power is a palatable form gained through associations and friendships. This type of power is particularly appropriate for higher education organizations, because few institutions enable lifelong friendships as completely as these organizations. Networks established in colleges and universities have always been traded for power and influence to gain jobs, work connections, and favor. The more influence one has to trade, the more power is gained. Old style associations (e.g., old boy and old girl networks) of the past have recently been supplanted with social media. These newer forms of connecting with friends and others expand people's reach that had been previously limited by time and distance. Asynchronous communication and access to global linkages are dismantling physical and temporal barriers. Ease of communication, links to friends of friends, and global connections have exponentially increased the possibilities of interpersonal alliances from which influence can be gained.

The Interrelationship of Power and Authority

Power and authority, although related concepts, are different. Authority is more formal than power and emanates from one's position (Morgan, 2006). As a result of social approval, tradition, or law, administrators possess authority to act that is defined by the position they occupy. Using authority, administrators, particularly executive leaders, can, among other responsibilities, hire and fire employees, determine budgets, and set goals. Authority is exercised in the influence of supervisors over employees and the

Chair of the Board of Trustees over the president. Although an important concept in organizational structures, higher education institutions and the people within them have significant limits on their authority. The presence of faculty governance structures, student organizations, and informal elements such as charisma and non-positional power means that no one has ultimate or limitless authority. Because the authority and ability to enact decisions is distributed across interest groups, coalitions, and power elites, power from a political perspective is limited and diffuse. Although many people assume that power is located primarily in the upper executive ranks (in other words, authority and positional power are equated), in higher education structures, "power is more diffuse, lodged with professional experts and fragmented into many departments and subdivisions" (Baldridge et al., 1978, p. 44). A college president, provost, or dean may have the authority to enact a decision, but lack the political power to make that change.

Understanding the limitations of authority and dynamics of power can help administrators avoid naïveté about their range of influence and effectiveness. Leaders are not immune from challenges to their authority and power. In addition to the issues that occur as a result of these challenges, power is distributed throughout the organization, even at levels where there is less positional authority.

> Lower level organizational members have, in reality, a great amount of power … in spite of the considerable degree of power possessed by lower level employees, these employees seldom attempt to exercise their power or to resist the instructions of their managers. (Pfeffer, 1991/2005, p. 291)

Employee strikes, faculty "work to rule" action, and student activism are ways that authority can be challenged and power exercised. Students, often erroneously viewed as powerless, express their voice and power through formal student governance organizations, collective action, and informal student activist groups.

Decision Making

Rationality is assumed to be the basis for decision making by those who believe that colleges and universities operate in orderly, methodical ways. From a political perspective, order and rationality are not assumed. Instead, it is assumed that "political constraints can seriously undermine attempts to arrive at rational decisions" (Baldridge et al., 1978, p. 36). Baldridge et al. (1978) devised a political model of decision making that assumed fluidity and complexity. Unlike the linear step-by-step procedures of the rational model, these higher education theorists believed that "*decision making is likely to be diffuse, segmentalized, and decentralized*" (Baldridge et al., 1978, p. 38; emphasis in original). They outlined the why, who, how, and which of decision making including the political controversy, compromises, and bargaining likely to occur within higher education institutions. The following questions can be used to assess successful ways to pursue decision making in a political climate:

1. *Why is a decision being made?* Political forces often bring the problem to someone's attention. Those political forces could be a downward shift in enrollment, the upcoming retirement of key faculty members, a president's retirement, or a host

of other issues. Because momentum and institutional procedures will carry an institution through the day-to-day decisions, it takes political pressure for larger scale decisions and change initiatives to capture the attention of administrators and faculty.

2. *Who should be making the decision?* "The right to make the decision often determines the outcome" (Baldridge et al., 1978, p. 38). Anyone can make a decision but it takes power and authority to implement it.

3. *How do you gain the advice of others?* The political model assumes that leaders will solicit input from colleagues (and foes, in some cases), gain support, and build ownership prior to making a decision. In higher education, this consultation often takes place through strategic planning committees, faculty governance bodies, and unofficial conversations.

4. *Which solutions are realistically available?* A solution may appear to be appropriate but unfeasible given the monetary, human, and time resources available. Some solutions are possible when an event, particularly a crisis, captures attention and makes a previously unpalatable decision inevitable.

The political perspective assumes that controversy, compromise, and bargaining are part of decision making. These are particularly in play when faculty are involved in the decision. Three types of faculty decision-making involvement have been identified: (a) *inactive,* employed primarily by faculty who concentrate their efforts on teaching and research; (b) *power elite,* used by senior faculty with the connections and longevity within the organization to unify other like-minded associates; and (c) *strategic,* initiated by faculty unions or other groups (e.g., college or school faculty groups) within the campus organizational structure (Baldridge et al., 1978). In general, a small group of faculty influences decision making while the majority of organizational members remains inactive and disinterested.

Internal and external stakeholder groups, including students, administrators, alumni, parents, and others, can carve out "spheres of influence" in which they make or influence decisions (Baldridge et al., 1978). In political organizations, it is the practice that groups outside a particular "sphere of influence" refrain from participating in decisions in that area. The character and range of the spheres shift depending on the environment, issue at hand, and type of campus. Administrators make decisions on a community college campus, for example, that would normally be executed by faculty at a liberal arts college. Political decision making depends on timing, finesse, and persistence. Administrators avoid curricular decision making; faculty eschew detailed budget decisions; student opinion is seldom exercised in long-term capital improvements. By establishing relationships, perfecting timing, and cultivating determination, faculty and administrators in political organizations can achieve their institutional purposes despite the inevitable setbacks and challenges.

Strengths and Weaknesses of the Political Perspective

Knowledge of the strengths and weaknesses (see Table 6.4) of the political perspective can assist faculty, students, and administrators involved in higher education to more effectively make decisions, set policy, and avoid undesirable associations.

Table 6.4   Strengths and Weaknesses of the Political Perspective

Strengths	Weaknesses
Provides a powerful analysis for decision making and policy making.	Can highlight divisiveness, competition, and other negative aspects of organizational life.
Clarifies organizational vision, mission, and goals.	Can focus institutional membership on immediate rather than long-term goals.
Provides attention cues for institutional leadership.	Can redirect attention onto tangential organizational goals.
Offers alternatives to the positional view of power and authority.	Can disempower the underrepresented and those with less access to power.
Explains the dynamic of relationships across bureaucratic levels.	Can diminish morale and healthy work environments.
Builds processes for change.	Can concentrate major decision making in the hands of an elite few.

NEXT STEPS: BRINGING THE THEORY INTO CURRENT USE

Critical race theory is suggested as a contemporary application of the political model (DeCuir & Dixson, 2004; Dixson & Rousseau, 2005; Ladson-Billings, 1998; Matsuda, Lawrence, Delgado, & Crenshaw, 1993; Solórzano, Ceja, & Yosso, 2000). This theory, first advanced in the mid-1990s in the legal studies literature, was further articulated in K-12 and higher education settings (Ladson-Billings, 1998; Patton, McEwen, Rendon, & Howard-Hamilton, 2007). The theory takes political, economic, and philosophical contexts of educational settings into consideration.

Critical Race Theory

Derrick Bell, a law professor at Harvard University, first advanced critical race theory (CRT) in his book, *Faces at the Bottom of the Well* (1992). The following principles define the theory, which can be used as a powerful interdisciplinary analysis and critique of the social and political contexts of educational settings.

1. Critical race theorists acknowledge that racism is normal and endemic to U.S. society. They expect to see expressions of racism and oppression throughout the institutions, including education, which make up U.S. society.
2. With recognition of the permanence of racism and its nature as a socially constructed dynamic, CRT proponents are skeptical about legal claims of neutrality, color-blindness, and objectivity. Instead, they articulate processes through which the political, economic, and social contexts, among others, are shaped by the racist dynamics early established in the United States.
3. Because racism and oppression underscore social structures, these dynamics affect the ways that group advantage and disadvantage are meted out.
4. Counterstorytelling is used as a methodology to convey the experiences of people of color and display the stark differences from the dominant master narrative.
5. An innovative and particularly useful principle in CRT is the idea of Whiteness as property. Many people view property as only applicable to tangible items. In contrast, CRT theorists articulate the ways that Whiteness can be bartered,

exchanged, and "cashed in" for other forms of capital. This could include money or more abstract forms of capital, such as social and cultural capital. Whiteness as property has particular application in educational settings where the color of one's skin can be exchanged for privilege, access to higher paying jobs, better neighborhoods, and higher quality schools; experiences that are then parlayed into additional property and capital.

6. CRT theorists seek to eliminate racism as a way to address all forms of oppression.

Although the application of CRT to higher education is nascent, Patton and her colleagues (Patton et al., 2007) offered insights into how this theory can be applied to college and university settings. They challenge the neutrality of theory used within higher education, address the way racism produces inequities including processes that render students of color invisible on college campuses, and expose the microaggressions prevalent on college campuses. (For additional information on CRT see DeCuir & Dixson, 2004; Dixson & Rousseau, 2005; Ladson-Billings, 1998; Matsuda et al., 1993; Patton et al., 2007; Solórzano et al., 2000).

The neutrality contested by CRT is most applicable to the political perspective through its challenge of the hypothetical unbiased political position advanced by theories and approaches with objectivity at their core. Counterstories as told by students of color and other oppressed groups on campus expose the aspects of higher education and political and social systems where inequalities and oppression exist. As opposed to possessing a "political agenda," a charge often leveled at CRT, critical theorists, and others adopting a social justice perspective to their educational work, CRT theorists discuss the ways that racism is a normal, everyday presence in U.S. society and, by implication, college campuses.

CONCLUSIONS

Despite the fact that the political model has been touted as particularly relevant for higher education, the approach may be one that many find distasteful. Others may find information about the model useful as they avoid politically charged associations and situations. Morgan (2006) offered some advice about situations to avoid when considering the political model. If one views these political games with insight, the efficacy of the political model can be revealed.

Being co-opted. Dissent can be quelled by inviting the dissenters into "official" ranks. Women faculty members with legitimate complaints about inequitable salaries are appointed as department chairs; student protesters are recruited onto presidential advisory boards.

Careerism. A long-established practice in political organizations is to establish oneself on a committee or in association with a person or group to advance one's career. With knowledge of how this political game is played, decisions that are advantageous to an individual but disadvantageous to an organization can be avoided.

Gamesmanship. Some people play the political game simply for its enjoyment. For those uninterested in this approach, it is best to avoid these people and the situations in which they operate.

Turf protection. The administrative overzealous defense of resources and power within a unit is a challenge to all organizations. This turf protection is particularly a problem in higher education institutions where individual colleges and schools compete for limited resources. When administrators or faculty concentrate on local goals at the expense of institution-wide purposes, all are disadvantaged.

Freewheeling. Organizational participants who loosely apply the rules, disregard policies seeking fairness, and play by "who you know" principles rather than equity create a negative political climate. Caution must be exercised to avoid being embroiled in this political game.

The positive aspects of the political model have much to lend administrators, faculty, and students seeking to better understand higher education institutions. Knowledge of the negative aspects of this model can aid those seeking to improve the organization through more collaborative and equitable means.

Questions for Discussion

- How does coalition building between faculty and students support activism within colleges and universities?
- How can conflict be viewed as a positive force for change in higher education settings?
- How can conflict be a negative force for change?
- How can political principles be used to affect change at the Board of Trustees level of an institution?
- How can CRT be applied to the political perspective?
- What political, economic, and cultural implications need to be exposed to reveal the liberatory potential of higher education?

Recommended Readings in the Political Perspective

Baldridge, J. V. (1971). *Power and conflict in the university.* New York: Wiley.

Bergquist, W. H., & Pawlak, K. (2008). *Engaging the six cultures of the academy* (2nd ed.). San Francisco, CA: Jossey-Bass.

Bruns, J. W., & Bruns, D. L. (2007). Effecting change in colleges and universities. *Journal of Leadership Studies, 1*(2), 53–63.

Hatch, M. J., & Cunliffe, A. L. (2006). *Organization theory: Modern, symbolic, and postmodern perspectives.* Oxford, England: Oxford University Press.

Kezar, A. (2010). Organizational theory. In J. H. Schuh, S. R. Jones, & S. R. Harper (Eds.), *Student services: A handbook for the profession* (pp. 226–241). San Francisco, CA: Jossey Bass.

Rhoads, R. A., & Liu, A. (2009). Globalization, social movements, and the American university: Implications for research and practice. *Higher Education: Handbook of Theory and Research, 24,* 273–315.

7

CASE

Coalition Building by the Board of Trustees and the Women's Faculty Caucus

The political perspective embraces interest groups as a normal occurrence within organizations. Interest groups often coalesce into coalitions to influence decisions, affect change, and exercise power. They particularly form when people do not have sufficient power on their own, so they combine their efforts. Interest groups and coalitions are particularly useful when resources, power, and valuable institutional assets are at stake. Because coalition members have agreed to cooperate, they are a group of individuals who act and can be treated as one (Cyert & March, 1959/2005). Interest groups and coalitions enable the less powerful to exert collective power as well as express their voices in the academic and administrative processes. Through bargaining and side payments, among other approaches, coalition participants exert influence, define objectives, and facilitate decisions.

Women's faculty caucuses, coalitions of administrators of color, and voting blocs among trustees all exert political pressure within higher education organizations. Interest groups and coalitions, particularly in higher education, which simultaneously acts as a public good and an elite feature of society, enhance the democratic nature of higher education (Baldridge, 1971b). Rather than a hindrance, astute members of political organizations must find "ways ... to create order and direction among people with potentially diverse and conflicting interests" (Morgan, 2006, p. 150). When input is solicited from neighbors in advance of new construction or opportunities are created for legislators to offer feedback about new majors, research centers, and campus programs, higher education administrators are following the political perspective. The needs, wants, and opinions of internal and external stakeholders are essential to the success of campus decisions, policies, and processes.

Political action and activism on college campuses through formal and informal activities of faculty and students is a long-standing tradition in U.S. higher education. The earliest colleges saw political action regarding student life (e.g., food service), curricular (e.g., faculty advising), and nationally focused issues (e.g., antiwar demonstrations) (Miser, 1988). Student activism has significantly affected national politics including action against the war in Vietnam in the 1960s, anti-Apartheid demonstrations of the

79

1980s, opposition to the Afghanistan and Iraq wars, and challenges to economic injustice through the Occupy Wall Street demonstrations of 2011.

================THE CASE================

The following case outlines a circumstance of coalition building among a faculty group and the political action taken to manage their influence. Using the political perspective, readers can consider the characteristics of that organizational approach including power, constituencies, attention cues, decision making, interest groups, and power elites.

Institutional Context

Countryside State University (a pseudonym), a research-intensive university with 2,000 faculty members, has long struggled to create gender equity among its employees. Despite efforts to recruit high quality women from the best programs in the country, the percentage of women on the faculty is 30%. This percentage lags nearly 20% behind the national average of 47% for all higher education institutional types (Institute of Educational Sciences, 2010).

Approximately 200 years old, Countryside is a land grant institution with a mix of professional and liberal arts colleges and schools with the former representing among the finest programs at the institution. The engineering school is particularly strong, an academic reputation that increases the male dominated nature of the institution. The paternalistic nature of the institution is further heightened by the recruitment of executive leaders from the medical school. There are few women administrators in that particular school, a fact not lost on women faculty aspiring to administrative positions. The practice of privileging males for leadership positions brings with it the tendency toward leadership styles that value expert authority and power, top-down decision making, and hard-hitting approaches to university business.

The Women's Faculty Caucus

The Women's Faculty Caucus, a group that has existed at Countryside State for 10 years, includes all full-time female faculty as its members. Concerned about diversity, equity, and social justice on campus, several senior women faculty established the Caucus to address these issues. Four or five women faculty serve on an organizing board, a loosely formed group that manages the Caucus's business. Membership on the board is open to anyone willing and available to come to meetings and join the discussion. The Women's Faculty Caucus was purposely organized with an informal structure including an absence of official recognition. The group lacks a budget, bylaws, or formal structure. It does not answer to any university administrative office or group. In this way, the Caucus is free to operate without the institutional parameters that define governance groups and administrative entities. The group was organized without the burden of a bureaucratic structure, ongoing agenda, or weighty overhead. There is no unwieldy administrative structure needing energy and resources to maintain it.

Questions to Consider

- How does the lack of formal structure enable the political success of the Women's Faculty Caucus?
- What is gained from a lack of formal structure?
- What is lost from a lack of formal structure?
- In what ways might the Women's Faculty Caucus be considered a power elite?

Regularly scheduled meetings of the Caucus are rare. Periodic meetings, often over lunch, are occasionally called when an issue presents itself. Anyone in the Caucus, essentially any female faculty member, could call a meeting of the board or Caucus. Despite the lack of organizing meetings, the interests and goals of the Caucus are clear: to promote diversity, equity, and social justice within the university's faculty and institution as a whole. Although by definition the Caucus's membership is made up of women, its equity and social justice mission extends to faculty of color, including men.

The Caucus has had several notable successes in its 10 years of existence. Activism by Caucus members has included letters to the president, provost, and executive officers signed by the most senior women on campus. Meetings with university officials outlining desired diversity efforts have resulted in several equal opportunity hires. Pressure exerted through motions to the Faculty Senate helped pass a diversity course requirement. At the urging of the Caucus, the institutional research office conducted two surveys to assess salary equity among women, faculty of color, and men on campus. They established a faculty mentoring program managed through the provost's office, an administrative office that, at the urging of the Caucus, held exit interviews for all departing women faculty and faculty of color. The Caucus successfully lobbied for periodic reviews of deans and vice presidents. They long advocated for family-friendly policies including family leave procedures and probationary (i.e., tenure) timeline extensions for family circumstances. Through e-mail communication that endorsed university and faculty senate committee nominees, Caucus members successfully supported female and feminist-oriented male candidates for faculty senate positions, including those of president and vice president. They endorsed like-minded candidates on college and school tenure/promotion and curriculum committees. An additional notable success of the Caucus was its campaign to mount a vote of no confidence in the president through a motion at the Faculty Senate. Although unsuccessful, this action precipitated the departure of two university officers, the former president and provost. These two officers were widely viewed as having taken inadequate action toward diversifying the faculty and creating equity throughout the institution. Through these actions, the Caucus affected significant change at the governance level of the university.

Questions to Consider

- What is the role of faculty caucuses and what political mechanisms can they use to effect change?
- How can other groups on campus (e.g., students, faculty of color organizations, faculty senates) form coalitions with caucus groups to effect change within institutions?

- How do academic freedom and tenure impact the role that faculty play in institutional activism?
- What power dynamics are exercised by groups such as the Women's Faculty Caucus?

Characters

Dr. Beth Deere: At the time of the Women's Faculty Caucus formation, Dr. Deere, a psychology professor, had worked at the university for 15 years. She had tenure and the rank of full professor. A political activist by nature, Dr. Deere had a keen sense of the power of political action and the strength of a well-formed strategy. She was not afraid of conflict and believed that struggle was one of the only ways that change was effected at traditional institutions such as universities.

Spurred on by the realization that the university was not sufficiently attentive to diversity and social justice, Dr. Deere organized the Women's Faculty Caucus. She felt that collective action was an effective way to address these issues. The informally appointed "head" of the organization, Dr. Deere had neither the title nor the legitimate authority emanating from an official position. Notwithstanding the lack of these bureaucratic trappings, Dr. Deere had substantial political power. She had the charisma to persuade small and large groups. She skillfully devised a strategy for the group that included dedication to a singular mission and avoided being distracted by issues that were not central to diversity and social justice. Her longevity at the institution provided a historical context and the understanding that even if the Caucus was not active for months or years, they could be called together through a few e-mails. In this way, the political action would pick up where it had previously left off.

The Women's Faculty Caucus Organizing Board: The organizing board of the Women's Faculty Caucus was a loosely collected group of five female faculty. Although predominantly from the College of Liberal Arts, there were female faculty from engineering, education, and social work who occasionally joined the board. The Caucus organizing board represented a wide range of women faculty across the university. Meeting every few months when the occasion called, meetings could be organized and run by any member of the board and, for that matter, any member of the Women's Faculty Caucus. In essence, any female faculty member with an issue could call a meeting of the organizing board.

The Women's Faculty Caucus as an interest group had issues to which they were committed. These included diversity within the faculty, pay equity for female faculty, and preservation of the academic core. The group felt that the recent increase in what they called "administrative bloat" put diversity and equity issues at risk. The increased salaries at the executive level increased the difference between the highest and lowest paid members of the institution and concentrated resources at the top of the bureaucratic hierarchy. The increase in administrative positions was accompanied by a concomitant decrease in the number of new tenure track lines available throughout the institution. Caucus organizing board members felt strongly that one of the ways to fight for diversity within the institution was to combat administrative bloat.

Dr. Thomas Urick, President: Dr. Urick had been president of Countryside State University for 7 years. He was hired and arrived at the university shortly after the resignation of the previous president. That president, Dr. Bogue, was the subject of a no confidence vote organized by the Faculty Women's Caucus. President Urick was therefore acutely aware of the power of the Caucus. Respecting this influence, he agreed to meet with Caucus members throughout his tenure as president. He did, however, limit the meetings to once a semester. More than that would imply that he was beholden to them for political approval and favor. While Urick was respectful of the Caucus's power and influence, he was puzzled by their organizational structure. He was accustomed to bureaucratic structures, particularly ones that reported to him. Through these structures, he communicated his vision, administratively gathered support for that vision, and managed efforts to achieve his goals. He was adept at organizing efforts using executive power toward the attainment of his vision and could not understand how a group operated without someone in charge. The president shared a set of interests in common with his executives, a group that formed a power elite on campus. They worked to maintain good relations with and support of the Board of Trustees, gain political support among institutional players, maximize their own and their close colleagues' salaries as a symbolic gesture of their worth, enhance the reputation of the institution through athletic championships, and exercise legitimate power to achieve the president's vision.

Urick had recently read an article that outlined five styles of conflict management: collaborating, compromising, accommodating, avoiding, and competing (Morgan, 2006). He was most comfortable with avoiding or competing. As a former business faculty member and dean, he could collaborate and compromise but preferred a more commanding approach. Urick was a decisive leader who liked to issue orders. The collaborative approach of the Women's Faculty Caucus was a mystery to him. How could anyone make decisions or achieve their vision if you had to consult with everyone first? The episodic nature of the Caucus's action particularly puzzled him. Each time he thought the Caucus had disbanded, he heard rumblings of its actions again. To this, he often thought, "here we go again."

Dr. Scott Lang: Dr. Lang had been the Chief of Staff through three presidencies at Countryside State University. He was extremely adept at his job and knew that his role was to minimize the political fall-out inherent in institutions like Countryside. He knew that he worked for the President and he protected Urick at all costs. Throughout his 12-year tenure at the institution, Lang had gained considerable political clout. He was a familiar face at Board of Trustees meetings. He knew how change could be effected—and stopped. Although Urick wanted to bring his administrative assistant from his previous institution, the chair of the Board of Trustees had insisted that Lang remain on as Chief of Staff. The chair could not imagine how Urick would be successful without Lang as his right hand man.

Lang's primary interests were the president's, whoever that person was at that moment in time. His secondary interests were personal and professional survival in the political climate of the university. He knew that university politics could be cutthroat and he was determined not to be a casualty of those machinations. He had survived two failed presidents and was determined to influence the success of the current president and survive that president's tenure if the success strategy failed.

Dr. Robert Bogue: Dr. Bogue was the president of Countryside State preceding Urick. The trustees had removed him and his provost after a failed vote of no confidence by the Faculty Senate. Currently on the history faculty, Bogue had returned to teach and conduct his research after a yearlong administrative leave. Bogue had used a collaborative style as president which some claimed was the downfall of his presidency. The chair of the Board of Trustees, in particular, saw Bogue's style as weak and indecisive. After 3 years with lackluster progress on recruitment gains, the vote of no confidence, failed or not, gave the chair of the Board a good excuse to ask for Bogue's resignation.

Bogue's interests had been to increase participation in the university governance bodies, create commissions that advised him on and distanced him from pressing university issues such as diversity and social justice, and to keep executive positions at a minimum to maintain the academic core.

Mr. John Rogers, Chair, Board of Trustees: Mr. Rogers, a lawyer in the local community and alumnus of the institution, was very proud of his work as a trustee. With the credibility of a governor-appointed position and knowledge gained through 10 years of experience on the board, he was very confident that the institution was on the right track. As chair of the presidential search committee that hired Urick, Rogers sought and hired a president whom he felt would provide the tough leadership the institution needed. The Board of Trustees had struggled through 10 years of two failed presidents. They were particularly displeased with the last president's collaborative leadership style, which betrayed lack of strength. Bogue had expended excess energy and resources on diversity hiring; energy that Rogers felt should have been expended on a strategic budget and long-range plan for the institution.

When the trustees were deliberating about how to dismiss Bogue, Rogers heard of the Women Faculty Caucus's plans to call a vote of no confidence. Although the Caucus's action provided trustees with the momentum to urge the resignation of President Bogue, Rogers was wary of the group. He did not want the Caucus to learn that their action had exerted any influence on the board. In Rogers's mind, Bogue and Urick could not be more different. Urick had a tough leadership style, exerted direction during critical decision making, and possessed all the qualities that one desires in an executive leader. Rogers had no desire to see a group of women, a minority of the faculty, take down the current president, Urick, in whom he had so much confidence. Therefore, the overlapping goal to remove Bogue was never openly discussed. Rogers felt that it would be inappropriate for his board to share goals with a radical group of female faculty. He also knew that participation in such groups as the Women's Faculty Caucus ebbed and flowed. If he, the board, and the president could wait the women out, their interest would, most likely, wane over time.

Rogers represents the interests of the Board of Trustees, a power elite at Countryside State University. Their interests are to maintain the legitimate power of the president, ensure the success of President Urick (at nearly any cost), uphold their fiduciary responsibility, and hire and retain the highest quality executive leaders to manage the institution. The board was in agreement that high salaries and a well-constructed package of incentives were necessary to attract the highest quality executive leaders.

Questions to Consider

- What kind of power does the Women's Faculty Caucus exercise?
- What kind of power does President Bogue exercise? President Urick?

- How is influence exerted through power elite groups such as the Board of Trustees?
- What styles of conflict management are effective among the various interest groups and administrative leaders?

Organizing Against Administrative Bloat

Typical of coalitions in politically oriented institutions, the Women's Faculty Caucus had been inactive for 18 months. After this relatively long period of inactivity, the organizing board met upon hearing concerns from women faculty about the level of administrative bloat at the institution. Countryside State University had traditionally operated from a "lean and mean" perspective with executive level costs historically held at modest levels. At the end of President Bogue's presidency, the president and provost offices shared a single executive assistant. There were only three vice presidents at the institution and they each had one associate vice president per office. Costs were contained and money was then invested in the academic mission.

With the hiring of President Urick, the mean and lean philosophy was replaced with a corporatization approach. Using this new philosophy, institutional leaders felt that executive staff assistants could be hired to manage many executive functions previously managed by a few administrative assistants. The deans of the colleges and schools followed suit by hiring chiefs of staffs within their areas. These newly established administrative positions were filled with highly qualified (e.g., doctorate holding) and liberally paid staff assistants.

The Women's Faculty Caucus saw the spread of administrative bloat as evidence of a negative effort to use corporate approaches to manage the institution. The provost's staff grew from one vice provost to four. The legal council's office expanded from two to six lawyers with a number of legal firms on retainer. Vice presidents grew from three to eight in number. Two colleges were split resulting in the hiring of an additional dean, bringing the total number of deans to 10. The Women's Faculty Caucus viewed these developments as a shift in philosophy away from unqualified support of the academic core to a corporate view of highly paid executives with complicated administrative support structures.

Questions to Consider:

- What organizational perspectives can help faculty understand the increase in the number of administrative positions needed to support institutional activities?
- What trends in higher education have resulted in an increased number of administrative positions?
- What attention cues should the president be attending to?
- What conflicting values in organizational perspectives (e.g., collegial and political) could explain the difference in point of view regarding the increased need for administrative positions?

In addition to the administrative bloat, the Caucus felt that excessive resources were being invested in nonacademically based student amenities (e.g., cable television in the residence halls, a new athletic facility with private exercise and weight facilities for athletes, a renovated student union, 24-hour food service). While the Women's Faculty Caucus understood the recruitment driven need for amenities to attract new students, they did not feel that these should be provided at the expense of a high quality academic mission. Investment in the academic mission must come first with nonacademic amenities following that initial investment. Dr. Deere, as the informal head of the Women's Faculty Caucus, had several conversations with female faculty who had concerns about the corporatization of the institution. They expressed their dismay at the deflection of resources away from the academic core and toward the executive salaries and student amenities.

Meeting with the President

Dr. Deere, the Women's Faculty Caucus organizing board, and four senior women faculty were highly engaged in the weeks leading to the fall Board of Trustees meeting. Devising a strategy for political action, this group (who privately named themselves the Anti-Administrative Bloat Committee) mounted a campaign to communicate their concern to the Board of Trustees about the rising levels of administrative staff and their accompanying salaries. Their first step was to meet with the president to express their concern to him about the trend he was pursuing. Following this meeting, which they did not expect to be satisfactory, they would meet with the Student Government Association to gain their support. Their next action would be a letter to the chair of the Board of Trustees. This letter would request time on the upcoming meeting agenda to discuss pay equity, lagging diversity among administrators and faculty within the institution, and administrative bloat. The women were particularly concerned about the lack of racial diversity within the executive leadership ranks at Countryside State. They did not expect their request to be honored by the board. Understanding that conflict is normal in political organizations such as the university, their next move would be to stage a protest at the Board of Trustees meeting, the only one in the annual schedule that was held on campus.

Upon entering the office for the meeting with the Women's Faculty Caucus, President Urick immediately asked, "Who's in charge of this group?" The women answered, "We all are." The president was clearly puzzled by this response and said, "You mean there is no one in charge here?" He turned to Dr. Deere and said, "I understand you are in charge" to which she responded, "Actually, I'm not. We all run the group together." Veterans of the Caucus had earlier explained to other organizing board members that over the 7 years of Urick's presidency, they had several meetings where he expressed dismay at the informal and collaborative structure of the Caucus. Each meeting with him started with the same question, "Who is in charge?" This was the case despite the fact that they gave him the same answer each time: "We all are." President Urick then said, "Surely there must be someone who calls the meetings and manages the group?" A different women from the first responder said, "No, we all do that." President Urick decided that since he had not gotten his answer that they should move on. He addressed his questions to Dr. Deere who he knew had the most longevity with the group, was a senior professor, and a former department chair. He assumed that she would be most able to understand the administrative structure and needs of the institution.

Questions to Consider

- What are differences in the style of the president and that of the Women's Faculty Caucus?

- What political practices does the Women's Faculty Caucus have at its disposal?
- What political practices does President Urick have at his disposal?
- What are ways that the president could "hear" the perspective of the Women's Faculty Caucus?
- What are ways that the Women's Faculty Caucus could "hear" the perspective of the president?

The meeting with the president went as the Caucus members expected. The women knew that the meeting was pro forma and would not result in any tangible results. Caucus members viewed the meeting as a step to put the president on notice that they were concerned with his hiring practices, and more fundamentally, his inaction regarding hiring a diverse faculty and staff. Their strategy was aimed at the Board of Trustees more so than the president. The president was not sympathetic to their cause, nor did he understand their structure or ways of operating. As a political caucus, their ways of operating differed from the managerial style that the president was accustomed to using. Though met with polite conversation, the women did not feel that their perspective was heard. This was particularly the case because the President had invited his chief of staff, Dr. Scott Lang, to sit in on the meeting with the Caucus. The women were amazed that the President had missed the symbolism of including the chief of staff at a meeting during which increasing administrative bloat was the topic of concern. The women interpreted this action as a sign that the highly paid executive staff member was tasked with managing the actions of the Caucus.

Over the 10 years of the Women's Faculty Caucus existence, presidents and deans had attempted to co-opt the group. Because the women faculty understood the political nature of higher education, members knew that any connection to a formal administrative structure would leave them beholden to the entity that granted them the privilege of a budget or administrative oversight. In this way, the Caucus women understood that they gained more power by operating outside the structure. Instead, they used their political and informal power to effect institutional change. This approach meant that this stance, though congruent with their political strategy and collaborative structure, came at a cost. Lacking a budget, the group solicited sponsorship from sympathetic deans, academic programs (e.g., women's studies), and departments (e.g., The Women's Center). They recognized the contradiction in their refusal to exist within the administrative structure and their simultaneous use of institutional resources. Although these contradictions existed, they were ones the Women's Faculty Caucus felt they could live with.

Meeting With the Student Government Senate

Following their opening salvo to the president, the Women's Faculty Caucus met with the Student Government Senate. The purpose of the meeting was to present a motion for the student group to support the request to the Board of Trustees to reduce administrative bloat at the institution. Prior to their meeting with the senators, the Women's Faculty Caucus committee met with the executive officers of the student government and felt they had solid support for their motion. They felt particular congruence with the students about keeping tuition costs as low as possible and maintaining the academic core. Based on the support expressed by the executive officers, the Women's Faculty Caucus members were surprised by the vehement resistance of the student government senators regarding their letter to the Board of Trustees. Although a minority, several student government senators voiced agreement with the Board of Trustees that faculty were overpaid for the amount of work that they performed in the institution. These senators were particularly concerned about the low quality of academic advising and lack of office hours held by many faculty. One senator felt that their resistance to the Caucus's request was a statement against faculty calls for increased salaries. They saw the calls for a decreased number of administrators on campus to be a ploy to increase faculty salaries.

Questions to Consider

- How can the Women's Faculty Caucus form a coalition with the Student Government Senate regarding their efforts to reduce administrative bloat?
- What attention cues could the Women's Faculty Caucus members have noticed? How might these been used to gauge the climate of the Senate?
- Lacking a coalition with the students, what other groups might the Women's Faculty Caucus approach?

Demoralized by their lack of success with the student government senators, the Women's Faculty Caucus committee members regrouped over a brown bag lunch. Because she knew that even the best laid strategy often went awry, Dr. Deere did her best to energize the group about the next steps in their strategy. She emphasized the successes gained with the Student Government Executive Committee. They decided that one person should talk to the president of the Student Government Association who they felt had supported their efforts. Although they had not received a positive vote concerning the motion they carried to the Student Government Senate, the support from the student government president and her executive officers could be useful in their efforts to decrease administrative bloat. A meeting between Dr. Deere and the student government president was held with disappointing results. Given the senators' vote, the student government president stated that she was required to abide by the vote of her constituency. While she agreed to informally talk to President Urick and members of the Board of Trustees, she would not take a public stance that contradicted the vote of the body over which she presided.

Letter to the Board of Trustees

Dr. Deere and her Faculty Caucus colleagues understood the strong support that President Urick had from the Board of Trustees. Despite this support, Caucus members felt that they must voice their concerns about the present direction of the institution. They felt that they could make their case if the Board of Trustees was convinced of the dire fiscal consequences of increasing administrative bloat. While this was a Caucus concern, it was not the primary one. Their first concern was the inattention to diversity and the erosion of the academic core. Through their discussions, they strategized that using arguments about diversity or academic core erosion would not persuade the board. This board had previously voiced disdain for faculty whom they saw as privileged members of the academy with limited workweeks and long vacations. They had previously voiced their opinion that faculty taught dated material out of step with the needs of today's business world. In their minds, faculty were anachronistic societal members who failed to understand the current state of U.S. higher education.

The Caucus knew they would never be granted a face-to-face meeting with the board chair or assigned time on the board's agenda. Because the board had lived through disruptions in their meetings by faculty and students, they had adopted a policy of tightly controlled meetings. Agenda items were set months in advance by the board executive committee. Speakers before the board were approved in advance and placed on a list by the president's office.

With the realities of how political systems worked within higher education, the Women's Faculty Caucus members composed a letter, which they sent to the chair of the Board of Trustees. Because they felt that staying within the sanctioned communication channels of the institution would yield the best results, they forwarded their letter to the institutional e-mail set up for the trustees. The letter outlined the issues as discussed with President Urick and student government officers and senators. The women felt they made a strong case against administrative bloat and a convincing argument about why the current institutional track disadvantaged the academic core and institutional reputation. Weeks after their letter was forwarded to the trustees e-mail address, the Caucus had received no response. They continued to meet and strategize ways for their message to get out to the board and others with power and influence in the institution. They knew that their effort would extend over the long haul and they were prepared to continue their efforts.

Unbeknownst to the Women's Faculty Caucus, the trustees' e-mail address was monitored by the president's chief of staff. This e-mail address was public and subject to all manner of unusual and inappropriate messages. Chief of staff Lang screened the messages from this e-mail address and forwarded only those messages to chair Rogers that he deemed essential for board business. Using the rationale that the agenda for the upcoming board meeting was already established, Dr. Lang decided that forwarding the letter to the trustees would have little effect beyond clouding already contentious issues.

Questions to Consider

- What political strategizing best explains Lang's decision not to forward the Women's Faculty Caucus's letter to the Board of Trustees?
- How can Lang's position of power be used as a way to explain his actions?
- What constituency does Lang serve?
- What are the competing interests that Lang is juggling with his decision not to forward the letter?

DISCUSSION

The political perspective through characteristics such as the normality of conflict, attention cues, presence of coalitions, power and authority, and power elites can explain a wide variety of action within higher education institutions. The perspective lends itself to an understanding of the political maneuvering and strategizing of administrators, faculty, students, and members of the Board of Trustees.

8

CULTURAL

What we cannot understand is respectfully assigned to the mysterious residual category of culture. (Marcus & Fischer, 1986, p. 39)

INTRODUCTION

Culture is a ubiquitous word on college campuses, with references to this elusive concept readily available. A culture of evidence, an entitlement culture, African American student culture, and faculty culture are phrases used in the higher education vernacular. These expressions attempt to define the character of an institution or perhaps the character to which the institution aspires. These depictions of institutional character and ways of operating convey the idea of "organizations as meaning systems" (Parker, 2000, p. 13); that is, meaning systems crafted by the people within them. This chapter uses the rich offerings from anthropology as a foundation from which to discuss culture as a way to view higher education organizations. This perspective can help make meaning of the rituals and ceremonies, architecture, sagas, language, and other features that exist within colleges and universities.

The interest in organizational culture began when Japan emerged as an economic power, particularly in the 1980s. That phenomenon, combined with the globalization of business and disillusionment with hard, quantifiable management, spurred managers and theorists to search for models of organizational functioning that better explained the less tangible aspects of institutional life: "The 'hard S's' of strategy, structure and systems needed to be supplemented by the 'soft S's' of style, skills and staff" (Parker, 2000, p. 21). Practitioners and theorists felt that the hard science approach crushed creativity and was inappropriate and ineffective in modern organizations. Using a cultural lens, organizational members sought to understand the ways that different perspectives impact day-to-day and long-range operations. Using a cultural perspective, faculty, administrators, students, and other stakeholders in higher education can achieve a richer, more complex understanding of organizations. This more nuanced and multifaceted approach is particularly useful during decision making, program development, and planning.

ANTHROPOLOGY AS A FOUNDATION
FOR THE CULTURAL PERSPECTIVE

Organizational culture theory can take two different approaches. The corporate culture approach advantages upper level administrators, assumes culture can be "managed," and holds executive leaders responsible for the substantial messages and meanings about culture. The second perspective, an anthropological framework, embraces an egalitarian approach. Anthropological models offer a deeper perspective on organizational life. From there, the less obvious complexities of organizational life can be better understood. In the anthropological perspective, all organizational members play a role in shaping culture and the construction of meaning from individual and collective experiences. In this chapter, the anthropological perspective is highlighted in the assumptions and discussion; concepts informed by the corporate culture literature that are congruent with the anthropological perspective are shared in the characteristics section of the chapter.

Anthropology as an underlying foundation for the cultural perspective on organizations provides a powerful means with which to view organizations. Several underlying assumptions include:

- A cultural group, over time, forms a unique culture made visible in its rituals, language(s), architecture, stories, and other tangible and intangible outcomes of cultural action (Kuh & Whitt, 1988).
- Organizations encompass unique cultures that can be understood and interpreted through ethnographic techniques such as interviewing, participant observation, and document analysis (Museus, 2007; Whitt, 1993b).
- Organizations, like cultures, are rehearsals, performances, and enactments (Turner & Bruner, 1986). The "mis-steps," gaffes, and faux pas are folded into the culture, history, and collective memory of the group.

The strengths and weaknesses of this perspective are summarized in Table 8.1. Clifford Geertz, a well-known interpretive anthropologist, provides a useful definition of culture, which can be used to understand higher education organizations:

> [Culture] denotes an historically transmitted pattern of meanings embodied in symbols, a system of inherited conceptions expressed in symbolic forms by means of which men [sic] communicate, perpetuate, and develop their knowledge about and attitudes toward life. (1973, p. 89)

Departing from the modernist approach, organizations are not "natural phenomena" inherently determined by forces outside the organization. Organizations from this view form through the actions of people who live and work within them. "Organizational culture is a process which is locally produced by people, but ... it can also be usefully talked about as a thing with particular effects on people ... it is both a verb and a noun" (Parker, 2000, p. 83). As a verb, culture is a medium through which people take action,

Table 8.1 Strengths and Weaknesses of the Anthropological Theoretical Perspective

Strengths	Weaknesses
Explains how organizational members make meaning within the day-to-day of organizational life.	May seem extraneous to the missions and priorities of higher education in the 21st century.
Illuminates possible connections to community, culture, and organizational life.	Provides limited explanatory value about economic priorities within higher education.
Clarifies how people become connected to entities, including colleges and universities, in meaningful and long lasting ways.	May situate higher education and its tradition in the past rather than the future.
Describes the importance and central role of ritual, tradition, and other higher education cultural artifacts.	Can appear out of step with current issues in higher education (e.g., affordability, globalization, and loss of the public trust).

create meaning, and achieve purposes. As a noun, culture builds congruence, gathers people as a community, creates clarity, builds consensus, and endows strength.

The uncertainty and idiosyncratic nature of human action means that organizations reflect human ambiguities. Complexity and ambiguity are as normal in organizations as they are in human living and, in the case of higher education institutions, are long-standing features. Rather than something to be fixed, complexity, multiple meanings, and paradoxical messages create opportunities for interpretation, clarification, and learning. They urge critical thinking and deep reflection. To understand college and university organizational cultures, one must learn to read and interpret the ways of operating, languages, and cultural elements within the setting. As institutions built on medieval structures (even new higher education institutions have vestiges of the earliest universities), these organizations are unquestionably culture bearing. Of all the modern organizations, higher education institutions fiercely maintain their underlying values through traditions such as graduations, convocations, and a myriad of other traditions that shape and build culture.

In contrast to the anthropological perspective of organizational culture, the corporate or managerial perspective treats culture as

> *a pattern of shared basic assumptions learned by a group as it solved its problems of external adaptation and internal integration, which has worked well enough to be considered valid and, therefore, to be taught to new members as the correct way to perceive, think, and feel in relation to those problems.* (Schein, 2010, p. 18; emphasis in original)

Culture from the corporate perspective is often described as "glue," the "stuff" that holds the organization together (Deal & Kennedy, 1982). From a corporate culture perspective, "there are better or worse cultures, stronger or weaker cultures, and … the 'right' kind of culture will influence how effective organizations are" (Schein, 2010, p. 13). Corporate culture theorists explain strong and weak cultures as follows: "A strong culture is a system of informal rules that spells out how people are to behave most of the time…. In a weak culture … employees waste a good deal of time just trying to figure out what they should do and how they should do it" (Deal & Kennedy, 1982, p. 15). From a corporate culture approach, higher education institutions are "weak cultures," lacking adequate cultural strength to be effective. Higher education institutions with their multiple goals, simultaneous organizational configurations (e.g., political and collegial, collegial and bureaucratic), and various missions are weak. Despite this supposed weakness, these institutions have stood the test of time and are among the most enduring organizations in history. Corporate culture definitions aside, higher education organizations have, by anyone's definition, rich and highly developed cultures. Competitive liberal arts colleges depend on intellectually centered cultures; Ivy League and near Ivy institutions use culture to market their strengths to prospective students; faculty culture is a formidable force for and against institutional change; student cultures are well documented in academic and popular texts and films. Though less frequently discussed, administrative culture is a meaningful force, particularly when technical and managerial expertise is essential.

In this chapter, the perspective taken is that culture does not *hold* the organization together so much as it *is* the organization. Although it contains some useful explanatory value, the corporate culture approach is an incomplete theoretical base from which to understand colleges and universities. Higher education as a marketplace of ideas and community of scholars values multiple and fiercely held and debated viewpoints. While the presence of these various points of view makes these institutions challenging to manage, a stance of top-down inculcation of values is inconsistent with the basic goals and purposes of colleges and universities. The (a) autonomy of faculty, (b) presence of multiple cultures, (c) high number of stakeholders, (d) existence of multiple and often conflicting goals, and (e) societal investment in public and private institutions make the corporate approach an inadequate framework for colleges and universities.

METAPHOR

Carnival and theater are two metaphors that portray the cultural perspective on organizations. Because both images imply performance, the dynamism and ever-changing nature of organizations are captured in these images. Carnivals and theaters have actors and audiences, performers and observers who exercise vital roles in culture building. With so many players, actors, and constituents composing, arranging, and living within organizations,

> sense-making is often contested, as organizational members defend alternative understandings of identity against the organization's attempt to reduce them to one-dimensional role players. Everyday life becomes a drama, a stage managed presentation with the continual danger of confusion lying beneath the surface. (Parker, 2000, p. 50)

STRUCTURE

From an anthropological perspective, "an organization is a set of meanings that people act out, talk out, and back up with their own armamentarium of forces—psychological, moral and physical" (Greenfield, 1986, pp. 145–154). Organizations as cultures are not isolated entities but institutions situated in a context that includes history, past players, and traditions that serve as the fodder for and backdrop to any culture building experience.

MAJOR CONCEPTS, CHARACTERISTICS, AND PRINCIPLES

Organizations as cultures are marked by several characteristics, concepts, and principles. Values and assumptions; subcultures; history, tradition, and context; priests, storytellers, and cabals; language; organizational saga; symbols; and architecture are briefly described below.

Values and Assumptions

Every organization has a set of values and assumptions, although contested in practices that can lead to clarification and change or disagreement and impasse. Values and assumptions pinpoint guidelines for everyday behavior, provide a common focus, and identify heroes and heroines. A homogeneous culture is not possible in colleges and universities. The presence of a highly professional staff (e.g., faculty, highly educated administrators), high societal expectations, and various constituent groups (e.g., alumni/ae, legislators, parents) guarantees the presence of numerous values and assumptions. The veracity of these assumptions changes depending on the vantage point used to view the organization. Whether formally built into the organization's structure through reward systems or informally through member-to-member communication, new affiliates quickly become familiar with the underlying values. If not, these new organizational members voluntarily or involuntarily leave the institution or stay and continually struggle to find their place within it.

Manning (2000) discussed values and assumptions from an anthropological context in her discussion of higher education rituals and traditions. Values and assumptions, espoused and enacted during ceremonies and rituals, are communicated through the messages and interpreted as meanings during those events. Messages are multivocal (i.e., people experience cultural events differently); meanings are individually and socially constructed. The complexity of higher education organizations can, in part, be attributed to the multiple messages and meanings that abound within these institutions.

Values and assumptions are particularly important to higher education institutions because they "are built into a college in tradition and legend, in administrative arrangements, in emphases of the curriculum" (Clark & Trow, 1966, p. 37). They are represented in the root metaphor and integrating symbols of an organization. These metaphors and symbols communicate the ways that groups evolve to characterize themselves, which may or may not be appreciated consciously, but that get embodied in buildings, office layouts, and other material artifacts of the group" (Schein, 2010, p. 16). Root metaphors that reflect the institution's values and assumptions can include leadership, environmental stewardship, and social justice. Their staying power and importance to organizational members is evident in the debates about institutional mascots, particularly enacted during athletic events. These mascots frequently embody outdated oppressive images (e.g., Confederate symbols) or disrespectful forms (e.g., Native American stereotypes). Likenesses of the mascot can literally be built into athletic stadiums and campus buildings. Arguments that these symbols simply have historical, not present-day, meaning are disingenuous to those who recognize that the oftentimes offensive values built into these symbols are perpetuated through daily enactment. Through protests, many mascots have been changed but many remain untouched.

The multivocal and multiple expressions of values, assumptions, messages, and meanings lend strength to higher education organizations, which have always existed in turbulent environments. The presence of numerous values enables organizational members to express multiple beliefs and quickly move to a latent or less emphasized set when the circumstance allows or requires. The presence of traditional assumptions and values (frequently represented by long-term faculty) and cutting edge assumptions and values (often represented by students) create a remarkable foundation upon which the institution can operate.

Organizations are not unitary phenomena with broad consensus across constituencies; people and ideas often conflict in organizations (Parker, 2000). Colleges and universities are sites of contestation, multiple meanings, and conflict. Though frustrating to many, others who value diverse perspectives revel in the fact that many institutional definitions and goals can exist simultaneously (Cohen & March, 1986). Birnbaum (1991) went so far as to attribute the success of higher education to the presence of multiple goals and stated that this characteristic enables colleges and universities to be highly productive organizations. For a university medical school, pure research on cancer may be the primary purpose of their work; in education, creating healthy, active learning environments for children and youth may be a goal; for student affairs professionals, creating programs, policies, and services that facilitate student engagement and success may be of utmost importance. No one goal need take precedence; all can exist simultaneously.

Subcultures

The anthropological and corporate approaches take distinctly different approaches on the topic of subcultures. Corporate organizational culture authors actively emphasize the dynamics between and among subcultures within an institution or organization. Executive leaders, entry-level staff, students, and alumni/ae each occupy, according to corporate culture authors, separate subcultures. Individual subcultures occupy a place in the power, influence, and status hierarchies within an organization.

The anthropological cultural perspective eschews rigid and deterministic hierarchical arrangements of human perspectives and behavior (Parker, 2000). Rather than subcultures, the anthropological perspective promotes the idea that there are many equally valid cultures within any organization. This perspective addresses a basic problem with the concept of subculture that "we immediately need to specify what kind of culture the subculture is subordinate to" (Parker, 2000, p. 84). A vivid example of this issue can be seen when students of color are said to occupy a "sub-culture" within the organization. This point of view positions them as "outside the mainstream"; visitors, a group never fully welcomed or part of the organization. When respectfully viewed as members of one of many cultures within an institution, the primacy of their perspectives, ways of being, and right to membership become transparent. Rather than a hierarchy of subcultures where one is more valid than another, one superior to a subordinate other, cultures within an organization are nested, embedded, and overlapped.

> People do not belong to a single subculture; their cultural identity is shaped by their gender, ethnicity, social class, sexual orientation, and age, among many other aspects of identity.... A single subcultural category is unlikely to capture the richness and diversity of organizational life in a college or university. (Bess & Dee, 2008, p. 387)

A complexity of cultures existing simultaneously in the same organization is an image that better fits institutions of higher education. Faculty, student, and administrative cultures weave together and exist separately, all at the same time. Although these cultures share some assumptions and values, their beliefs also diverge. Administrative culture values efficiency, faculty culture values autonomy, student culture values experimentation.

History, Tradition, and Context

Colleges and universities possess delightfully varied cultural forms that evolve over time through the actions of cultural inhabitants. Through habit, repetition, and socially constructed organizational forms (e.g., decentralized and centralized structures, religious and secular affiliations), a cultural context takes shape.

> A college is not simply an aggregation of students, teachers, and administrators. Although the character of a college is greatly influenced by the nature of its staff and students, it also has qualities and characteristics which are to some extent independent of the people who fill its halls and offices at any given moment. (Clark & Trow, 1966, p. 18)

Since culture is created through human action, organizations are rich places for meaning and culture building: "Clothes, spaces, symbols, games, roles and rituals are seen to be deployed and arranged in complex constellations" (Parker, 2000, p. 50). These constellations form a unique perspective on an organization reflected in its history, mission, and stories. It is literally built into the architecture and physical features of the institution.

For culture to form, human action is required. In other words, while humans create culture in the moment, they also re-create the culture enacted in the past and foretell the culture of the future. Architecture, language, ceremonies, stories—the physical, mental, and symbolic elements of organizational life—become the raw material for culture building. For the culture to have long-term, significant meaning for the organizational members, the organizational elements and actions should be grounded in the organization's values and assumptions. This culture building process could perhaps be monitored for purposes of intervention and influence (Parker, 2000), but precise management, overt influence, and purposeful manipulation is impossible. From an anthropological perspective, human action is simply not that malleable or predictable.

Priests, Storytellers, and Cabals

While culture cannot be explicitly "managed," it would be wrong to assume that leaders and other organizational members cannot intentionally and unintentionally shape meaning, and, with that, shape culture. Everyone plays a role in shaping culture, although some institutional participants, because of increased power, visibility of position, and longevity within the organization, exert more influence. Deal and Kennedy (1982) point to "spies, storytellers, priests, whisperers, [and] cabals" (p. 85) as members who create hidden hierarchies of power, communication, and influence. People who occupy these roles are culture bearers—people within the organization who take on various roles as communicators, creators, and perpetuators of culture during their organizational tenure. These roles require "imagination, insight, and a sense of details" (Deal

& Kennedy, 1982, p. 88). In higher education organizations, these roles are particularly visible during faculty senate meetings. At any one meeting, storytellers regale attendees with sagas of past deeds. Whisperers exert their influence through side conversations and postmeeting "clarifications." Cabals form voting blocs to slow undesirable innovations. Spies travel back and forth between department offices and executive suites as information is bartered for future favor. Using ethnographic techniques of observation, organizational members can learn about institutional culture by noting the actions of these culture bearers.

Language

Language within an organization is more than simply a means to communicate. Language is a fundamental and highly symbolic aspect of culture. It represents and re-creates habits of thinking, mental models, and organizational paradigms (Schein, 2010). Taught to newcomers through socialization processes, the jargon of a field, terms employed within a group, and expressions considered professional or appropriate distinguish membership and cultural belonging. WEAP LANGUAGE.

> Language, in its most general sense, is central, since an organization's culture is manifested in and through its local languages. Slang, jargon, acronym and technicality hence become exemplifiers of cultural processes because they are ... illustrative of the kinds of communities that organizational members inhabit. (Parker, 2000, p. 70)

In addition to signals about membership and belonging, language has the capacity to shape reality. "Language is power. It literally makes reality appear and disappear. Those who control language control thought, and thereby themselves and others" (Greenfield, 1986, p. 154). The use of first names for executives, the custom of addressing people as "doctor" or "professor" during meetings, and evocation of traditional phrases during graduation and campus ceremonies convey and shape the power of administrators, faculty, and students. Although allowances are made for students and others unfamiliar with established practice, breaches of protocol are discouraged (e.g., student protests during trustees' meetings, excessively emotional expressions during meetings).

Organizational Saga

Language is powerfully used by storytellers and within saga to convey organizational culture (Kuh, Schuh, Whitt, & Associates, 1991). Values and assumptions are communicated to those new to the organization through these myths and sagas (Bess & Dee, 2008). Clark defined saga within higher education contexts as "a collective understanding of current institutional character that refers to a historical struggle and is embellished emotionally and loaded with meaning" (1986, p. 82). These cultural artifacts serve many purposes including (a) establishing normative behavior, (b) creating standards for excellence, (c) honoring founders, and (d) communicating core values (Birnbaum, 1991). "Saga reveals values held deeply by current organizational members, and identifies acceptable behaviors that are likely to contribute to the desired direction for the future of the organization" (Bess & Dee, 2008, p. 367). Saga tells the tales of the organization's heroes and heroines. For example, there are stories told of Mount Holyoke College's founder, Mary Lyon, and her efforts to collect small amounts of money from local farmwomen, and these shape community ideas about fortitude and persistence in hard times. The values of egalitarianism, equality, and openness are relayed through the saga of Notre Dame University students, who late at night upon seeing the office light of former President Hesburgh, climbed the fire escape to speak to the famous university president. Through telling and retellings, sagas become explanations and shape expectations of the "way things are done here." The people whose activities are repeated in sagas need not be institutional leaders in the positional leader sense. Dining service workers often exemplify powerful institutional values regarding student-centeredness and an ethic of care (Kuh, Kinzie, Schuh, Whitt, & Associates, 2005). Sagas can erupt at any location within the organization and carry their messages throughout the institution.

Symbols

Every action contains meaning within it that refers to or symbolizes something else. Everything is symbolic (Parker, 2000) and all actions are symbolic acts. The complex nature of symbols is particularly evident in higher education organizations, which encompass multiple cultures in the same institutional space. Academic regalia at a university ceremony could symbolize curricular excellence to faculty members, the achievement of a career goal for students, or elitism to a local community member. A statue of the founder on the campus green could represent pride for one group and outmoded values to another. Diplomas represent an obligation to family for a traditionally-aged undergraduate and the fulfillment of a lifelong dream to an adult learner. Used effectively, symbols can set expectations and provide messages that shape meaning. When a college president uses a convocation address to convey who "we" are, she shapes expectations for community building. A significantly different message is conveyed when an interim president moves into the president's quarters. One is about communal action; the other about establishing power and presence. As with all cultural forms, symbols have the potential to express mixed messages. Symbols that are meant to include can inadvertently exclude. Action meant to set expectations for excellence can chafe against student expectations of adult freedom and independence.

Architecture

The architecture of a campus immediately communicates the values, aspirations, and character of an institution (Bergquist & Pawlak, 2008; Kuh, Schuh, Whitt, & Associates, 1991; Kuh & Whitt, 1988). These qualities may be explicitly expressed in mission statements and include beliefs about academic excellence, leadership, and access. Less explicit ideals are also conveyed through the built culture of a college campus. The physical space of colleges and universities, when placed, for example, on top of a city hill or sequestered behind forbidding walls conveys exclusion, elitism, and separation. The physical height of bell towers, steeples, and administration buildings communicates the desire to pursue lofty ideas (Bergquist & Pawlak, 2008). Campuses that choose less conventional approaches to their physical space (e.g., classes in a local high school) are communicating an equally valuable approach (e.g., access) to higher education and academic achievement. Physical space can enable and constrain an institution's values. Civic engagement may chafe against a college campus built at a distance from local communities. In contrast, global citizenship may be tangibly conveyed through art and architecture reflecting the styles of several countries.

The direction that buildings face, placement of parking, and position of academic buildings in relation to other structures tangibly convey institutional values and intentions. Residential campuses often focus inward, community college and commuter-based campuses project outward (Bergquist & Pawlak, 2008). A quick tour of a campus provides students with an impression about what is important to a campus, how they will be treated, and what kind of community they can expect.

Where buildings are placed, what they look like, and how they are maintained, the amount of open space provided, the care taken to provide places for large and small groups to interact, the priority given to space for students, and the amount of control students have over their setting can be viewed as demonstrating the institution's commitment to community and student life (Kuh, Schuh, Whitt, & Associates, 1991, p. 91).

While it is expected that colleges and universities will have distinctive architecture, higher education institutions of the 21st century are using a wide variety of physical forms. Campus configurations range from the traditional ivy covered buildings, central campus greens, and bell towers to virtual spaces absent of traditional classroom spaces and accoutrements. The sprawling space and multiple campus arrangement of a research extensive campus, accessible buildings of community colleges, and tightly packed buildings of an urban college each speak to a distinctive sense of place. Each aptly communicates institutional goals and purposes. For-profit campuses, community colleges, and institutions with highly specialized curricular offerings often rent space in office buildings, schools, and other settings that do not resemble traditional colleges. While these spaces are often erroneously called "nontraditional," the "non-campus-like" physical space communicates the message that all students, adult, first-generation college students, returning learners, are welcome. In this way, students become connected to the campus and link their purposes to an entity larger than themselves (Manning, 2000). Regardless of the style of the college or university, campuses evoke a sense of place (Gruenewald, 2003) that remains with students for years after graduation.

In addition to institutional values and purposes, campus architecture defines managerial expectations about power dynamics, communication habits, and authority. Faculty offices—how big they are, whether they are shared, how clean they are, how well they are appointed—may shape the communication patterns that emerge among faculty colleagues and between faculty and students (Bess & Dee, 2008, p. 365). In the same institution, student affairs staff may occupy egalitarian imagined cubicles while faculty have private offices occupied for only a few hours a week. Separate dining spaces for faculty and students are a campus staple and fodder for debate. The presence of students in faculty space can spark discussion and resolutions at faculty senate meetings. The nature of work, individual or group, can be determined by a quick perusal of that person's space. Conference space available for group work conveys one style of work; individual offices walled off for independent, autonomous activities convey quite another.

STRENGTHS AND WEAKNESSES OF THE CULTURAL PERSPECTIVE

The cultural perspective, similar to all organizational perspectives offered in this book, contains strengths and weaknesses regarding its implementation within higher education (see Table 8.2).

Table 8.2 Strengths and Weaknesses of the Cultural Perspective

Strengths	Weaknesses
Provides understanding of intangible aspects of organizational life.	May conflict with the budget- and enrollment-driven emphasis of today's higher education institutions.
Enables organizational participants to infuse meaning into their daily lives.	May not appeal to students who view rituals, sagas, and other cultural artifacts as unnecessary or off-putting.
Fits well with the pomp and circumstance of higher education.	May give the impression that higher education emphasizes the superficial at the expense of substance.
Creates meaning beyond the expediencies and bureaucratic aspects of organizational life.	May seem frivolous or unnecessary to organizational members who see their role as administrative.
Provides alternative views of leadership that create more equitable environments for a wider range of people.	A more diverse and open view of leadership may clash with board of trustees members' view of direction.

NEXT STEPS: BRINGING THE CULTURAL PERSPECTIVE INTO CURRENT USE

A significant aspect of organizational culture is the presence of a wide diversity of cultural groups among faculty, students, staff, and administrators. Higher education, from an international perspective, has always been a diverse enterprise. But the traditional monocultural and dominant culture principles (with the exception of women's colleges, historically Black institutions, Hispanic serving institutions, and tribal colleges) upon which colleges and universities in the United States were founded are being challenged in favor of egalitarian, inclusive, and socially just values.

Multicultural Leadership and Organizational Development

In a discussion of organizational theory, Bordas (2007) portrayed characteristics of multicultural and mainstream leadership styles from a cultural perspective. Using different foundational principles upon which to build the different approaches, she outlined an inclusive, community oriented, and pluralistic approach to leadership. Although Bordas framed her work in the context of leadership expressed in African American, Latino/a, and Native American communities, multicultural leadership can be applied in any setting where inclusion, collaboration, and justice are desired. Bordas suggested that multicultural leadership is collective, contains an other-centered orientation, and works for the community good. Mainstream leadership, by contrast, is competitive, individualistic, lives in the present, and embraces capitalism. Table 8.3 details the differences between these two different styles of leadership.

The increasing numbers of students of color, adult students, and first generation college students, as well as the appeal for more equitable organizations, warrant a different approach to higher education leadership than has been used to date. The heroic, command and control style of leadership does not enable the flexibility needed to address the

Table 8.3 Characteristics of Multicultural and Mainstream Leadership

Multicultural Leadership	Mainstream Leadership
Collective orientation.	Individualistic orientation.
Leadership as community action and social activism.	Leadership as command and control with vision emanating from the top.
Seeks egalitarian pluralism.	Values meritocratic approaches.
Addresses the social structures that hinder peoples' progress.	Creates hierarchy.
Embraces public values.	Embraces private virtues.
Privileges community and justice concerns including widespread participation.	Privileges power elites as more knowledgeable and able to lead.
Seeks the good of the whole.	Seeks individual advancement and achievement.
Relies on moral authority.	Uses legitimate and positional authority.
Encourages active, visible citizenship.	Isolates leaders from the public.
Builds interdependency.	Sustains rugged individualism.
The group enlists leaders.	Individuals seek out leadership positions or are appointed by a small group of elites.
Builds community capacity and group empowerment.	Concentrates privileges and power in the top group.
Seeks full participation and consensus building.	Top down, command and control style of decision-making.
Engages people to find community-oriented solutions.	Profit and individual or limited institutional advancement as main concerns.

(Bordas, 2007)

challenges to higher education institutions in the 21st century (see Table 8.4). Bordas's conceptions of multicultural leadership, feminist approaches to organizational management, and new science and spiritual applications to organizations can aid higher education faculty and administrators to conceive of leadership styles that can better equip colleges and universities to meet the current challenges.

Table 8.4 21st-Century Challenges

Globalization and internationalization including massification.
Economic challenges including decreased state funding and ongoing tuition increases.
Shift of higher education as a public to private good.
Increased competition and market-driven emphasis.
Changes in management, administration, and teaching due to technological innovations.
Increased power to administrators due to need for advanced budget and management expertise.
Diversification of students including increased students of color and women's degree attainment.

CONCLUSIONS

The cultural perspective offers a helpful analysis with which to view colleges and universities. Older concepts of the cultural perspective as elucidated by Burton Clark and others can be combined with the newer ideas related to multicultural organizational development to obtain a contextually-rich view on organizational theory and leadership. Either as a singular perspective or in combination with others offered in this text, this perspective can assist organizational members to invite all to exert leadership in ways that can better guide their institutions through the current challenges.

Questions for Discussion

- What are some of the enduring symbols that have endured throughout the history of higher education?
- What cultural artifacts (e.g., symbols, traditions, rituals) would you expect to experience within the U.S. and the international context of higher education?
- What higher education cultures are the sources of tensions within college and university systems?
- How can the cultural perspective be used to understand complexity within higher education?
- How can the cultural perspective be used to address contemporary higher education pressures such as loss of public trust, low graduation rates, and low college-going rates of certain groups of students?
- How do cultural artifacts and the historical cultural practices of higher education exacerbate allegations of elitism?

Recommended Readings for the Cultural Perspective

Cameron, K. S., & Quinn, R. E. (2006). *Diagnosing and changing organizational culture: Based on the competing values framework*. San Francisco, CA: Jossey-Bass.

Keyton, J. (2011). *Communication and organizational culture: A key to understanding work experiences* (2nd ed.). Thousand Oaks, CA: Sage.

Kezar, A. (2011). Organizational culture and its impact on partnering between community agencies and postsecondary institutions to help low-income students attend college. *Education and Urban Society, 43*(2), 205–243.

Martin, J. (2002). *Organizational culture: Mapping the terrain*. Thousand Oaks, CA: Sage.

McMurray, A., & Scott, D. (2003). The relationship between organizational climate and organizational culture. *Journal of American Academy of Business, 3*(1), 1–8.

Ravasi, D., & Schultz, M. (2006). Responding to organizational identity threats: Exploring the role of organizational culture. *The Academy of Management Journal, 49*(3), 433–458.

Schein, E. H. (1991). What is culture? In P. J. Frost, L. F. Moore, M. R. Louis, C. C., Lundberg, & J. Martin (Eds.), *Reframing organizational culture* (pp. 243–253). Newbury Park, CA: Sage.

Schein, E. H. (1990). Organizational culture. *American Psychologist, 45*(2), 109–119.

Schein, E. H. (2009). *The corporate culture survival guide*. San Francisco, CA: Jossey-Bass.

Tierney, W. G. (2008). *The impact of culture on organizational decision-making: Theory and practice in higher education*. Sterling, VA: Stylus.

9

CASE

Campus, Student, and Faculty in a Clash of Cultures[1]

The last 50 years in higher education have witnessed significant changes in regard to access for previously underrepresented student groups. Changes in federal laws, campus policies, and demographics have resulted in increased access for women, people of color, and students of limited financial means. The Land Grant Acts of 1862 and 1890, the original G.I. Bill from 1944 and its recent modifications, the Higher Education Act of 1965, and the growth of public colleges and universities during the golden age of higher education of the 1960s were federal and state policies designed to increase access for a wide range of the U.S. population. In addition to U.S. citizens, access has increasingly been granted to international students (Institute of International Education, 2011). The presence of significant numbers of international students has been used as proof of the strength of the U.S. system of higher education. A large number of theories and models are available to understand the complexity of diversity initiatives on college campuses. Aguirre and Martinez (2006) offered two views, co-optation and transformation, as approaches to view leadership and management regarding campus diversity.

CO-OPTATION

Co-optation involves selective leadership practices in responses to diversity that often benefit those in positions of power rather than the intended beneficiaries (Aguirre & Martinez, 2006). The goal of co-optation "is to change diversity to fit the dominant group's interests" (p. 57). Rather than fundamental change, co-optation absorbs people of color, women, and other underrepresented groups into the existing leadership and power structure. True organizational change fails because the underrepresented members obtain token leadership positions or nominal programs and services. These initiatives often appear, particularly to dominant group organizational participants, to benefit the underrepresented groups but instead perpetuate the power dynamics in the organizational structure. This approach may result in changes to the social structure, but rarely are they the types of change that enact more equitable distributions of power or privilege. This approach is an example of what Freire (1970/1997) called false generosity.

When a co-optation strategy is used, the maintenance of the existing organizational culture and power structure is paramount. Any group or individual that threatens the organizational stability is to be co-opted or absorbed into that structure in ways that engender organizational loyalty, distract the underrepresented group member from the original goals of equity or transformation, and reward the person for adhering to the leadership and organizational structure of the institution. Examples of co-optation strategies (adapted from Aguirre & Martinez, 2006) include:

1. Training programs with a focus on individuals' biases, but that neglect to address the institutionally embedded biases within the organizational structure;
2. Curricular changes that "study" underrepresented groups, but do not fully recognize or incorporate their contributions to the larger higher education knowledge base;
3. Staff and faculty recruitment efforts that maintain the dominant culture attitude that people from underrepresented groups are affirmatively hired at the expense of dominant culture members; and
4. Provision of programs, services, or approaches that recognize diversity, but do not reshape the power structure to more equitable forms.

Co-optation methods seek to control, maintain the organization's mission, and stabilize its purposes. Regardless of whether co-optation is intentional or unintentional, the impact is similar: members of the underrepresented group are marginalized, their input diminished, and the organization power structure remains inequitable.

Transformation

In an approach diametrically opposed to co-optation, Aguirre and Martinez (2006) borrow language about transformational leadership from James McGregor Burns's (1978) classic work, *Leadership*. Transformation entails a top-down approach with upper level administrators leading diversity efforts. With a nod to the role that everyone plays in promoting diversity, Aguirre and Martinez's discussion falls short of the true promise of a transformation model of diversity within higher education. Their concept of transformation will be expanded as a theoretical foundation for this case using Kezar, Carducci, and Contreras-McGavin's (2006) definition of transformational leadership:

> Transformational leadership is typically defined as a power and influence theory in which the leader acts in mutual ways with the followers, appeals to their higher needs, and inspires and motivates followers to move toward a particular purpose. (Kezar et al., 2006, p. 34)

Kezar and her colleagues, following Burns, discuss the ways that transformation leadership engages ethics and morals. For diversity to be achieved in organizations, leaders can use transformational leadership to "develop and cultivate vision [and] empower rather than manipulate" (Kezar et al., 2006, p. 37). This approach is particularly important when a sense of justice and fairness is sought, people's livelihoods and quality of life are at stake, people have invested their life's work in an organization, or interaction among people marks organizational functioning.

Freire's (1970/1997) discussion of transformation also provides further insight about moving organizations to more diverse forms. He suggests a pedagogy of the oppressed in which everyone involved, leaders and followers (in fact, those terms have limited meaning in this context), are committed, through praxis, to the liberation of all. This transformational approach to organizational change is represented in attempts within the institution to honor the cultural ways of being and voices of all organizational members, diminish the inequitable staff/faculty or executive leader/staff dichotomies, and enter into solidarity with all within the institution. Through praxis, or action and reflection to transform the world, higher education institutions can become more inclusive, equitable, and empowering. Through dialogue and trust engendered by the belief that a more socially just organization benefits all, transformation and nonoppressive structural forms are possible (Freire, 1970/1997).

Management and Leadership

Aguirre and Martinez (2006) outline four possible leadership or management styles related to co-optation and transformation: (a) bureaucratic management, (b) reactive leadership, (c) change-oriented management, and (d) transformational leadership. Bureaucratic management and reactive leadership are co-optation approaches; change-oriented management and transformational leadership are transformational approaches.

Bureaucratic Management

In this approach, the existing bureaucratic organizational structure and ways of operating are used to established programs and services for underrepresented groups. Mentoring programs, feeder institution partnerships, and academic and student services programs that serve the needs of underrepresented groups are examples of programs established through bureaucratic management. Positional authority and power remain intact while management establishes programs that incorporate a diversity of people into the organization without changing the monocultural nature of the institution. These programs nominally serve the needs of people from underrepresented groups while maintaining the underlying monocultural assumptions and institutional power structure. Bureaucratic management is a form of co-optation as the programs are folded into the existing dominant institutional culture and power structure: "Although it seeks to promote diversity in organizational structure, it does not promote diversity as a social force capable of transforming organizational culture" (Aguirre & Martinez, 2006, p. 51). While bureaucratic management style initiatives are often a necessary first step on the road toward an inclusive institution, they fall short of the transformation that addresses social justice issues within today's higher education.

Reactive Leadership

This approach involves "leadership that seeks to bring about organizational or environmental changes to protect the privileged status of the dominant group" (Aguirre & Martinez, 2006, p. 76). Organizational change resulting from student activism, faculty appeals, and environmental pressures can be categorized as reactive leadership, another form of co-optation. Examples include diversity courses disconnected from an academic home, underfunded affinity group offices, and diverse student admissions efforts without accompanying retention planning. Efforts like these add diversity initiatives to an organization but do not build equitable systems into the institution.

Change-Oriented Management

Proceeding from a technical rational approach, change-oriented management assumes that knowledge, particularly about organizational improvement, can result in a more efficient working and organization relationship. Through professional development and other educational means, workers and leaders learn optimal techniques for managing higher education institutions as complex, diverse organizations. This approach reflects the corporate approach to organizational culture whose proponents believe that culture can be managed. From this approach, diversity can also be managed through employee-focused professional development activities, goal-oriented organizational change, and strategic planning. Depending on the emphasis, change-oriented management can be co-optation or transformation.

Transformational Leadership.

From a transformational position, the "purpose of leadership in higher education then is to promote social justice principles that promote diversity as a transformative force in higher education and as a social change agent in society" (Aguirre & Martinez, 2006, p. 55). Proponents of this approach recognize that higher education is contested terrain where groups that have traditionally held the power and control continue to manipulate the organization in ways that maintain their power while conceding token changes within the organization. Following Burns (1978), transformational leadership has a moral component such that the needs of all are recognized. This contrasts with transactional leadership, which is functional: "Transformational strategies respond to the demands for social justice regarding the incorporation of racial and ethnic minorities [and other underrepresented groups] in the institutional fabric of society" (Aguirre & Martinez, 2006, p. 57).

=================THE CASE=================

The aftermath of 9/11 and the U.S. involvement in Iran and Afghanistan wars heightened prejudice about Muslims. Islamophobia is evident on college campuses as Muslim war refugees and immigrants attend college. Anti-Muslim feelings are evident in the Birther Movement aimed at Barack Obama and the attacks on Islamic community centers. This case explores diversity and Muslim students including policies regarding religious expression at a public institution.

Institutional Context

Classic University is an institution of 12,000 undergraduate students and 3,000 graduate students located in Springfield, the state capital and largest city in the state. Located in a major city of 3 million people, Classic University was established in 1827. Originally, a highly competitive liberal arts institution, the university had expanded since its founding to become a research intensive institution. The university attracts highly motivated undergraduate students who work closely with faculty and doctoral students on research projects.

With a long-standing commitment to diversity, Classic administrators, students, and faculty worked diligently over the last 20 years to expand programs and services that created a more inclusive campus environment. The institution has a history of curricular reform starting in the 1960s, which continues today with faculty-led colloquia on building inclusive classrooms, teaching diverse students, and transforming curricula. The student affairs division has taken extensive steps to recruit diverse staff, expand programs for students from underrepresented groups, and reform their systems to create more equitable and just systems. These efforts included major changes in the residence halls and discipline systems.

Because the university was located in a city designated as a refugee resettlement community, it was not unusual to see a diversity of peoples within Springfield. Many of the refugees and their children took advantage of tuition subsidy programs to attend the institution. This population added to the U.S. students of color and international students recruited in efforts to diversify the university undergraduate population.

Characters

Ms. Hadiya Kanasani, Student and President, Muslim Student Association: Ms. Kanasani is the President of the Muslim Student Association at Classic University. When she was elected president of her group, she lobbied the administration to establish a female-only swim hour. As a Muslim student who practices her religion by wearing a hijab, Ms. Kanasani has worked hard to improve the academic and social climates for Muslim students.

Dr. Aazim Solaimani, Professor: Dr. Solaimani is a professor of world religions who has worked at Classic University for 10 years. A long-time advocate for Muslim students, both at this campus and his previous employer, Dr. Solaimani is the adviser to the Muslim Student Association. He worked hard with Ms. Kanasani to obtain a female-only hour designated in the on-campus pool. He feels that this acknowledgment of the practices of Islamic women will help recruit additional Muslim students to the campus.

Dr. Loren Tustin, Vice President for Administration and Facilities: Vice President Tustin has worked at Classic University for 10 years. Before coming to Classic, he had minimal experience working in higher education. His background is in K-12 education, particularly as Commissioner for Education in the state. He became employed at the university after being approached by chair of the Board of Trustees. After firing the vice president for administration and facilities due to inappropriate purchasing procedures, the trustees wanted a vice president whom they could trust to better manage the university's financial and budgeting systems. Well-versed in K-12 educational practices, Tustin found the university campus exhilarating and challenging at the same time. While he had extensive experience with parents, legislators, and school staff, the presence of activist students was a new experience for Tustin. He found that he enjoyed the contact he had with students and relished the opportunity to work with Ms. Kanasani and her group. He had recently met with more students after the elimination of the vice president for student affairs position in an effort to cut costs. Student affairs responsibilities were divided among the remaining vice presidents. Student issues with facilities regularly came to Tustin to resolve.

President Jerome Lynch: Lynch had been at Classic University for 10 years and was feeling that it was time to move to a new institution. He had thoroughly enjoyed his time at the university but felt that he had achieved the goals he had set out to meet. He also knew that president–trustee relations tend to deteriorate after several years. He wanted to move to a new position before a crisis on campus, student protest, or faculty work action tarnished his record.

President Lynch had a strong record regarding diversity. He had doubled the representation of faculty of color. These employees now represented 20% of the faculty. He had urged stronger recruitment of students of color and international students. The result was a 10% gain in students of color (for a total of 22% of the total undergraduate student population) and 3% gain in international students (for a total of 7% of the total undergraduate student population). He knew that much of the success for the undergraduate population gains concerning diversity was a result of efforts by the Division of Student Affairs. This was one of the many reasons why it pained him to eliminate the vice president for student affairs position. But Lynch believed that Classic had advanced as an institution to the point where attitudes and assumptions about diversity were engrained in the institutional fabric. Extraordinary efforts by any one department were unnecessary because diversity was integrated everywhere. The elimination of the vice president for student affairs position not only saved money but was a better fit with Classic's designation as an academic-centered institution. The provost, provost office, and the vice president for administration and facilities had absorbed the different areas of student affairs and could handle the issues that arose.

Ms. Rachael Austerberry, Reporter, The Post: Ms. Austerberry had covered the university beat as the education reporter for *The Post* for 2 years when she heard about the female-only swim hour. As someone who fought for women's rights in the workplace, she took offense at any programs or services that implied that women needed special treatment. She had taken particular interest in Title IX and wrote newspaper stories about any attempt to treat men and women athletes differently. She was about equality, period.

Mr. Tyler Duckers, Male Senior Undergraduate Student: Tyler Duckers enjoyed swimming in the old pool located on the edge of campus as part of his regular exercise routine. The pool was convenient to his off campus apartment. In addition to the convenience, he enjoyed the fact that he often had the pool completely to himself. An avid swimmer from high school, it was not unusual for him to swim for 6 or 8 hours of the 20 hours a week that the pool was opened.

Questions to Consider

- What are some ways that organizational culture works to enhance the diversity of undergraduates and faculty on a university campus?
- What are some organizational culture aspects of Classic that may interfere with the efforts to recruit a diverse group of students?
- In what ways does the university represent a co-optation approach to diversity?
- In what ways do the university efforts regarding diversity represent a transformational approach?

Creating an Inclusive Campus Climate for Muslim Students

Ms. Kanasani was determined to establish a time that women who practiced the Islamic faith could maintain their values about modesty. Even the most modest bathing suit would not meet the Islamic restriction that prevented all but immediate family members from viewing a woman's hair. After a year of discussion with Dr. Tustin, the administrator in charge of athletic facilities, Hadiya Kanasani's efforts to designate a female-only hour of swim time were successful. Out of the 20 hours of open swim time available in the old pool facility, 1 hour was designated for women. The Muslim Student Group and Vice President Tustin reached the agreement in part because the pool in question was located in an old facility not used extensively by students. Although Ms. Kanasani felt that the more centrally located pool was a better choice and better matched the institution's commitment to cultural inclusion, she was thankful that this first step was taken. Tustin saw this as a way to increase the pool usage while accommodating students who had religious restrictions or simply a personal desire to swim in a same-sex environment. He felt that many Muslim and non-Muslim female students would take advantage of the female-only swim hour.

Questions to Consider

- How is the designation of a female-only swimming hour a symbol of Classic University's commitment to diversity?
- What are the values and assumptions that drive a decision to create a female-only swim hour?
- What are the values and assumptions that exist within a college community that may conflict with the decision to create a female-only swim hour?
- How is the Muslim student group being treated as a subculture of the institution?

Turned Away from Exercise

Tyler Duckers was disappointed to go to the pool for his regular exercise only to be turned away by a female lifeguard. He was told that this was the female-only swim hour. He recalled seeing several women with headscarves entering the locker room and inquired whether the hour was reserved for Muslim students. He was told, no, the hour was reserved for any woman wishing to swim in the presence of women only.

Furious that he had been kept from his regular exercise, Tyler alerted Rachel Auterberry, a reporter whose work he had read in the local paper. He called *The Post*, asked for her specifically, and suggested that she talk to university officials about their position on this manner. Tyler did not like the fact that the impetus for the female-only swim hour was the religious preferences of Muslim students. He had nothing against Muslim students. He only wanted fairness and equality to be upheld at the university.

The female-only swim hour had been in effect for approximately 3 months when a story about the initiative appeared in the local newspaper. For the story, Ms. Auterberry interviewed Vice President Tustin, Tyler Duckers, several other students whom Tyler had recommended, and Ms. Kanasani. She attempted to get a statement from President Lynch but was unable to reach him prior to her deadline. The story was a short piece but she felt that it had impact.

The Newspaper Story

Muslim Students Demand Restricted Swim Hour

Rachel Auterberry, *The Post*'s Education Reporter

Classic University, in keeping with its long history of accommodating minority students, has instituted an accommodation in an effort to enhance the multicultural nature of the institution. In deference to Muslim students, a female-only swim hour has been allocated in a University pool. According to Mr. Loren Tustin, Vice President for Administration and Facilities, the female-only swim hour was established after the Muslim Student Association petitioned him. He stated that the rationale for the initiative was "to ensure that our Muslim female students were as comfortable exercising as were students from other religions. The Muslim religion forbids women to show their hair to anyone other than family. We felt that the establishment of this hour would enhance their attempts to stay healthy while maintaining their religion's traditions." When asked about Title IX and if a male-only swim hour would be established, Mr. Tustin admitted that no such plans were under discussion. He also admitted that prior to the establishment of the restricted swim hour, the general student body had not been consulted. The students who regularly used the pool in which the female-only hour was established were also not surveyed or consulted to obtain information about their exercise habits.

Classic University is not the only institution to accommodate Muslim students. Accommodations established in institutions across the country include designated prayer rooms for Muslim students, footbaths designed for pre-prayer rituals, and gym hours for women. Dr. Aazim Solaimani, a professor of world religions at Classic University, commenting on the changes on other campuses stated, "the accommodation of Muslim students will enable more students from our religion to come to U.S. institutions. Now they can practice their religion while studying. This is a significant step in creating a multicultural university."

Although non-Muslim women can use the swimming pool or gym facilities during the female-only designated times, the impetus for the changes have been to accommodate Muslim students. Mixed reactions abound from on- and off-campus. Lorenzo Smith, a local businessman and Classic University alumnus, disagreed with the policy stating, "I don't think campus facilities should be designated for any one religious group—particularly a religion that represents a minority in this country. I worry about where this might lead." Tyler Duckers, a senior student who routinely uses the pool involved in the controversy, said, "Why should someone feel that they couldn't swim with members of the opposite sex? What religion would require that? I think everyone should be treated equally. No one group should take precedence over another." Other students interviewed for this story echoed Mr. Duckers's sentiment about there being no need for a female-only swim hour.

Ms. Hadiya Kanasani, a junior at Classic University and president of the Muslim Student Association, initiated the demand for a female-only swim hour. Ms. Kanasani, an international student from Turkey, expressed her pleasure at the establishment of the swim hour. "This is a great move on the part of the University and we really appreciate the accommodation."

Questions to Consider

- What multiple meanings can be discerned from the establishment of a female-only swim hour?

- What campus cultures are involved in the clash over the establishment of a female-only swim hour?
- What options are available to a university when campus cultures possess competing values and assumptions?
- What messages were conveyed about the female-only swim hour to represent the core values of the institution?

Competing Assumptions and Values

President Lynch was not in the habit of intervening in the business of his vice presidents. Particularly in matters involving controversies over student policies, he believed that the resolution of such matters was best left with the experts. Unfortunately, this was the first student controversy that occurred since the vice president for student affairs position was eliminated. Although dubious at first, Lynch was convinced by Vice President Tustin's arguments that the remaining offices on campus could adequately administer the student affairs functions.

Lynch was concerned that the institutional value of equity and fairness was competing with the special accommodation being made for the Muslim women. After several calls from Board of Trustees members, parents, local alumni/ae, and current students, he asked Tustin to eliminate the female-only swim hour. It was becoming a lightning rod and distraction for the other multicultural efforts he was attempting. He felt that he had to go with the majority opinion and do what was best for all students.

Questions for Discussion

- In what ways could the establishment of a female-only swim hour be used to implement a transformational approach to institutional diversity?
- What elements of the co-optation approach to diversity are evident in this case?
- How might this situation and the final decision become part of the organizational saga of the institution?
- If you were president of the institution, what assumptions of the culture would you rely upon to make your decision about the female-only swim hour?

DISCUSSION

The establishment of an accommodation to a student group that represents a culture different from the dominant institutional culture is certain to create conflict on campus. Dominant groups rarely see their perspective as one of many ways to operate, but instead as the correct way. The power structure and ways of operating within an institution often provide support for this point of view. As higher education institutions seek to diversify their student bodies, faculty, and administrative ranks as well as attract international students, shifts and potential transformation in the institutional culture will be necessary to welcome and serve students whose norms differ from those of the dominant culture.

NOTE

1. This case was inspired by reports of a female-only swim hour at George Washington University. The details and names were changed to portray organizational culture theory.

10

BUREAUCRACY

There is the principle of fixed and official jurisdictional areas, which are generally ordered by rules, that is, by laws or administrative regulations. (Weber, 1946/2005, p. 73)

INTRODUCTION

Organizations, from a bureaucratic perspective, are "rationally ordered instruments for the achievement of stated goals" (Selznick, 1948/2005, p. 125). Bureaucratic principles are so inculcated into modern living that they are often considered inherent parts of daily life. In reality, bureaucracy is just one of many ways to organize collective human behavior. "Virtually all colleges and universities have been organized at least partly along bureaucratic lines, so it is important to understand their advantages and disadvantages" (Bess & Dee, 2008, p. 203). Though many decry the red tape and glacial pace of bureaucracies, it is difficult to imagine administrative operations without this form. Bureaucracy is an undeniable and enduring perspective through which to view organizational functions in higher education. While this book describes a number of ways to view organizations, aspects of bureaucracy either shape a number of those perspectives or exist as the norm against which other forms are compared. Despite the dominant and ubiquitous nature of bureaucracy in institutions of higher education, the presence of this dominant organizational form was not always the case.

Early universities, if one can call those early organizations by that term, were not bureaucracies. Operating with an informal paternalistic style, scholars set up shop in a cafe or public establishment and attracted paying students. Scholars were deemed as such because they owned the book; the technology of the time that made learning possible. These early scholars were not associated with an institution but were self-employed, independent scholars. While non-institution-affiliated scholars exist in today's higher education system, they are the exception rather than the rule. In modern day colleges and universities, rank, title, and employment with an organization are formalized.

Many take these organizational elements for granted, but each is based on bureaucratic principles as defined by early theorists such as Max Weber and Henri Fayol. Students, like professors, find their place in higher education institutions through their association with a formal educational institution. Through this connection, they earn credits and, ultimately, a degree. Using bureaucratic principles of standardization and specification, learning is classified into majors, degrees, and certificates.

MODERNIST ASSUMPTIONS AS A FOUNDATION FOR THE BUREAUCRATIC PERSPECTIVE

Max Weber, the father of bureaucracy, made this organizational form decidedly modern by emphasizing precision and efficiency (Merton, 1957/2005): "Weber's ideas were based on his presumption of the importance of rationality, impersonality, and objectivity in decision making and in the application of rules" (Bess & Dee, 2008, p. 204). Borrowing from the Enlightenment, Weber built the modernist assumptions of logic and progress into his theory of bureaucracy. These underlying principles endure in today's bureaucratic forms (see Table 10.1).

Weber built rationality into every principle and characteristic of bureaucracy (Merton, 1957/2005). This rationality is particularly expressed in the goal orientation that underlies all organizational activities. True to the modernist perspective, people in bureaucratic organizations assume that progressive movement toward goals is essential. Movement toward organizational goals is achieved by the competent action of the people who fill the ranks of institutional staff and management. Progress is also reflected in principles about growth that underscore modern organizations. Bigger is better in bureaucracies as, in the case of higher education institutions, student bodies grow in size, majors are added, and new ways of teaching are developed.

Today, those who work in bureaucracies, use their services, or consume their products often have a negative view of this organizational form. The cumbersome, time-consuming procedures common in bureaucracies are the source of frequent complaints. Despite its current problems, bureaucracy was a revolutionary and forward thinking concept when Weber first theorized its principles. Prior to this organizational

Table 10.1 Strengths and Weaknesses of the Modernist Theoretical Foundation

Strengths	Weaknesses
Provides a familiar way for people to view organizations.	Discourages innovation through the imposition of order and rationality.
Seeks to build order and rationality by imposing a structure from external sources.	Assumes an ideal type of organization, eliminating other possible forms.
Can provide measurable units for accountability and planning processes.	Cannot account for the less tangible, hard to measure products of organizational systems.
Eliminates duplication of effort through reductionism and specialization.	Lack of redundancy places organizations at risk for catastrophic failure.
Allows people to adjust slowly to incremental change.	Does not account for the ways that organizations and systems change in sudden and revolutionary ways.

innovation, paternalism was the predominant style of organization. Early organizations relied on leadership approaches emphasizing authoritarianism and arbitrary treatment of employees. The Great Man Theory (i.e., leaders are born, not made) (Carneiro, 1981), outdated by today's egalitarian standards, was firmly rooted in the early paternalistic higher education organizations. These early and in some cases current paternalistic organizations lacked consistent policies and procedures. The organizational leader operated as the "head of the family" with unlimited power and arbitrary, at times capricious, rule. Bureaucracy was invented to revolutionize the excesses, favoritism, nepotism, and lack of procedures of paternal organizations. Credentials replaced favoritism; standard operating procedures traded for opinion; and objectivity supplanted subjectivity.

METAPHOR

Quintessential bureaucratic organizations include the military, Catholic Church, and McDonald's. Each conjures the image of a well-oiled machine (Morgan, 2006). In McDonald's, every action—from the way customers are greeted to the salt on the fries—is routinized. Consistency is assured through standard operating procedures. A McDonald's franchise whether in Paris, France, or Bloomington, Indiana produces the trademark product with minor variations. This worldwide standardization is possible because individual staff choice is eliminated. Any McDonald's staff member, trained in the procedures, can substitute for other staff members. Each employee is a cog in the wheel of the machine created from a central corporate location and, as such, is expendable (Ferguson, 1985). Standardization as illustrated on an organizational chart dictates "'A place for everything and everything in its place'" and "'A place for everyone and everyone in his [sic] place'" (Fayol, 1916/2005, p. 57).

STRUCTURE

Bureaucratic theory holds that organizations should follow an ideal, natural, or perfect order (Fayol, 1916/2005; Ferguson, 1985), one in which human action follows the hierarchy of nature. Following this natural, ideal order, bureaucracies adopt a hierarchical, pyramid shaped structure. Mimicking the simple to complex forms found in nature, early proponents of bureaucracies used authority and responsibility as a way to vertically organize organizations. Bureaucracies are "natural" in their organization from simple to complex, lower to higher, and smaller to greater. They are complex because employees with more complicated jobs are positioned near the top of the organization. They are higher in the ways that responsibility increases as one goes up the hierarchy. Greater in the ways that power is concentrated at the top of the hierarchy. Although many are tempted, bureaucratic theorists advise against changing the structure to accommodate individual personalities. To do so interferes with the rational order and can result in a Byzantine organization that lacks logic and objectivity.

MAJOR CONCEPTS, CHARACTERISTICS, AND PRINCIPLES

Ferguson (1985) outlined the major characteristics of bureaucracies as originated by Weber:

A complex rational division of labor, with fixed duties and jurisdictions; stable, rule-governed authority channels and universally applied performance guidelines; a horizontal division of graded authority, or hierarchy, entailing supervision from above; a complex system of written record-keeping, based on scientific procedures that standardize communications and increase control; objective recruitment based on impersonal standards of expertise; predictable, standardized management procedures following general rules; and a tendency to require total loyalty from its members toward the way of life the organization requires. (p. 7)

For the purposes of this introductory text, only the basic characteristics of bureaucracies are discussed in this chapter (see Table 10.2). Bureaucratic concepts that may be of interest but which are not discussed in this chapter are outlined in Table 10.3. Additional information on bureaucracies is located at the end of the chapter.

Despite advice by early bureaucratic theorists (Fayol, 1916/2005) about the need for flexibility and artful application of principles, bureaucratic organizations tend to "fossilize." Their ways of operating and standard operating procedures become an impediment, a sea of red tape that frustrates everyone associated with these organizations.

APPOINTMENT OF STAFF

The move away from the nepotism and patronage systems of the pre-bureaucratic, paternalistic organizations introduced meritocratic organizational practices. In a meritocracy, one gains a position because one has the necessary qualifications (Weber, 1946/2005). In other words, people are hired as employees and paid to fill an office. Objective credentials and qualifications are used to judge whether the candidate is suitable for hiring, theoretically regardless of personal connections or family background.

Being hired into an office is one of the major ways that employees are viewed as cogs in the mechanistic wheel of bureaucracies. When an office becomes vacant, another

Table 10.2 Basic Characteristics of Bureaucracies

Concept	Description
Structure	Hierarchy.
Appointment of Staff	Appointed to their office by expertise and credentials.
Authority	Concentrated at the top of the hierarchy.
Communication	Formal vertically and informal laterally.
Decision Making	Rational and top down.
Ways of Operating	Standard operating procedures.
Labor Organization	Division of labor and specialization.
Span of Control	Number and range of direct reports.
Stability of Personnel	Constancy of staff that enables effectiveness and efficiency within the organization.
Centralization/Decentralization	Location and focus of power and/or control of organizational processes.

Table 10.3   Additional Bureaucratic Concepts

Concept	Description
Unity of direction	"One head, one plan."
	Unity and coordination of action among the employees in a given area is a goal of bureaucracies (Fayol, 1916/2005).
Unity of command	One employee, one supervisor.
	"Nothing but confusion arises under multiple command" (Gulick, 1937/2005, p. 83).
Remuneration of personnel	Employees should receive a salary based on the cost of living, availability of personnel, business conditions, and economics (Fayol, 1916/2005).
Individual interest subordinated to the general interest	The interest or interests of one employee or group should not take precedence over the interests and concerns of the organization (Fayol, 1916/2005).
Scalar chain	Line of authority.
	"The chain of superiors ranging from the ultimate authority to the lowest ranks" (Fayol, 1916/2005, p. 56).

"part" (e.g., employee) theoretically and easily fills the vacancy. If the structure is well constructed, employees are interchangeable. Organizational success is not based on personal qualities but on a set of time and performance-based criteria. Rational action is thus built into human organizations (Selznick, 1948/2005). By removing the personal and emphasizing the functional, organizational success is independent of the person, but rather, depends on the way the organization or bureaucracy is organized to withstand ups and downs in staffing. This objective, impersonal process assures the continuation of the organization, regardless of those who occupy it.

The bureaucratic principle of appointment to a role was and is best exemplified in assembly lines and fast-food companies such as McDonalds. Weber, however, theorized that the position should be held for life, as a vocation, not a "job." Lifelong, vocational style employment is a bureaucratic principle widely applied in higher education institutions where tenure for faculty and disciplinary loyalty are widely accepted. These characteristics of employment apply equally to administrators and staff who are often difficult to fire and who occupy their positions, or ones similar to them, for life.

The meritocratic principles of appointment imply that the "best" person, based on objectively determined criteria, is hired to fulfill an identified role. Although this principle of merit exists theoretically, it is rarely enacted in practice. Critical race theorists (Ladson-Billings, 1998) and feminist theorists (Ferguson, 1985) have debunked the assumptions of objectivity and merit. In reality, favoritism, propinquity (i.e., hiring someone because he or she shares similar characteristics to one's own), and gender, racial, sexual orientation, and other prejudices exist within all organizations. While the value of subjectivity versus objectivity can be debated, the solely merit-based philosophy does not work in practice.

Authority

The efficient and effective operation of an organization depends on authority; the authority to plan, organize, staff, direct, coordinate, report, and budget (Gulick, 1937/2005).

In bureaucracies, managers and executives, referred to as line officers, possess the formal authority to execute these responsibilities: "Authority is the right to give orders and the power to exact obedience" (Fayol, 1916/2005, p. 49). Also called bureaucratic authority, formal authority is attached to the office or position held by the employee (Morgan, 2006). Bureaucratic or formal authority is vastly different from charismatic, political, expert, or reference power. "Distinction must be made between a manager's official authority deriving from office and personal authority, compounded of intelligence, experience, moral worth, ability to lead, past services, etc." (Fayol, 1916/2005, p. 49). Higher education organizations, as seen from the bureaucratic perspective, contain considerable authority in the executive offices of the president and provost. Despite the "ideal" authority embedded in bureaucratic positions, authority cannot be exercised unless subordinates agree to be led and influenced. Authority emanates from the position or office, but real power comes from those being supervised, directed, or governed.

> To the extent that authority is translated into power through the assent of those falling under the pattern of command, the authority structure is also a power structure … authority becomes effective only to the extent that it is legitimized from below. (Morgan, 2006, p. 168)

Authority and its related concept, power, must be earned. Organized in order of the authority imbedded in organizational roles, positions are hierarchically organized from lowest to highest order of importance. In classic bureaucracies, the number of positions decreases and authority increases as one moves up the hierarchy (see Figure 10.1).

Authority, power, and responsibility are interrelated concepts in organizations. One can have responsibility with the required authority but lack the power to execute the role. A college president, for example, can possess the responsibility of his or her office without the accompanying personal power to effectively execute the duties of the position. Responsibility and the exercise of authority to achieve goals are more difficult as one proceeds up the chain of command due to increasingly complex work, larger numbers of workers, and tasks for which the results are more elusive (Fayol, 1916/2005). Authority without responsibility to exercise it is wasted; responsibility without authority is unproductive.

Authority and power have long been sources of tension on college campuses. The presence of academic freedom and tenure, student activism, and administrative professional power create a complicated mix of circumstances regarding how authority and power are exercised. In professional and educational environments such as higher education, successful management depends on the delegation of responsibility within the organization. Traditional bureaucratic theory defines authority and power in ways that do not adequately express the dynamics of colleges and universities.

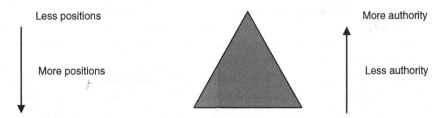

Figure 10.1 Relationship between Positions and Power

The prevalence of bureaucracies persuades many that the existing authority configuration is the only choice available. But, powerful counterstories about a wider variety of organizational forms challenge traditional notions of authority by illustrating collaborative, generative, and more equitable approaches (Bordas, 2007; Ferguson, 1985; Helgesen, 1995; Ladson-Billings, 1998). Authority, according to these countertheorists, is possessed and exercised by all in the organization.

Communication

Communication patterns in bureaucracies are determined by the vertical and horizontal direction of its flow (Guetzkow, 1965). The vertical form includes top-down communication; for example, supervisor directives to subordinates, executive missives to the entire institution, and activities involving multiple levels of the organization. This formal communication type represents a major task of administrators as they oversee subordinates, plan and execute goals, and direct organizational purposes.

Communication patterns, in keeping with the objective, rational nature of bureaucracies, are formal and prescribed. Rules governing bureaucratic communication, each of which is dictated by the role, status, and power held by the speaker, include the following:

1. Subordinates respect the chain of command by only communicating directly with their bosses. It is unacceptable and precarious to skip levels (e.g., talk to your boss's boss).
2. Requests must be made "in writing."
3. Incidents, procedures, and consequential actions (e.g., firing) must be documented through a paper trail.
4. Meetings include protocols about who is allowed to speak (and who can speak out of turn), the length of time one can speak, and tolerance for side conversations.

These communication patterns are predominantly one-way with limited opportunity for dialogue, feedback, or dissent. "In order to do business with bureaucrats, one must engage in conversation with them; this requires that one learn their language, play their game, and come onto their turf" (Ferguson, 1985, p. 15). Communication in bureaucracies becomes real in the form of written documents, through commands given by those in authority, and within prescribed and formal channels. In reality, communication also flows horizontally through rumor mills and a variety of informal means (Roethlisberger, 1941/2005; Simon, 1957; Taylor, 1947; Weber, 1947).

Communication within organizations has changed dramatically with the advent of electronic mail, the Internet, social networking groups, cellular phones, and other instantaneous and advanced means of communication. Technology has enabled more widespread access to information accompanied by the means to communicate across bureaucratic levels. Etiquette within bureaucracies continues to dictate older patterns established by the classic organizational theorists, but new forms have radically changed how information is controlled and communication achieved.

Communication is intricately connected to authority, specifically, the office that has the legitimacy to control the frequency and nature of communication. Administrators at higher levels within the hierarchy have wider and more formal means of communication (Guetzkow, 1965). These administrators possess a wide range of organizational resources (e.g., calling meetings, writing memos, utilizing distribution lists) through which to disseminate their messages. For example, organization-wide e-mail distribution lists are tightly controlled through the president's office, human resources, or public relations. Only a few in a university (e.g., president, provost, faculty senate president) could effectively call a community-wide meeting that people would actually attend.

Horizontal communication is less formal and more "independent of the formal structural size of the organization as a whole" (Guetzkow, 1965, p. 541). This form takes place primarily across similar bureaucratic levels (e.g., between secretaries, among faculty). The strength of the horizontal communication is measured by the initiative it engenders within the staff (Fayol, 1916/2005). The success of this method depends on the network of personal contacts held by the administrator. On the negative side, horizontal communication can undercut superiors and cause confusion among the lower ranks.

Decision Making

In keeping with the assumptions of power and control with bureaucracies, the leader or leaders in a bureaucracy are charged with making rational choices. Theoretically, bureaucratic decision making proceeds through seven steps: (a) identify the problem or opportunity, (b) gather information, (c) analyze the situation, (d) develop options, (e) evaluate the alternatives, (f) select an alternative, and (g) act on the decision (Simon, 1955, 1979). The belief in the efficacy of this model has been so strong that administrators often "retrospectively" construct these steps for a decision that may have actually been achieved differently, even subjectively, haphazardly, or through "drift." "From the gut" or subjective decisions, although commonplace, are discouraged by a bureaucratic mind-set.

Simon (1956) recognized that the rational model of decision making was more myth than fact. He suggested that decisions are more often made through a process of satisficing. Rather than an exhaustive process that explores options, most bureaucrats find a solution that is "good enough," one that satisfies sufficient parameters of the decision situation. This solution is adopted and perhaps adapted. In this way, time, a valuable commodity within organizations, is not wasted on identifying solutions that will never be enacted.

Ways of Operating

Most organizations have accepted standards for the ways they are to function. "The management of the office follows general rules, which are more or less stable, more or less exhaustive, and which can be learned" (Weber, 1946/2005, p. 74). These standard operating procedures (SOPs) are represented in higher education organizations through staff and faculty manuals. Elements of standard operating procedures are often codified in faculty and other union collective bargaining agreements. Hiring and firing procedures, timelines for tenure and promotion, and schedules for budgets are often strictly and legally maintained through SOPs. In organizations such as hospital emergency rooms and the military, where variation can have dire consequences, these standard operating procedures strictly dictate behavior and action.

Labor Organization

People make sense of an organization's structure, lines of authority, and reporting configuration by examining its organizational chart. These charts represent the ideals of specialization and division of labor (Fayol, 1916/2005; Gulick, 1937/2005). From this familiar image, a job applicant, new employee, or seasoned organizational member can determine the areas of responsibility for administrators within the organization. In fact, one could drill down through various division and department organizational charts to see the roles and responsibilities of nearly everyone within the institution.

In bureaucracies, tasks and responsibilities are systematically divided into offices and among people. With efficiency as the goal, organizations work to avoid repetition, map out clear lines of communication and effort, and delineate responsibility: "The object of division of work is to produce more and better work with the same effort" (Fayol, 1916/2005, p. 48). Efficiency is achieved because this approach allows management to (a) take advantage of employees' different skills and aptitudes, (b) eliminate lost time when people are assigned only the tasks for which they are trained, and (c) better utilize lower skilled workers (Gulick, 1937/2005). An important function of the division of labor and specialization is the separation of thinking as performed by management versus doing as performed by staff. This division of labor becomes the justification for salary, power, and status differences within the organization. The separation of thinking and doing is evident in the division of labor and specialization among faculty, administrators, and staff in higher education organizations.

The organization of faculty and their academic work also represents specialization and division of labor. Disciplines (e.g., English) are divided into specializations (e.g., African American literature) and subdisciplines that are then represented in the departments that make up the academic structure of a college or university. The myriad departments and programs representing disciplinary specialization is more complex today than when the University of Vermont established academic departments in 1826, the University of Wisconsin in 1836, and the University of Michigan in 1841.

Span of Control

The bureaucratic concept of span of control refers to the number of departments, staff, and areas of responsibility coordinated by an administrator who is a specialist hired for her or his expertise in those areas. The manager's knowledge limits and that person's time and energy limits the span of control. Most people can adequately direct only a few people (Gulick, 1937/2005). The supervisor's limitations on knowledge are more significant today than when Gulick wrote about span of control. The wide range of technologies and specialties required to manage a modern college or university are substantial. Higher education executives often manage broad spans of control. It is not unusual, in fact it is commonplace, for a director to supervise employees who are proficient in areas unfamiliar to the supervisor. Provosts, in particular, can be responsible for academic affairs (through coordination of a number of deans or directors), institutional finances, teaching and learning initiatives, student affairs, diversity initiatives, and any number of areas. Although close supervision is not an expectation at that level, the wide span of control can threaten effective and strategic management of a college or university.

Space and physical facilities are additional complicating elements regarding span of control (Gulick, 1937/2005). Coordination, even with a broad span of control, is easier when all personnel are located in one space. The introduction of branch and satellite campuses, including international campuses, significantly impacts span of control, coordination, and effective management. Technologies such as electronic mail and video-aided telecommunications augmented with regular local and international travel are now standard expectations of many higher education administrators.

Stability of Personnel

Stability and constancy within bureaucracies occur through consistency of personnel.

> Time is required for an employee to get used to new work and succeed in doing it well … If when he [sic] has got used to it or before then, he [sic] is removed, he [sic] will not have had time to render worthwhile service. If this be repeated indefinitely the work will never be properly done. (Fayol, 1916/2005, p. 58)

Unless hired on a temporary basis, most administrators and staff are employed with the expectation that long-term employment is possible and desirable. Retirement and medical benefits, vacation accrual, and the promise of advancement are elements that shape the expectation that stability rather than instability is expected. This stability allows the employee to become familiar with the organization and work of the unit, gain experience useful to the organization, and build loyalty to and connection with the institution.

Centralization/Decentralization

The choice whether to centralize authority in one or several offices or to decentralize and share authority across a wider range of offices is a difficult one for any organization. "Centralization is not a system of management good or bad of itself, capable of being adopted or discarded at the whim of managers or of circumstances; it is always present to a greater or less extent" (Fayol, 1916/2005, p. 55). In higher education, with its multiple goals and purposes, the centralization–decentralization dilemma is particularly acute. The professional and disciplinary expertise of deans and faculty exacerbate the centralization-decentralization tensions in academic bureaucracies. Centralization enhances standardization, control, and consistency. Decentralization can allow multiple purposes to exist within the organization because oversight is less vigilant. Leadership across a wider range of offices and units is possible because responsibility is diffuse, located away from the center of the organization. An advantage of decentralization is that "local" management can make up for leadership deficiencies at the executive (e.g., president and provost) level. But, too much decentralization can be detrimental to organizations. Goals become too disparate, waste results from duplication of effort, and power struggles erupt throughout the organization.

> Unless the sentiment of general interest be constantly revived by higher authority, it becomes blurred and weakened and each section tends to regard itself as its own aim and end and forgets that it is only a cog in a big machine, all of whose parts must work in concert. It becomes isolated, cloistered, aware only of the line of authority. (Fayol, 1916/2005, p. 57)

The size and nature of higher education institutions, except for the smallest of colleges, drive these organizations to a more decentralized form. It is a rare dean or department chair who takes orders in the way envisioned by the original bureaucracy theorists.

Table 10.4 Strengths and Weaknesses of the Bureaucratic Perspective

Strengths	Weaknesses
Seeks to minimize patronage, favoritism, and nepotism through standardization and objectivity.	Breeds alienation among employees who may feel infantilized and misused in a system that does not recognize their full potential.
Provides a means to organize complex tasks.	Routinization and standardization can quickly lead to red tape, which interferes with responsiveness and adaptability.
Works well in settings where routinization of task is needed to produce a standard outcome or product.	Cannot quickly adapt to the changing environments typical of higher education institutions.
Pursues the goal of fairness through objectivity and impartiality.	Fails to take into account the human element within organizations.

STRENGTHS AND WEAKNESSES OF THE BUREAUCRATIC MODEL

The bureaucratic model is perhaps one of the most highly criticized organizational approaches (Briskin, 1996; Ferguson, 1985). As with all organizational perspectives, this perspective contains strengths and weaknesses (see Table 10.4).

NEXT STEPS: BRINGING THE BUREAUCRATIC PERSPECTIVE INTO CURRENT USE

Bureaucracy is an older perspective that warrants consideration of the ways that its original premises remain relevant to today's higher education. A contemporary application of the bureaucratic perspective is strategic management as articulated by Toma (2010, 2012). Strategic management follows the tradition established by George Keller (1983) in his classic book, *Academic Strategy*.

> Keller (1983) argues that strategy is grounded in an institution shaping its own destiny, focused on keeping pace with the current environment, influenced by markets and competition, oriented toward action, both rational and tolerant of ambiguity, and obsessed. With the fate of the institution, it considers the traditions and values of an institution, as well as its aspirations and priorities, while taking into account strengths and weaknesses, both academic and financial, and the external environment. (Toma, 2012, p. 121)

In bureaucracies, a long-standing tension has existed between the goals of efficiency and effectiveness. Strategic management addresses this tension by emphasizing capacity building as a means to achieve the vision and purposes of higher education institutions.

> Strategy is not only a plan toward attaining missions and achieving aspirations but is also a pattern and thus consistent over time; a position, locating particular products in particular markets; a perspective, or the fundamental ways an organization does things; and a ploy, a specific maneuver intended to outwit an opponent or competitor. (Toma, 2012, p. 121)

Stating that building organizational capacity is an administrative foundation of any institution, Toma (2010) discusses the ways that capacity building is essential if an organization is to achieve its vision. Systems thinking, particularly understanding how parts of an organization are interrelated with and affected by all other parts is a significant element of strategic management. This approach considers the integration and synchronization of different elements of the organization: purposes, structure, governance, policies, processes, information, infrastructure, and culture (Toma, 2010). The integration of organizational elements using systems thinking enables college or university leadership to identify gaps, disconnects, and areas lacking the resources necessary to achieve the purposes being undertaken. For example, if a university wants to establish a new doctoral program in electrical engineering, strategic management using systems thinking can assist the leadership to determine existing faculty resources, market availability, extramural funding, and other components that must be in place for the program to be successful. Without adequate resources, the institution may not have the capacity to meet its goals. Lacking this capacity, the program may fail to meet enrollment, quality, or revenue generating goals.

Structure, particularly as expressed in hierarchy, power dynamics, and reporting lines, is a particular feature of the bureaucratic perspective. Strategic management expands ideas built into the early bureaucracy literature in its shifted perspective about the ways organizations function. Rather than a simple hierarchy, strategic management theorists imagine organizations as webs (Toma, 2010). A web conveys the interrelationships among the parts and the important ways that one part can positively and negatively affect other parts. In this way, alignment and coordination are considerations in strategic management.

Strategic management considers the structural elements articulated in the bureaucratic perspective as leadership assesses the ways that a structural aspect does or does not support the goals of the organization or initiative undertaken. Strategic management expands the bureaucratic perspective as the method considers the interrelationships among the parts. Knowledge of these interrelationships can assist leaders to better align the parts in ways that build capacity. Using systems thinking, administrators can evaluate where weakness or breakdown in one area will potentially affect other areas, even areas at a distance from the breakdown. Although the bureaucratic perspective addresses interrelationships, these are largely one way (e.g., horizontal communication, scalar chain) with inadequate discussion about the ways that structural elements at a distance from one another, communication patterns outside rigid bureaucratic prescriptions, and inadequate performance by organizational officers can affect the organization's capacity to achieve its goals. Strategic management addresses these organizational elements in ways that provide additional insights and facility to lead. Finally, strategic management expands the bureaucratic perspective in its use as an analytic tool. The approach can help leaders determine future goals, actions, and initiatives because they are guided by knowledge about the capacity of the organization to undertake those plans (Toma, 2010).

CONCLUSIONS

Bureaucratically organized institutions are more effective in stable, unchanging environments than in volatile, constantly changing ones. Unfortunately, the former do not exist in higher education. Despite this fundamental conflict, effective work in higher education institutions warrants an understanding of bureaucracy and how this type of organization operates. Even the most skeptical of critics concerning this organizational form will find elements of it everywhere, even in the most loosely organized college or university. But proponents of bureaucracies might take heed of an observation by Stephenson (2010) concerning the efficacy of this form. She claims that bureaucracies "demand constant tending and feeding to be sustained; awe arises because they are mercurial, magically summoning power from unknowable depths to kill an innovation or destroy a career with aplomb" (p. 1). If higher education is to achieve its current purposes and rise up to meet future challenges, the energy expended to maintain the bureaucratic form may be better invested in other places.

Questions for Discussion

- Are the ideas and techniques of classical bureaucracy relevant to contemporary higher education?
- How can higher education leaders use the concepts of strategic management to effect change within their institution?
- How do bureaucratic principles enable higher education effectiveness? How do they constrain effectiveness?
- Why do bureaucratic ways of organizing persist in contemporary higher education institutions?
- How do bureaucratic ways of organizing enhance higher education leaders' ability to transform society? Constrain their ability?

Recommended Readings in the Bureaucracy Perspective

Blau, P. M. (1956). *Bureaucracy in modern society.* New York: Crown.

Butler, B., Joyce, E., & Pike, J. (2008). Don't look now, but we've created a bureaucracy: The nature and roles of policies and rules in Wikipedia. *Proceedings of the 26th Annual SIGCHI Conference on Human Factors in Computing Systems.*

du Gay, P. (2005). *The values of bureaucracy.* Oxford, England: Oxford University Press.

Keeling, R. P., Underhile, R., & Wall, A. R. (2007). Horizontal and vertical structures: The dynamics of organization in higher education. *Liberal Education, 93*(4), 22–31.

Olsen, J. P. (2005). Maybe it is time to rediscover bureaucracy. *Journal of Public Administration Research and Theory, 16*, 1–24.

Pinchot, G., & Pinchot, E. (1994). *The end of bureaucracy and the rise of the intelligent organization.* San Francisco, CA: Berrett-Koehler.

Powell, W. W. (1990). Neither market nor hierarchy: Network forms of organization. *Research in Organizational Behavior, 12*, 295–336.

Simon, H. A. (1947). *Administrative behavior.* New York: Macmillan.

Weber, M., Gerth, H. H., & Turner, B. S. (1991). *From Max Weber: Essays in sociology.* New York: Routledge.

11

CASE

Executive Leadership and the Corporatization of Higher Education

The corporatization of higher education has been a topic of noteworthy interest in recent years. Higher education has been pushed toward corporate-inspired ways of operating by the rise in tuition, decreased levels of public funding, increased emergence of higher education as a private good, and demands for accountability, among other trends (Andrews, 2006). The common use of the term chief executive officer (CEO), applied to higher education presidents, points to the current practice of applying corporate ideas to higher education. The corporatization of higher education, as argued by Aronowitz (2000), Bok (2003), Giroux (2002), and Levine (2000a), among others, is a deleterious development in higher education; one that is shifting the very foundation and values of these long standing institutions.

For opponents of higher education corporatization, business practices such as branding, cost savings through decreased employee benefits, and use of nonacademic amenities to recruit students are viewed as negative higher education management trends. Andrews (2006) provided a checklist against which faculty, the focus of that author's attention, can compare their institution (see Table 11.1). Answering affirmatively to these questions can provide information about the extent to which an institution is adopting corporate practices.

Questions to Consider

- What are several internal and external pressures on today's higher education that are driving corporatization?
- What long-standing values and traditions of higher education must change when an institution adopts a corporate approach?
- What value is attained when colleges and universities are operated "like a business"?
- What is gained with a corporate approach to higher education management?

Income generation through auxiliary services, online and distance learning, and fee-for-service programs has become a required means to keep institutions solvent.

Table 11.1   A Corporatization Checklist

- Is your college or university hiring low-paid, non-tenured contingent faculty to replace departing tenured and tenure-track faculty?

- Has your institution decreased need-based financial aid? Has there been a corresponding increase in merit-based scholarships?

- Are high corporate-level salaries (especially when compared with faculty salaries) being paid to administrators?

- Is there an increasing reliance on search firms—expensive and inadequate substitutes for an appropriately constituted, well directed, and faculty-dominated search committee?

- Are faculty members' teaching and service contributions being devalued while pressure to obtain external funding for research is increasing?

- Have health and retirement benefits for faculty decreased in an environment in which the costs of health care and retirement are rising rapidly?

- Have courses and curricular programs formerly regarded as essential to a college education been eliminated? Are for-profit courses being established without regard to their long-term educational value?

- Is there an increasing emphasis on intercollegiate athletics as a selling point for admissions and fund raising? Is this trend complemented by increased spending on teams that is not matched by increased spending on teaching, research, or financial aid?

Adapted from Andrews (2006).

Outsourcing as a way to economize and develop new services, including residence halls, is common. Multimillion dollar and complex financial models require additional staff to undertake cost-benefit analyses, responsibility centered budgeting, and other financial processes borrowed from the corporate world. College and university presidents, responsible to a wide array of intra- and extra-institutional stakeholders, must juggle the medieval academic structure of the collegium and the corporate structure of a modern bureaucracy. The rapid rate of change that exists on today's college and university campus is congruent with a corporate approach to management but incongruent with traditional models of higher education organization.

Bergquist and Phillips (as cited in Bergquist & Pawlak, 2008) suggested structure, process, and attitude as three organizational development domains related to change within higher education institutions. Organizational change, a frequently sought goal, can be affected by influencing structure, process, and attitude. Changes in organizational charts, reward systems, and institutional policies and procedures result in structural changes. When communication configurations, decision-making approaches, conflict management methods, or management styles change, process adaptation follows. Attitude, the third domain of organizational development, entails "how people feel about working" in the structures and processes of the organization (Bergquist & Pawlak, 2008, p. 82). All three domains work together; attitude is affected by structure and process. Process is influenced by attitude and structure.

A search for a new president, or chief executive officer (CEO) in corporate parlance, is a particularly salient opportunity for change. A new president can bring change in all three domains of process, structure, and attitude. Particularly during the honeymoon period of a president's new administration, changes are possible that are difficult if not impossible to institute in later stages of the presidency. Existing senior administrators often tender their resignations; new administrators are hired. Departments and divisions shift into new configurations. Programs are eliminated. New communication, management, and decision-making styles are brought into institutional practice.

Questions to Consider

- What structural changes might a new president make to solidify a base of support for new initiatives?
- What process changes might be necessary to garner support for a new vision for an institution?
- How does loyalty among staff members impact the success of a new president?
- How does objectivity and distance by presidents inform the principles of bureaucracies?

The bureaucratic principle of unity of command (Morgan, 2006), stating that each person should receive orders from one source, is most evident during presidential searches. With the chair of the Board of Trustees as the titular or actual chair of the search committee, the reporting line between the president and Board becomes abundantly clear. With all deference to stakeholders notwithstanding, the president's definitive "boss" is the Board of Trustees. While members of the Board of Trustees normally use closed executive sessions to issue presidential evaluations and directives, presidential searches are regularly conducted using the democratic processes of representation, open forums, and abundant feedback.

Boards of trustees, regents, or visitors, as they are sometimes called, have four primary purposes on college campuses: hire and fire the president, review programs for introduction or termination, exercise fiduciary responsibility for the institution by reviewing the budget, and assure the mission and direction of the institution (Chaitt, Holland, & Taylor, 1996; Kezar, 2006; Tierney, 2004). This case discusses bureaucratic principles involved in a presidential search. Particularly illustrated are the concepts of line and staff, division of labor, stability of personnel, responsibility as endowed in the office, and scalar chain.

THE CASE

Institutional Context

Prize University is a very high research activity institution as designated by the Carnegie Classification (Carnegie Foundation, 2010). The flagship institution located in a state of approximately 25 million people; Prize University is part of a complex system of higher education institutions. Of the 25 institutions in the state, Prize University has the highest admissions standards, attracts extremely qualified faculty, and boasts the highest rate of research funding of all universities in the state. After 9 years of uninterrupted presidential leadership, Prize University is searching for a new chief executive. Citing health concerns, the former president resigned a year ahead of schedule; the vice president for administration and finance stepped in as interim president.

Characters

Frank Harrison: Mr. Harrison, a retired CEO of a local Fortune 500 firm, served as the chair of the Board of Regents of Prize University for 5 years. A veteran of university politics, Mr. Harrison felt that the president of this institution with its $3 billion budget needed to have an executive leader with business experience. As a member of the board for 7 years prior to becoming chair (12 years total), he was consistently puzzled by the University faculty's insistence that the president be an academic. In Harrison's mind, the provost could manage the academics. The president needed to be a CEO, someone familiar with the intricacies of financial planning, personnel management, and leadership. Leaders from the corporate world or government sector could manage the substantial budget. The job was unsuited for someone with a career spent in academia.

In addition to serving as board chair, Harrison led the presidential search committee, a position he took seriously. While past search committee chairs allowed the president's executive assistant staff to manage the committee, he was extremely involved in the process. While some administrators and faculty complained that his approach was micromanaging, he felt that he was exercising his legal and fiduciary responsibility as board chair.

Interim President John Creamer: Creamer had served as a vice president of the institution for 25 years. He had filled a variety of roles including associate vice president for finance, director of human resources, and, most recently, senior vice president for administration and finance. An alumnus of the institution, Creamer had spent his adult life at Prize University. He was extremely loyal to the institution and enjoyed his role as interim president. He had served under the most recent president, Dr. William Hunter, a strong academic leader who had minimal understanding of the intricacies of the budget. Dr. Hunter had made it clear from the start that he delegated the financial matters to Creamer. As such, the vice president had a free hand with how money was allocated throughout the institution. This approach resulted in a disconnection between the academic, research, and administrative functions of the institution. When he assumed the interim president position, Creamer had promised not to apply for the job. On the urging of numerous administrators in the institution and government officials outside the university, however, he was regretting that decision. His plan was to talk to Chair Harrison and see if he could become a candidate, even at this late stage of the search.

Dr. Gary Kegan: A veteran of three presidents, Kegan was the executive assistant to the president. A veteran of university administration, Dr. Kegan was on the committee or had staffed three presidential searches. In addition to his experience with these essential university search functions, he had also staffed a number of provost and vice presidential searches. He was familiar with Mr. Harrison's desire to be an active search committee chair and he welcomed his involvement, but in his experience, trustee chairs were usually figureheads. They were chair in name but left it to the staff to manage. This search promised to be very different. Kegan was looking forward to the change.

Dr. Mary Glazer: Glazer was a relatively new faculty member at the university. She was recruited from her old institution because of the substantial research dollars she brought with her. Her work in molecular biology was cutting edge and left her little time for university service. When she was invited by interim president John Creamer to be on the committee, she reluctantly agreed. She knew that Creamer was using her international reputation as a way to recruit top candidates. Despite her misgivings about serving on the committee, she agreed because she feared that the corporatization of the university was eroding the research mission. While she understood that research dollars were viewed as a substantial revenue source for the university, Glazer had a purist view of the research enterprise. Her academic career was dedicated to the pursuit of new knowledge. She felt strongly that the next president needed to fully understand the research mission of an institution like Prize.

Authority and Power

Dr. Kegan was a traditionalist regarding presidential leadership. A student of bureaucracy and advocate of its use, Kegan believed in separating the person from the office. As a first hand observer of several Prize University presidents, Kegan had seen the good results when an administrator's personal and public personas were unconnected, as much as that was possible. His first president, Steven Curtis, a man of considerable talent, had gotten himself into trouble when he let his personal beliefs interfere with professional business. An unenlightened administrator regarding diversity, Curtis had based his hiring on the racial and gender identities with which he was comfortable. The consistent practice of hiring White men was met by challenges from students and faculty and became a primary reason for Curtis's early retirement.

Similar to Kegan, Chair of the Board Harrison also adhered to bureaucratic principles. He believed that legitimate power was the most effective way to achieve change within an institution. Harrison struggled with faculty claims about expert power and believed that true power came from the authority endowed in a position or office. University presidents, like corporate CEOs, were at the pinnacle of power and, therefore, were most able to effect organizational change. As Board chair, Harrison took his authority role regarding the president seriously. He and the other Board of Trustee members were the boss. They were invested in the success of the institution and used the means at their disposal to exercise power and communicate their vision. Budget approval and vision, mission, and strategic plan authorization were their major means to keep the institution on track. They delegated the day-to-day operation and other responsibilities to the president and his staff and then held him responsible for assuring that their identified course of action was followed.

In conversations during the presidential search committee retreat, it became clear that Harrison and Kegan were like-minded concerning presidential leadership. Both felt that leadership and management acumen needed to take precedence over academic credentials. At the urging of the Board, substantial progress on financial reform had been achieved under Interim President Creamer's leadership. This was accomplished without the need to explain financial management details to the president. They had had years of financially inexperienced presidents who lacked the necessary knowledge and background for fiscal management. On-the-job training and nationally sponsored professional development helped but did not alleviate the need for trustee intervention when the president did not have all the skills necessary to lead a multibillion dollar operation.

Questions to Consider

- What conflicts can you envision between the academic-related qualities of the president and the bureaucratic responsibilities and expectations of that executive position?
- What qualities and skills gained from a president's experience as an academic and scholar enhance that person's ability to undertake the presidential role?
- What qualities and skills necessary for presidential leadership are not gained through experience as an academic and scholar?
- What do you envision as the skills necessary for a president over the next 20 years in higher education? How can those skills be taught to today's academic leaders?

Traditional Views of the Office of the President

The search committee was deep into conversation during their off-campus retreat. The group was evenly split between people who believed that traditional bureaucratic principles were the best means of leadership and those who believed that a more academically oriented, collegial approach was necessary. The collegial group, led informally by Dr. Glazer, felt the institution would benefit from a president who was socially and personally more accessible to administrators and faculty. Glazer felt strongly that interim president Creamer lacked knowledge of the importance of knowledge generation and research as central to the university's mission. From her perspective, he understood how research dollars through indirect costs flowed into the institution, but lacked an understanding of how basic research, even the most arcane, advanced knowledge in today's society.

Board Chair Harrison led the bureaucratically inclined group that felt it was necessary for the chief executive officer to exercise authority and strong management. This approach involved a decisive leadership style, distance from employees to convey authority, and logistical use of the presidential accoutrements to convey power and leadership. Harrison knew that vision flows from the president's office, often in consultation with others, but ultimately directly from the chief executive officer.

Questions to Consider

- How do power and privilege intersect in bureaucracies? How are both expressed through the presidential role?
- What is the relationship between the trappings of the president's office and presidential authority?
- How are the symbols of the president's office viewed from a bureaucratic perspective? From a collegial perspective? From a cultural perspective?
- How does presidential authority from a bureaucratic perspective create the opportunity for change? How can this authority create barriers to change?

Presidential Qualifications

Administrative and staff hiring in bureaucracies, including higher education institutions, is based on qualifications and criteria. Whether a presidential search is managed externally through an executive search firm or internally via committee, qualifications are determined as a first step in the recruitment process. Often symbolized in the job description, the qualifications only tell part of the story about the qualities sought in a president.

At their retreat, the presidential search committee at Prize University determined a list of requirements for the position. Using presidential job descriptions from competing institutions, materials from past searches, and information from the higher education literature, the following qualifications were included in the job description.

1. Experience as an academic of high (e.g., full professor) rank with impeccable teaching and scholarly experience;
2. Proficiency in fund raising;
3. Understanding of strategic planning, problem solving, financial management, and executive administration processes;
4. Possession of a vision with the capability to communicate this to the university community;
5. Prior experience managing a multimillion or multibillion dollar institution;
6. Understanding of internal and external institutional politics in a state university environment;
7. Knowledge of how to work with internal and external stakeholders including state legislators, elected city officials, alumni/ae, parents, and local businesspeople; and
8. A change-oriented approach matched with an understanding of institutional administrative practices.

A recent posting for a presidential search at the University of Utah had summarized the herculean qualities desired of a president. The search committee agreed that the presidency of Prize University demanded similar heroic attributes:

> Ideal candidates must have broad administrative and management experience, a proven record of administrative and scholarly achievement in higher education, experience and success in fundraising, and leadership qualities essential for the administration of a large, culturally diverse, and complex academic and research institution. (*The Chronicle of Higher Education*, 2011)

This paragraph exemplifies the tension existing for today's college and university presidents: they must have spent significant time honing their academic credentials and scholarship while simultaneously gaining the requisite management skills to oversee a multimillion or billion dollar institution. Few other contemporary organizations require such a wide array of qualities for its chief executive officer.

Questions to Consider

- If you were to write a job description for the presidential search at this institution, what qualifications would you include?
- How can strong academic credentials be balanced with the need for executive management skills?
- In what ways can structure and administrative personnel be used to balance the skills needed within an administration of a university?
- What are the necessary skills for the next generation of presidents?

Interviews, Open Forums, and Community Input

The presidential search committee spent weeks reviewing applications, informally checking references, and determining the pool of candidates for in-person interviews. After interviewing 10 candidates in airport conversations (i.e., a process whereby the search committee travels to a central location and interviews multiple candidates in short meetings), the on-campus interview pool was whittled down to four candidates. Because the search was entering a more public phase, candidate materials (e.g., vitas) were posted on a presidential search website. The committee knew that conflicting opinions being played out on the committee would be amplified through campus community input.

Dr. Glazer was looking forward to the open forums. Through numerous conversations with faculty and staff on campus, she knew that people wanted a change from the traditional bureaucratic approach to presidential leadership. Her colleagues were interested in a president who was less bureaucratic and more collaborative. She believed you could be an effective administrator while being open, participative, and exercising first among equals leadership. While several committee members agreed with her, others, most notably Board Chair Harrison, believed that a top-down, decisive, and commanding style of leadership was needed at this point in the institution's history. In his mind, leaders who portrayed vision from the top, who set the tone, were strong, and decisive had served the institution well in the past. Glazer believed that these traditionalists could be swayed if campus community members shared their alternative point of views about leadership and administration. She encouraged many to attend the open forums and express a more up-to-date way to lead; one that was collaborative, participative, and empowering.

The existence of two different approaches to presidential leadership, bureaucratic and collegial, was well represented on the search committee and among the candidates, who were split evenly into two groups by leadership style: two candidates exemplified "command and control" leadership and two exhibited a collaborative approach.

Questions to Consider

- What campus practices dictate the inclusion of community input in presidential appointments?
- In what ways does campus-wide inclusion reflect (or not reflect) a bureaucratic approach to administration?
- In what ways does campus-wide inclusion reflect (or not reflect) a collegial approach to administration?
- Which style of leadership and administration most resonates with your approach to higher education management and organization?

Four presidential candidates visited the university for on-campus interviews. Much to the disappointment of search committee members, the open forums for each candidate were sparsely attended. Although committee members had encouraged involvement from the community, people voiced the opinion that the ultimate decision on who was hired was determined by the trustees. They felt that their opinion would not be heeded in the open forums or follow-up evaluation. With the burden of too much work to be completed, they told her, "What's the point? The trustees are going to appoint whomever they want. It's a waste of time for us to attend the meetings and provide input."

Questions to Consider

- In what ways do bureaucracies disempower the voice of those lower on the hierarchy?
- What communication patterns exist in bureaucracies that encourage the flow of communication between hierarchical layers?
- How do power, position, and privilege overlap in bureaucratic structures?
- Who is responsible for hiring the president in a bureaucratic organization?

The search committee met for their final meeting to determine an unranked list of candidates with narrative about each individual's strengths and weaknesses. This list was presented to, and a final decision made by the Board of Trustees. The committee's role was to give recommendations, not select the candidate. In this way, the lines of authority between the president and Board of Trustees were clear. The search committee was advisory; the ultimate decision rested with the Board.

The committee, as reflected in previous deliberations and discussions, was split in their opinions about the best candidate or candidates. Many felt strongly that the candidate with a strong research record and recent experience, as a provost at an institution similar to Prize University, was the most likely choice. This coalition of committee members, led by Dr. Glazer, lobbied hard for this candidate to be discussed in a manner that highlighted his obvious strengths as an academic and researcher. Board Chair Harrison and his contingent had other plans for the list. His choice for president was clear: the candidate who was a sitting president at an institution similar in size and scope, but not reputation, to Prize University. In this way, Prize would benefit from the administrative and managerial expertise of a seasoned professional and the candidate would be attracted to the academic excellence of Prize. Although the deliberations were lively, even heated, Harrison knew his perspective would prevail. It was his responsibility to carry the unranked candidate narratives to the Board. In a closed-door session, he would give his perspective on the strengths and weaknesses of each candidate and his opinion on what was best for the institution. His choice for the next chief executive officer would need to tackle the issues facing Prize: a complex budget situation, a marketing plan that portrayed the institution effectively, and an imperative to contain costs through salary savings and outsourcing. Harrison knew that his choice would command a high salary and an attractive contract, including a severance package at the end of his tenure, but the outcome would be worth the price.

The Board of Trustees met to determine the outcome of the presidential search with Harrison's candidate as the obvious choice. They felt that the process had maintained the integrity of the search process by creating opportunities for input and a democratically-oriented search committee. They were confident in their choice.

Questions to Consider

- Using a bureaucratic perspective, how might you influence the search as a member of the search committee?
- Using a political perspective? Using a collegial perspective?

- What are the strengths and weaknesses of the bureaucratic leadership perspective?
- What are the strengths and weaknesses of a collaborative, participative approach to leadership and administration?

DISCUSSION

Depending on the perspective of the viewer, a presidential search committee can be viewed as a fait accompli, the inevitable outcome of bureaucratic principles laid down in earlier decades. Or, the appointment of a new president can be an opportunity to transform leadership styles, institutional trajectory, and organizational practices. As with all perspectives, each has its positive and negative aspects. There is stability and constancy in bureaucratic procedures that offer continuity over time. In bureaucracies, the lines of authority and power are very clear. Each entity, from the boards of trustees to the lowest staff member on the hierarchy, has a job description and operating procedures that, at maximum, dictate or, at minimum, shape the rules of operation. Presidential searches are an opportunity to observe the written and unwritten rules of an organization at work. Assumptions become more evident, reporting lines are revealed, and power becomes visible. This case sought to illustrate some of the tensions within bureaucracies when a new executive is chosen. In the current world of higher education, a significant tension exists between the desire of the Board of Trustees to hire an experienced executive and the faculty (and others) who wish to hire an academic or researcher. This tension, played out for decades, promises to continue into the future.

12

NEW SCIENCE

If we want to transform the structure and leadership of our organizations, we have to address change at the fundamental paradigmatic level. We have to change the thinking behind our thinking. Leaders who want to initiate real change processes must become aware that they have been acting out of a paradigm. They must see the origin and nature of this existing paradigm and its effect on their management. And they must get to a point where they can feel the reality of an alternative paradigm—or the creative excitement of standing at the edge between paradigms. (Zohar, 1997, p. 25)

INTRODUCTION

There can be no doubt that the internal and external higher education environment has increased in complexity over the last 25 years. A volatile economic climate, complicated policy environment, heightened societal expectations, and complex management conditions have increased the challenges to leaders within colleges and universities. Some have responded with calls for a new way of leading, a new paradigm. In the context of this book, the term paradigm denotes a mental model, mind-set, or conceptual framework (Zohar, 1997). Older paradigms emphasizing rationality, certainty, and control fail to provide the theoretical, philosophical, and practical depth needed to address today's challenges. "One ... paradigm is not adequate to the task of understanding the network of the intricate and ambiguous human relationships making up educational practice" (Kincheloe, 2006, p. 86).

This chapter applies to higher education organizations the paradigm often referred to as emergent, new science, and quantum (Allen & Cherrey, 2000; Clark, 1985; Lincoln, 1985; Wheatley, 2007, 2010; Zohar, 1997). The principles of the older, Newtonian paradigm no longer fit a postmodern world characterized by complexity, interrelationship, and uncertainty. Although there are many circumstances, such as hospital emergency rooms, where the standard operating procedures of the Newtonian paradigm are appropriate and essential, higher education institutions are not among that paradigm's success stories. Institutional complexities, the presence of diverse populations, and high professional status among faculty and administrators are situations that argue for supplanting the traditional paradigm with a new one. The quantum model is one that better explains the environments in which higher education exists today. The complex organizational structures, multiple power configurations, and elaborate networks of stakeholders require the flexible and creative approach of the quantum paradigm. In this chapter, the theorists Stephenson, Wheatley, and Zohar are particularly highlighted as a foundation upon which to explain how new science perspectives can be effectively applied in higher education.

ASSUMPTIONS OF THE NEW SCIENCE PERSPECTIVE

The new science or quantum model is among the most recent organizational perspectives to emerge among organizational and leadership theorists. Margaret Wheatley most notably introduced this approach in her books, *Leadership and the New Science* (2010) and *Finding Our Way* (2007). Taking the pop and business literature by storm, Wheatley introduced a new way to think about organizations. The quantum perspective was not new to the social sciences. Thomas Kuhn (1962) had introduced the emergent or new paradigm in the 1960s.

The ruminations of Thomas Kuhn (1962), published in *The Structure of Scientific Revolutions* and applied to a wide variety of settings, including higher education, are well known. Kuhn speculated that paradigms or worldviews dominate until they can no longer explain phenomena. The phenomena left unexplained can include research findings and organizational functioning. When that occurs, a new paradigm takes its place and the evolutionary process of building and replacing recurs. Talking about scientific methodology, Kuhn stated that when

> the profession can no longer evade anomalies that subvert the existing tradition of scientific practice—then begins the extraordinary investigations that lead the profession at last to a new set of commitments, a new basis for the practice of science. (1962, p. 6)

Identified paradigm shifts include Galileo's discovery that the Earth circles the Sun and Einstein's theory of relativity. The new science assumptions, also called postpositivism, emergent paradigm, or postmodern are a recent paradigm shift. Zohar articulated these assumptions in marked contrast to the positivist assumptions that preceded this paradigm shift (see Table 12.1).

These underlying assumptions result in organizations that are complex and interrelated; thoroughly connected to the context and environments in which they exist; concerned with process and product; and open to a wide variety of styles and possibilities. Similar to the other theoretical foundations discussed in this book, the philosophy of science perspective carries strengths and weaknesses that inform organizational practice (see Table 12.2).

The phrase quantum leap is perhaps the most common reference to the ideas about the new science paradigm.

Table 12.1 Zohar's Characteristics of the Positivist and Post-Positivist Paradigms

Positivist	Post-Positivist
Determinism	"Radically" indeterminate
Dualistic (i.e., either/or)	Non-dualistic (i.e., both/and)
Competitive	Cooperation
Fragmented	Interrelated
Reductionistic	Wholistic
Certainty	Uncertainty
Prediction and Control	Control is an illusion
One reality	Multiple realities
Simple	Complex
Cartesian split (mind and body separate)	Mind, body, and spirit inseparable
Linear	Non-linear
Uni-causality	Multiple causality

Quantum leap … means not just a big leap, but a leap from one kind of reality to another … it means a leap from a world we understood and could manage to one where at first nothing makes sense. A leap that requires us to rethink our basic categories and strategies, to alter our most cherished and deeply unconscious assumptions. (Zohar, 1997, p. 41)

Quantum leaps entail paradigm shifts. They are uncontrollable, unpredictable, and full of opportunity. Higher education institutions currently exist in volatile environments. In such circumstances, administrators and faculty often yearn for prediction. How many students will accept admission? Will the legislature rescind the state allocation? Will the price of heating oil to heat the buildings increase? Despite the search for objectivity and certainty, administrators, faculty, and students experience opportunities to make quantum leaps everyday. Zohar and others argue that what is missing from our experiences is the shift in assumptions that comes with a quantum leap. The shift to a new paradigm involves understanding that these environments can be understood though

Table 12.2 Strengths and Weaknesses of the Philosophy of Science Theoretical Foundation

Strengths	Weaknesses
Provides a powerful theoretical analysis through and with which to view organizations.	May emphasize intellectual over practical approaches to organizational functioning.
Better explains the environmental volatility and uncertainty of organizational life.	May paralyze those uncomfortable with ambiguity.
Enables people within organizations to be more flexible and adaptable.	May appear as if "anything goes."
Allows people to accept the idiosyncrasies of organizational life.	Can be used as an excuse for not making meaningful progress on organizational goals.

not controlled, that there are many possible outcomes to the situations presented, and there is more going on than objective measures reveal.

The quantum paradigm theorists acknowledged that the presence of human beings, inevitable disorder of natural and human systems, and the holism present in all systems introduces indeterminacy into organizational life. Organizational participants, regardless of how hard they try, cannot predict or control outcomes. Neither can they identify a singular right way to proceed. Wheatley suggested that it is the managers' and leaders' assumptions about organizations that make them seem unmanageable, not the organizations themselves. Her main premise is that "there is a simpler way to lead organizations, one that requires less effort and produces less stress than the current practices" (Wheatley, 2010, p. xxix). It was time for a paradigm shift from Newton to Einstein (see Table 12.3). The quantum paradigm emphasizes interrelatedness, mutual and multiple causality, multiple realities, uncertainty, and control as an illusion.

Interrelatedness

The Newtonian paradigm reduces everything to its parts. The epitome of this approach was scientific management, an approach advanced by Frederick Taylor and put into practice most vigorously with Ford's assembly line. Human beings were similar to the car parts being assembled. All were interchangeable and anonymous cogs in a wheel. Higher education was not immune from this reductionist approach.

> We broke knowledge into separate disciplines and subjects, built offices and schools with divided space, developed analytic techniques that focus on discrete factors, and even counseled ourselves to act in fragments, to use different "parts" of ourselves in different settings.... Until recently we really believed that we could study the parts, no matter how many of them there were, to arrive at knowledge of the whole. We have reduced and described and separated things into cause and effect, and drawn the world in lines and boxes. (Wheatley, 2010, pp. 18–19)

Table 12.3 Differences between the Newtonian and Quantum Paradigms

Newtonian Paradigm	Quantum Paradigm
The Universe is viewed as a machine, divided into parts.	The Universe is viewed as a complex system of relationships.
Only elements comprehended through the physical senses can be known.	Creativity, insight, and intuition are additional ways of knowing and discovering.
Understanding emerges from an examination of cause and effect.	Multiple and mutual causality provide more complex explanatory power regarding human functioning, particularly in organizations.
Progress is made through incremental changes.	Self-organizing occurs when a system faces change and disorder requiring a new way of operating.
Reality is based on natural laws which, when discovered, could be used to predict and control phenomena.	Uncertainty, ambiguity, and complexity underscore nature and human behavior.
Organizations can be reduced to their parts, which can be changed out when necessary.	The organization is holistic; it is more than the sum of its parts.

(Clark, 1985; Gleick, 1987; Wheatley, 2007, 2010; Zohar, 1997)

The quantum world does not view parts as separate, discrete objects separate from the whole. Instead, interrelationships make up reality: "relationships are not just interesting … they are *all* there is to reality" (Wheatley, 2010, p. 25). Taking their lead from physics where scientists discovered that particles took on meaning (e.g., as a wave or a particle) depending on how they were viewed, the quantum organizational theorists postulated that relationships form the core of reality in institutions. Organizations did not exist as entities separate from human behavior that operated on "natural" laws determined from outside that system. Rather, humans and their relationships *were* the organization. In practice, quantum-assuming organizational members understand that leaders and other personnel cannot be swapped out like machine parts. The absence of one person has a ripple effect on the entire system as relationships shift, change, and re-form. Adjustment time may be necessary and considerations taken into account when organizations transition to a new leader or lose a pivotal member. Opportunities to effect long-awaited changes may emerge. Relationships among coworkers may take different shapes. Work routines may traverse different paths.

Mutual and Multiple Causality

Organizational theorists and leaders adhering to the Newtonian perspective often search for the silver bullet, the singular solution that is the definitive answer to problems. From the Newtonian perspective, effects have singular causes in a chain of events, which, with enough information, can be predicted and controlled. Quantum theorists and their organizational proponents operate from the assumption that multiple causality better explains events within an organization. No one cause can predict events across different times, contexts, and circumstances. Large and small changes occur resulting in Greek philosopher Herclitus's saying, "you can never step in the same river twice."

Multiple causality is expressed in practice when quantum leaders abandon the practice of holding postmortems in an effort to ferret out *the* cause of a problem or *the* "one right response" to an issue. Instead, these discussions seek ways to build adaptability and flexibility into organizational systems to achieve responsiveness and nimble action. With the recognition of multiple and mutual causality comes the understanding that situations cannot be controlled. Instead, multiple paths and answers are possible and sought with an eye for context and finding several appropriate solutions. From a quantum perspective, administrators seek to broadly understand a situation and determine ways to use the myriad of skills and talents of the staff and faculty.

Multiple Realities

Higher education institutions are extremely complex organizations. A singular view of reality fails to account for this complexity and can leave leaders with an incomplete view of their organizations. The quantum perspective assumes that there are multiple realities possible in any circumstance. The specific reality that is ultimately expressed is a result of an intricate interplay with, and relationship among, for example, organizational members, context, and environment. The multiple stakeholders within higher education will certainly have different perspectives about the organization. But, the quantum model takes this dynamic one step further. Quantum theorists argue that different realities, not simply different perspectives, exist. Alumni members of boards of trustees are pertinent examples of the existence of multiple realities in colleges and universities. The college from which the alumna graduated may be vastly different from the one about which she is making decisions as a trustee. Regardless of the fact that decades may have passed since the alumna graduated, her view of the institution may remain in that past reality. This view, though very real for the trustee and the basis upon which she acts, may no longer correspond to the reality as expressed by others in the current day institution. Regardless of that disconnect, her obsolete reality may be the one upon which she bases her policy decisions. Without recognition of the existence of multiple realities on the board of trustees, throughout the administration, and among faculty, decision making is incomplete and ineffective.

Uncertainty

Zohar calls for leaders to use the quantum perspective as a way to create new organizations, ones "that can thrive on uncertainty, can deal creatively with rapid change, and can release the full potential of the human beings who lead and work or live within them" (1997, p. 5). Organizations, similar to the living organisms, are in a constant state of change. Their structure must be flexible and malleable enough to adapt to the changing internal and external environment. If rigid, the organization will be ineffective at best and archaic at worst.

Higher education exists in a particularly uncertain environment. Rapidly changing political environments on state and federal levels, economic volatility, and changing student preferences are a few of the circumstances that create an uncertain and ambiguous climate. This uncertainty means that administrators, faculty, and others involved in colleges and universities must exercise flexibility and openness. This need for adaptability is particularly important during institutional planning. In an uncertain environment, you cannot account for everything; therefore, an organization must be nimble enough to rapidly change course or adjust when faced with anticipated circumstances or an unforeseen opportunity.

The budget crisis of 2008 left many colleges in a precarious position regarding their endowment and earning rate. This circumstance showed that a large endowment could be a blessing and a curse. With significant income generated through endowment earnings, an institution can become overly dependent on that revenue as a major source of income. The sudden and astonishing drop in endowment earnings meant that revenues were severely affected. While, in good times, a large endowment provides exceptional nimbleness, in bad times, the same endowment can lead to lack of adaptability.

Control as an Illusion

In bureaucracies, managers and others look "for the laws inherent within each organization. Find those laws, understand the machinery of the organization, and a leader can exercise control" (Zohar, 1997, p. 49). The quantum view of organizations holds no such illusion about the possibility of control. The myriad of contingencies that impact a situation means that no formula or algorithm will accurately predict the outcome in all situations. When one abandons the illusion of control, it does not mean forsaking the possibility of influence. Administrators, including those adopting a quantum perspective, need to plan appropriately, skillfully craft organizational functioning to achieve at the highest levels, and manage the organization so its members and stakeholders benefit. One must do so with the knowledge that the best planning may fail, unforeseen circumstances will surely intervene, and educated guesses may be as valuable as the most detailed of analytical models. One can never plan for all elements in a particular situation. From a negative perspective, a hurricane during semester opening, or, in a positive sense, a large, unexpected gift from a donor, could radically change a situation and make prior planning irrelevant.

When organizational members give up the illusion of prediction and control, unexpected benefits accrue. When one abandons the idea that people are predictable, they become surprising. When strict consistency of behavior is no longer expected, than the realization that "each of us is a different person in different places" emerges; "this doesn't make us inauthentic; it merely makes us quantum" (Wheatley, 2010, p. 27). Rather than control, administrators using a quantum perspective look for order. The search for order from within a system like an organization is a leap of faith. Imposing control on the order that exists is more comforting but foolhardy in today's complex organizations. Flexibility and adaptability, although they may decrease the efficiency of an organization, increase its effectiveness. "The more controlled the parts of a system, the less they contribute to the system and the less they are part of the whole" (Zohar, 1997, p. 49).

METAPHOR

Several metaphors have been used to describe quantum organizations: a hall of mirrors where the view shifts with each position change; a hologram where the whole is contained in the parts; woven fabric to convey the warp and weave of complex inter-relationships; and, perhaps most provocatively, the "world as a great thought" (Wheatley, 2010, p. 38). These metaphors and images portray shared purpose, dynamism, connection, and relationship (Allen & Cherrey, 2000). The imagery of this approach to organizations challenges basic assumptions about leadership, prediction, and control.

STRUCTURE

Networks and heterarchy are the organizational forms associated with the quantum perspective. The term *heterarchy*, often evoked in quantum organization writings, was first used by Ogilvy (1977). Hierarchies emphasize, perhaps to excess, the vertical connections within an organization, heterarchy emphasizes the vertical *and* horizontal connections (Hedlund, 1986). Both hierarchy and network characteristics exist in these configurations. Networks are critical components of heterarchies. Karen Stephenson, a leading theorist on heterarchy and social networks within organizations, uses her anthropology, chemistry, and art backgrounds to paint a complex picture of organizations. With relationships at the center of the perspective, networks enable connections to form and change to occur. Heterarchy "is an organizational form somewhere between hierarchy and network that provides horizontal links permitting different elements of an organization to cooperate" (Stephenson, 2010, p. 2). In higher education, these heterarchies could be different divisions, academic departments, and schools/colleges in the same institution or a group of institutions within a system or consortium.

While some might welcome the demise of pure hierarchies, heterarchies include this all too familiar structure while also incorporating the interrelationships and connections of networks. Heterarchy theorists do not propose to replace hierarchy but to understand that this widely accepted structural form tells only part of the organizational story.

> Hierarchy is an important aspect of an organization's structural integrity. It is, in fact, half of the knowledge equation. But hierarchy's power cannot be confused with that of the equally real and relevant social networks that account for so much organizational knowledge. In the final analysis, hierarchy and networks should be yoked together to ensure balance and accountability. (Stephenson, 2005, p. 263)

Stephenson's image of heterarchy contrasts sharply with the image of hierarchies in which people on different layers, particularly as depicted on an organizational chart, can be blind to the full impact of the rich array of connections between and among the layers. When leaders and other organizational members are unaware of these connections, they fail to understand that managing institutions is difficult, often impossible.

Heterarchical structures can be imagined as a double helix in which hierarchy and networks influence and benefit each other to create more effective organizational structures (Kleiner, 2003).

> Any network can unravel a hierarchy and any hierarchy can crush a network. Hierarchy without network is austere; network without hierarchy is anarchy. Together they form a natural tension in the dance of discovery. (Stephenson, 2001, p. 5)

Without a structure such as hierarchy, it is difficult to imagine how networks form and endure. Without networks built on trust to humanize hierarchy's form, organizational purposes could not be achieved. Heterarchies depend on networks, connections, and, most importantly, trust for their organizational form and effectiveness. "Networks are built from trust and trust is invisible and ubiquitous" (Stephenson, 2004, p. 2). Stephenson (2005) warns of the dire consequences that can ensue when trust-based networks are ignored.

Heterarchy as an organizational form is a helpful concept to explain college and university structures. Higher education institutions have a side-by-side structure of hierarchy and collegium. The collegium acts as a powerful social network while the hierarchy provides a structure upon which to manage administrative tasks. Colleges and universities are separate heterarchical structures that cooperatively network in a loose state and federal structure with formal and informal networks. Individual colleges and universities are further connected through faculty disciplinary associations, professional associations, and consortia. The goals of each structure combine to form a regional, federal, and global system that offers higher learning, enacts social change, enables class mobility, and realizes social justice. Any one college or university alone could not achieve these societal goals. They can only be realized through the cooperation and networked efforts of the entire higher education system.

MAJOR CONCEPTS, CHARACTERISTICS, AND PRINCIPLES

If one were to adopt a quantum perspective on higher education organizations, several elements would become obvious: their nondualistic nature, trust and cooperation, communication, power, and leadership.

Nondualistic

The Newtonian paradigm emphasizes dualism, either-or thinking. Managers and leaders are either right or wrong, win-lose situations are common, and public (or work) and private (or home) personas are separate. In contrast, new science thinking emphasizes both-and (Zohar, 1997). This approach includes the absence of a Cartesian split among mind, spirit, and body. From a quantum perspective, these human elements are recognized as an indivisible whole. "There are no either/ors. There is no need to decide between two things, pretending they are separate. What is critical is the *relationship* created between two or more elements" (Wheatley, 2010, p. 27; emphasis in original). Organizations viewed from a dualistic perspective are efficient or nonefficient, profit or nonprofit, public or private. The quantum theorists eschew these dualisms in favor of an approach where both ends of the continuum can exist simultaneously. Efficiency and inefficiency could both have their place in the same department. A college could contain characteristics of for-profit and nonprofit organizations. Some higher education institutions are a mix of public and private elements. The adoption of a nondualistic viewpoint opens opportunities and possibilities. Rather than only one way to proceed, many ways of operating become available.

Trust and Cooperation

Stephenson and others link networks, relationships, and trust to the real power within organizations.

> The association between trust and learning is an instrument of vast, if frequently untapped, organizational power. The act of reconnecting and talking with a trusted colleague generally triggers a resurgence of mutual memory, opening the gates to fresh learning and invention.... Because networks of trust release so much cognitive capability, they can (and often do) have far more influence over the fortunes and failures of companies from day to day and year to year than the official hierarchy. (Kleiner, 2003, p. 3)

Networks are crucial to modern organizations because of the existence of the information age. In the past, tangible goods may have been the currency of power and achievement. Today, knowledge is the currency of power. Stephenson discerned seven networks within organizations: work, social, innovation, expert knowledge, career guidance or strategic, learning, and decision making (2005). One can picture these networks on multiple layers with connections among and between them forming a grid of relationships. These seven networks are held together through relationships and trust. With such an emphasis on the power of relationships and value of human capital, it is difficult to imagine the era when people were devalued as only cogs in the bureaucratic machine. Today, relationships are closely linked to value because knowledge and learning must be featured for an organization to succeed. Knowledge exchange and organizational learning can only occur in an atmosphere characterized by trust.

The principle of cooperation underscores the quantum perspective because in networks everything is interdependent (Kleiner, 2003). All parts of the organization are integrated and interrelated to all other parts. When the notion that an organization is made up of "things" is abandoned and supplanted with the practice of thinking about relationships, connections, and influences, organizational culture, ethos, and vision make sense. Creativity and trust emerge (Zohar, 1997).

A continuum that radically distinguishes the Newtonian and quantum approaches is competition versus cooperation. Newtonian theorists and their organizational proponents assume that competition makes organizations stronger. Competition among organizational members is encouraged with the belief that rivalry increases productivity and morale. Higher education has several examples where competition has negatively affected the entire system. To increase admissions and retention competitiveness, higher education institutions have built more facilities: recreation centers, student unions, state-of-the-art classrooms, and residence halls. The competition to build bigger and better facilities to attract students has created a higher education arms race. The bar is continually raised and expectations increased beyond what most institutions realistically can and perhaps should provide. Competition between and among institutions has resulted in individual institutions pricing themselves out of their market. Quantum theorists reject competition and instead embrace cooperation as a way to make the organization stronger and more profitable. Cooperation creates more networks, shapes a more humane work environment, and accomplishes complex, difficult to achieve goals.

Higher education organizations contain reservoirs of power, trust, networks, and relationships waiting to be tapped. In some ways, colleges and universities are *only* about relationships and networks. These institutions build lifelong relationships with students who become alumni/ae, contain professors who often dedicate their life's work to one institution, and form communities that become the context in which learning occurs. The networks of disciplinary colleagues, former employees, lifelong learners, and loyal alumni/ae are formidable. The learning that takes place within higher education institutions extends to corporations, nonprofit organizations, and other colleges and universities. The most interesting learning within colleges and universities occurs when faculty and students form relationships characterized by trust and cooperation. The application of the principles of Stephenson's networks and Zohar and Wheatley's quantum relationships can further the goals of these organizations because "the organization's ability to implement any new strategy depends primarily on the way knowledge courses through its networks" (Kleiner, 2003, p. 13).

Communication

The epitome of the interrelatedness, cooperation, and trust engendered in networked and quantum organizations is communication. Stephenson (2005) identified different roles (hubs, gatekeepers, and pulse takers) that people use in networks to communicate and achieve their goals. People who are *hubs* are very well connected. They keep information flowing and possess a very high level of trust. *Gatekeepers* have or control access to critical people and link different groups or networks throughout the organization. They transmit ideas and serve as knowledge brokers. *Pulse takers* are indirectly linked to people across networks without necessarily being at the center of them. Their relationships enable them to monitor the health and direction of the organization (Gladwell, 2000; Kleiner, 2003; Stephenson, 2001, 2005).

Higher education institutions have many who fill the hub, gatekeeper, and pulse taker functions. Staff members are particularly well-positioned to be hubs. Faculty and administrators in governance roles easily become gatekeepers. And, campus coffee shops and faculty dining rooms become places where pulse takers ply their wares.

Although these roles exist, their impact is perhaps dampened by the fact that colleges and universities are made up of buildings and physical facilities built over long periods of time. Long corridors and cramped office spaces can hinder communication and knowledge sharing. The use of e-mail, websites, and other technology as well as attention paid to the physical location of people in the hub, gatekeeper, and pulse taker roles could enhance the trust building, knowledge sharing, and connection building functions within the institution. Attention to these communication patterns is particularly important because of the independent nature of faculty work. With a majority of faculty work (e.g., class preparation, grading, research) conducted autonomously and often off campus, faculty have little interaction with colleagues and administrators. Trust is difficult to develop under these circumstances and knowledge sharing and the resulting innovation are lost.

Power

Power from a quantum perspective is substantially different from conceptions of power in the Newtonian paradigm. The first difference is that power is a capacity (Wheatley, 2010). This aspect of organizational life is not a finite entity but an infinite force available to anyone within the organization. From a quantum perspective, power increases as one gives it away. Power becomes less about managing tasks than about cultivating relationships. Rather than using coercion and "power over," leaders cultivate power "with" based on the understanding that power cannot be taken, only given. A second difference is that power is not absolute but changes with the context. Power that exists for an administrator or faculty member in one circumstance may be useless in a different, though similar circumstance. A third difference is that power is not limited to the legitimate authority conferred by the position. In an organization that depends on networks of knowledge, all members possess power and have contributions to make. With this more equitable type of power, one person or group does not have all the power, knowledge, and answers. Power springs from many centers and exists in many places throughout the organization (Zohar, 1997). As one thinks about the networks that exist in organizations, "the actual power of an organization exists in the structure of a human network, not in the architecture of command and control superimposed on it" (Stephenson, 2005, p. 245).

From a quantum perspective, power is about dialogue, not debate; it is about respect, not control; and about cooperation, not competition (Zohar, 1997). In a networked world, the locus of power, knowledge, and intelligence is no longer controlled by a few. Information, communication, and resources formerly available to a limited number of people are now accessed by a wider array of institutional members (Allen & Cherrey, 2000, p. 4). One is advised not to underestimate the power or authority that remains in the bureaucratic structure, but there is also a more equitable and organization-wide distribution of power shifts, leadership, responsibility, and ownership throughout the organization.

Leadership

Stephenson (2005) recommends that leaders today must "lead with trust." The double meaning in this statement cannot be overlooked. Adaptability, flexibility, and tolerance for ambiguity are valued leadership skills in complex, uncertain, and dynamic quantum organizations. "Quantum leadership implies that control give way to some more subtle, intuitive feel for the situation and the creative potential of its indeterminacy" (Zohar, 1997, p. 51).

When leadership is viewed as a relationship, then the leadership exerted by the "followers" is as or more important than that exerted by positional leaders. Leadership from a quantum perspective is a process diffused throughout the organization. The leader-follower distinction is blurred as leadership becomes a relationship between and among people, not a quality any one person possesses (Rost, 1993).

> We may fail to honor these leaders more formally, trapped as we are in our beliefs about hierarchy and power, but we always know who the real leader is and why we are willing to follow.... They emerge from the group, not by self-assertion, but because they make sense, given what the group and individuals need so that they can survive and grow. (Wheatley, 2010, p. 11)

The distributed nature of quantum organization leadership means that leadership is more distributed and exerted more vigorously because it emanates from everywhere. If one assumes, as is done in the Newtonian model, that the most important and essential leadership is exerted at the executive level, then only a limited number of people can be leaders. If the quantum assumptions of leadership are adopted, there are more leaders within the organization and more leadership exerted. Table 12.4 summarizes ideas shared by Allen and Cherrey (2000) about leadership in Newtonian and quantum organizations.

STRENGTHS AND WEAKNESSES OF THE NEW SCIENCE MODEL

The new science perspective, similar to all organizational perspectives offered in this book, contains strengths and weaknesses regarding its implementation within higher education (see Table 12.5).

Table 12.4 Leadership Elements in Newtonian versus Quantum Organizations

Leadership Element	Newtonian Organizations	Quantum Organizations
Style	Decisive, aggressive, autonomous, "great man"	Collaborative, inter-related, "great people"
Decision making	Top down, in the hands of a few	Democratic, consultative
Control orientation	Rigid	Flexible
Communication style	Controlled, one way, up and down, formal, "information is power"	Information widely shared, uni-directional, power comes from everyone being informed
Power	Positional power, finite	Power earned through trust and respect, infinite
Structure	Hierarchical or quasi-hierarchical	Heterarchy, networked, round, flat, web
Change	Incremental, step by step, logical and rational	Systemic, can be episodic (e.g., revolutionary), strategic in a systemic way
Resources	Based on finite, consumable elements (e.g., fossil fuel)	Based on infinite, human centered elements (e.g., employees)

(Allen & Cherrey, 2000; Rost, 1993)

Table 12.5 Strengths and Weaknesses of the New Science Perspective

Strengths	Weaknesses
Creates opportunities regarding leadership, organization-wide collaboration, and extending human potential.	Requires a shift in perspective away from well-established and accepted traditions.
Better explains the complexity and uncertainty of today's post-modern organizations.	Requires a high level of cognitive complexity to manage the full impact of environmental complexity and uncertainty.
Promotes buy-in regarding the institution's vision and mission.	May create the impression of weakness on the part of executive leaders.
Enables the expression of multiple voices and perspectives within the organization.	May be a difficult transition for boards of trustees and others who see accountability as expressed in quantifiable, concrete terms.
Allows the "softer" elements of organizational life (e.g., hope, trust, connection) to be developed and used.	Can be viewed as irrational and unstructured.

NEXT STEPS: BRINGING THE NEW SCIENCE PERSPECTIVE INTO CURRENT USE

Complex systems theory, a related extension to the new science literature, is the most current application of this organizational perspective. A substantial body of literature has emerged in the last several years concerning complex systems and complexity science. This body of literature is fruitfully applied to organizations like higher education institutions that defy the logic adopted from simple systems, "systems with [a] small number of well-understood components" (Amaral & Uzzi, 2007, p. 1033). In contrast, "complex systems typically have many components that can autonomously interact through emergent rules" (p. 1033). Complex systems theory can be used as a tool with which to gain a richer understanding of how higher education institutions work as systems that, though loosely connected, operate on rules and practices that have emerged over time. Complex systems have expanded upon the principles of the new science (e.g., uncertainty, self-organization, ambiguity, holism) to offer powerful explanations for how organizations work in the real world of practice.

> Complex systems arise whenever there are populations of interacting agents (persons, organizations, or communities) that act on their limited and local information. That is, the agents and the larger system in which they are embedded operate by trading their resources without the aid of a central control mechanism or even a clear understanding of how actions of (possibly distant) agents can affect them. (Amaral & Uzzi, 2007, pp. 1033–1034)

The lack of a central organizing system need not imply lack of leadership. Instead, complex systems theory enables organizational actors to explore the ways that coordination and action are possible in the absence of the traditional organizing mechanisms (e.g., hierarchy, central coordination), practices thought to result in highly effective organizations. Instead, the absence of a central organizing mechanism creates space for creativity, innovation, and redundancy, which can correct errors and maintain vibrancy.

Complex systems theory includes, among other concepts, connectivity and self-organization (Amaral & Uzzi, 2007; Cooper, Braye, & Geyer, 2004). Theorists use the concept of connectivity to discuss the ways that all organizational parts and elements influence each other. Connectivity implies interdependence, the ways in which parts of the system, including people, depend on one another and coordinate their efforts. With complex organizations such as colleges and universities, the number of relationships among the various elements is high, thereby increasing the complexity and decreasing people's ability to manage the various connections and relationships. Complex systems theorists discuss the ways that control is not possible; leadership is affected by knowing where to influence rather than how to control. Similar to the connectivity characteristic, the self-organizing nature of complex systems relates to the ways that all persons and parts influence each other. Tradition, time, and practice combine to suggest rules that determine action, including future planning. Rather than overdependence on a central leadership structure, leadership and action emerges from all parts of the organization. However, this action is unpredictable and lacks the rationality expected by traditional organizational thinkers who assume that leadership emanates from a top-down hierarchical structure.

Complex systems theorists discuss organizational characteristics that are all too familiar in higher education. They recognize that both the internal system and its external environment are inconstant; change is inevitable. College and university staff, students, faculty, and administrators are creative decision makers, closely attached to each other and their attendant actions. Uncertainty and paradox are expected features of these organizations. Problems, even the most intractable ones, can be "moved forward." Solutions can be, often must be, crafted from minimal information rather than exhaustive analysis. Small changes can have important effects. And, finally, behavior is patterned and not necessarily random (Fraser & Greenhalgh, 2001).

Complex systems and complexity science are highly applicable to higher education settings in two additional ways. One, as complex organizations, the simple, rational models of the past cannot supply the knowledge, skills, or capabilities needed to lead these important societal institutions. "The complex real world is made up of messy, fuzzy, unique, and context embedded problems" (Fraser & Greenhalgh, 2001, p. 801). Second, as educational institutions and drivers of social change, complex systems and complexity science can lead our educational practices away from the transmission of knowledge and toward capability building. Fraser and Greenhalgh (2001) distinguish between competence, a long held goal of educational systems, and capability, a necessary component to effectively operate in complex systems. Competence is "what individuals know or are able to do in terms of knowledge, skills, attitude"; in contrast, capability is the "extent to which individuals can adapt to change, generate new knowledge, and continue to improve their performance" (Fraser & Greenhalgh, 2001, p. 799). Transformational, relational, and nonlinear learning are ways that students can build capability, a concept that goes beyond the knowledge and skill acquisition of previous educational teaching, including teaching and learning in higher education institutions.

CONCLUSIONS

The quantum or new science perspective, particularly through the writing of Margaret Wheatley, has gained significant attention and notoriety. The popularity of this approach signals the need for an approach to management and leadership within higher education that decreases the reliance on command and control leadership, power driven actions, and competition. The complex issues facing higher education cannot be solved through old paradigm methods. Only through joining our efforts can societal issues be addressed through the education provided at colleges and universities.

Questions for Discussion

- How can the uncertainty inherent in the new science perspective be used to effect societal transformation through higher education institutions?
- How can the new science perspective guide an understanding of complexity and effectiveness in institutions of higher education?
- In what ways does the new science perspective explain change in higher education?
- How is the new science perspective useful in explaining the ever-accelerating pace in higher education?
- What areas of higher education are best explained by the new science perspectives? Which areas are least well explained?

Recommended Readings for the New Science Perspective

Ancona D., Malone, T. W., Orlikowski, W. J., & Senge, P. M. (2007). In praise of the incomplete leader. *Harvard Business Review, 85*(2), 92–100.

Kilmann, R. (2001). *Quantum organizations: A new paradigm for achieving organizational success and personal meaning.* Boston, MA: Nicholas Brealey.

Luthans, F., & Youssef, C. M. (2007). Emerging positive organizational behavior. *Leadership Institute Faculty Publications.* Paper 8. Retrieved from http://digitalcommons.unl.edu/leadershipfacpub/8

Morgan, G. (2006). Learning and self-organization: Organizations as brains. In G. Morgan (Ed.), *Images of organization* (pp. 71–114). Thousand Oaks, CA: Sage.

Ng, P. T. (2009). Examining the use of new science metaphors in the learning organization. *Learning Organization, 16*(2), 168–180.

Senge, P. (2006). *The fifth discipline: The art and practice of the learning organization.* New York: Currency Doubleday.

Senge, P., Smith, B., Kruschwitz, N., Laur, J., & Schley, S. (2010). *The necessary revolution: How individuals and organizations are working to create a sustainable world.* New York: Random House.

Spears, L., & Lawrence, M. (2004). *Practicing servant-leadership: Succeeding through trust, bravery, and forgiveness.* San Francisco, CA: Jossey-Bass.

Wheatley, M. J. (2006). Leadership lessons from the real world. *Leader to Leader, 41*, 16–20.

Wheatley, M. J. (2007). Leadership of self-organized networks lessons from the war on terror. *Performance Improvement Quarterly, 20*(2), 59–66.

Wheatley, M., & Frieze, D. (n.d.). Using emergence to take social innovation to scale. Retrieved from www.berkana.org

13

CASE

Getting Ahead of the Disruption[1]

TRENDS IN HIGHER EDUCATION

In 2000, Arthur Levine wrote an editorial for *The Chronicle of Higher Education* titled "The Future of Colleges: 9 Inevitable Changes" (2000b). He discussed the ways that "shifting demographics, new technologies, the entrance of commercial organizations into higher education, the changing relationships between colleges and the federal and state governments, and the move from an industrial to an information society" (p. B10) were changing the nature of higher education in the United States. He foretold the rise of free online course offerings through groups such as MITx and the Khan Academy. In essence, education is evolving with the rise of technology that has made the acquisition of knowledge as easy as reaching for a smart phone. Levine's nine trends included the following:

- Higher-education [sic] providers will become even more numerous and more diverse ...
- Three basic types of colleges and universities are emerging ... "brick universities," or traditional residential institutions; "click universities," or new, usually commercial virtual universities ... and "brick and click" universities, a combination of the first two ...
- Higher education is becoming more individualized; students, not institutions, will set the educational agenda ...
- The focus of higher education is shifting from teaching to learning ...
- The traditional functions of higher education (i.e., teaching, research, and service) could become unbundled ...
- Faculty members will become increasingly independent of colleges and universities ...
- Degrees will wither in importance ...
- Every person will have an educational passport ...
- Dollars will follow the students more than the educators. (2000b, pp. B10–B11)

While Levine's list outlines many challenges within higher education, absent from his list are the profound changes occurring internationally. Levine concluded his editorial with a statement expressing his fear that either because of complacency or the slow speed of higher education decision-making processes, the opportunity to shape tomorrow will be missed.

BORDERLESS EDUCATION

"Privatization" is the name often given to Levine's trend referring to the increase in numbers and types of higher education providers (Observatory on Borderless Education, 2011). Public and private spheres within higher education are blurring as joint ventures, international partnerships, student "swirl," and entrepreneurial ventures become commonplace. Fueled by the call for lifelong learning and higher education as an engine of worldwide economic development, the need for efficient and readily available education is increasing. Students are attending numerous institutions as a way to decrease costs, accelerate educational progress, and attend courses not available at their main institution. The desire for varied college experiences through study abroad and international internships, among others, is fueling increased student mobility. With more extensive movement among students and scholars as a goal of the Bologna Process, an agreement between many European countries, this worldwide movement promises to increase in the next several years.

IMPROVED TEACHING AND LEARNING

Increased options for higher education paired with high-priced tuition have fueled a switch in emphasis from teaching to learning. Students who now have advanced access to knowledge through sophisticated technology (and the skills to use it) are increasingly intolerant of didactic style (e.g., lecture) approaches to teaching. Techniques that engage students in the learning process are increasingly used because there is a shift in student expectations about how knowledge is acquired. The emphasis on learning as opposed to teaching is a practiced concept for traditional liberal arts colleges. These institutions are known for their efforts to engage students in the learning process. Through small classes, high quality interaction between faculty and students, and an emphasis on quality, these institutions are at the forefront of excellence in U.S. higher education. Relying on the earliest model of learning within higher education, traditional liberal arts colleges in the United States were fashioned after the Oxbridge model of England: small seminar classes, on-campus residential communities, and emphasis on the life of the mind and learning for learning's sake. Questions have been raised about whether traditional liberal arts and the financial model upon which it is based is sustainable given the current trends. Because many of these well-established institutions have generous endowments and alumni/ae support, they may not as yet be experiencing the financial challenges faced by their public institution counterparts.

The case below discusses ways that the liberal arts sector of U.S. higher education is discussing options at institutional and sector-wide levels to try and get out ahead of the impending changes. The challenge is to maintain higher education's historic mission as expressed by the traditional liberal arts colleges while guaranteeing their future by creating a more sustainable financial model. Responding to these challenges, Nikias and Tierney (2011) called for bold rather than modest action. These authors called for a revalued and reshaped traditional undergraduate experience, preservation of quality, a redefined undergraduate curriculum, and an active role by scholars beyond their narrow disciplines. Their call for action echoes the spirited ambition that underscored the founding of American higher education and sustained it as the preeminent higher education system in the world.

THE CASE

The challenges currently facing higher education necessitate new ways of organizing and thinking about organizational structure. In an age where information is ubiquitous, time asynchronous, and knowledge highly accessible, the principles of the new science perspective (e.g., interrelatedness, uncertainty, mutual and multiple causality, multiple realities, and control as an illusion) can serve as a means to achieve the evolution of the traditional liberal arts model.

Questions to Consider

- How can the idea of multiple realities encourage college administrators to imagine innovative ways of operating?
- Does the uncertainty inherent in the future point to the futility of strategic planning?
- If control is an illusion, how do faculty and administrators plan?
- How can interrelatedness be used as a way to forge new and unexpected connections?

Institutional Context

Peaceful Setting College is a highly competitive liberal arts institution located in a Midwestern U.S. state. The pastoral setting of Peaceful Setting College and location in a small college-centric town contributes to the institution's impression as a place of academic excellence and higher learning. With a substantial endowment and healthy application pool, Peaceful Setting enjoys the enviable position of having the financial resources to see the institution through difficult financial times. They also have a very active alumni/ae base that gives generously to the annual fund.

A critical issue facing the college is the fact that the per-student cost is significantly higher than that of the nearby state institution. Peaceful College's "high tuition/high aid" model has led to dependence on a small number of full pay students as a significant revenue source to support the generous tuition discounting. Although the college is not currently in financial crisis and has the resources to weather difficult circumstances, administrators are concerned that their financial and educational model is no longer sustainable. Similar to other colleges with a residentially based liberal arts mission, Peaceful Setting College administrators are interested in exploring innovative ways to approach the education they deliver now and in the future.

Questions to Consider

- How is the history of highly competitive liberal arts institution intertwined with the history of American higher education?

- What societal expectations exist for a highly competitive liberal arts institution such as Peaceful Setting?
- What are the mechanisms for funding a high tuition/high aid model? What are the advantages and disadvantages of this model?
- For your region, what enrollment trends influence the continued use of the high tuition/high aid model?

Characters

Dr. Margot Laurent, English faculty member: Dr. Laurent has worked at Peaceful Setting for 23 years. The college has been the site of her life's work and she has no plans to work anywhere else. She was honored when the Dean of the College asked her to chair the Subcommittee on the Future of the Liberal Arts.

Dr. Claus Schulz, Dean of the College: Dr. Schulz has been the Dean of the College at Peaceful Setting for 5 years. He has thoroughly enjoyed his time as dean, particularly because his position has allowed him to assure the institution's dedication to the traditional liberal arts mission. He is fortunate to work with faculty who are highly motivated and produce an exceptional level of quality in their disciplines. They take the education of students seriously and are very committed to the liberal arts mission of the institution. As Dean of the College, Dr. Schulz chairs the Strategic Planning Committee that meets monthly to undertake institutional long-range planning. The Subcommittee on the Future of the Liberal Arts is a subcommittee of the Strategic Planning Committee.

Dr. Odelia Turner, Consultant, Assembly of Liberal Arts Colleges: For the last 2 years, Dr. Turner has consulted with the Dean of the College and others at Peaceful Setting College on the role of the liberal arts and the future of colleges with that emphasis. As a nationally recognized scholar on the future of the liberal arts in U.S. higher education, Dr. Turner has consulted extensively with institutions such as Peaceful Setting. Highly committed to the long-standing model within higher education, Dr. Turner is a realist. She knows that the model needs to evolve or it will die as a viable one within U.S. higher education. Dr. Turner was pleased to be hired on as a consultant to Peaceful Setting. Because of its academic excellence and long-standing commitment to the liberal arts, the college is an excellent test case for crafting the future of liberal arts institutions.

Questions to Consider

- What leadership principles from the new science or quantum perspective could be applied to the complex, interrelated task of determining a sustainable model for liberal arts education?
- What new science perspective principles could Peaceful Setting College faculty, trustees, and administrators use to balance the uncertainty of future events with the need to undertake planning?
- What elements of the heterarchic form can assist the college faculty, administrators, students, and trustees as they seek to innovate and create a new model?
- How can the interrelationships between and among institutions be used as strengths in determining a new model?

Traditional Liberal Arts Model

The Dean of the College, in consultation with Peaceful Setting's faculty, the Board of Trustees, student groups, and other college constituents, was convinced that the liberal arts model, long the hallmark of Peaceful Setting and institutions like it, had to change. Their singular approach to higher education had been in effect for the 200 years of the college's existence and the nearly 400 years of American higher education. The liberal arts tradition was the original college model and went back to the *trivium* of grammar, logic, and rhetoric and *quadrivium* of arithmetic, geometry, astronomy, and music (Brubacher, 1990).

The conversations about the viability of the liberal arts model were spurred by the realization that the traditional residential campus, high tuition/high aid, and low faculty–student ratio approaches upon which the liberal arts model was predicated was financially unsustainable. The high cost of tuition was severely affecting access, a longstanding commitment of the institution; shifting demographics were shrinking the potential pool of full pay students; and employee salary and benefit costs were outpacing the college's ability to raise tuition. It was becoming evident that the small classes (average class size at Peaceful Setting was 18), limited courses and majors (including courses of study with extremely small enrollments), rigid class schedules requiring full-time enrollment, and student enrollment limited by the residential nature of the college was no longer financially sustainable. As a way to get out ahead of an impending crisis, Dr. Schultz wanted to explore new models predicated on the same innovation that originally ushered in the liberal arts model. Since introducing the formation of the Subcommittee on the Future of the Liberal Arts, Dr. Schulz spent considerable time explaining that he did not want to eliminate the liberal arts but to help it evolve. Without this evolution, the model and college were at risk of extinction.

Questions to Consider

- How is evolution from a liberal arts tradition to a new model in keeping with the principles and practices of the new science perspective?
- What are examples of the multiple realities embraced by different constituencies on campus?
- How might those multiple realities affect planning for the evolution of the liberal arts model?
- What expectations do traditionally aged students and parents have for colleges such as Peaceful Setting?

The Changing Face of Higher Education

Reworking the liberal arts model at Peaceful Setting College required adaptation, not abandonment. The model had served the institution well and many were solidly against substantial changes. In fact, many faculty and administrators at the college argued that their tradition emphasizing the liberal arts gave them the critical thinking capacity and analysis skills to face current changes. Globalization and interconnectedness are changes that require the nimbleness of thinking and adaptation taught through a liberal arts curriculum. It was not the liberal arts model and the goals underscoring the model that needed change, but the financial model (e.g., residential based learning, low faculty–student ratios).

College officials felt that five trends were driving the need to change to a new financial model: (a) the existence of a globally connected world, (b) the need for a sustainable financial model that took the interrelationships of private and public funding into account, (c) changes in the national and international conversations about decreasing the number of years to attain an undergraduate degree, (d) the capability to offer a Peaceful Setting College education through technological advances, and (e) shifting demographics driving the recruitment of a type of student not previously enrolled at Peaceful Setting College.

Questions to Consider

- What demographic trends are driving enrollment? How will demographics shift over the next 10 years?
- What new science principles and characteristics are helpful in thinking about the ways that the shifting demographics, financial state of higher education, and global nature of higher education interact?
- How can new science assumptions be brought to bear to effect the changes necessary to build a more sustainable model for liberal arts institutions?
- Which characteristics of the new science perspective are less helpful in considering a new liberal arts model?

Long Range Planning About the Future of the Liberal Arts Tradition

The Future of the Liberal Arts Committee, chaired by Dr. Laurent, began their discussions about a new model that could sustain the institution into the future. The committee was energized by the discussion because it promised to build upon the creativity and innovativeness that characterized the college's founding. Committee members were buoyed by the fact that the college was not in a financial crisis so they could pursue ideas with less urgency and more creativity.

Dr. Turner, the consultant from the Assembly of Liberal Arts Colleges, was a welcomed resource regarding the committee's task. Because of her past work with the institution, she was familiar with the strengths and weaknesses of Peaceful Setting College. She knew that they embraced the traditional, competitive liberal arts model. Her organization had been working nationally and internationally to maintain the best of the liberal arts tradition while building a more sustainable financial model. The decreases in federal financial aid, competition for students, and increased costs of running a campus meant that this tried and true model was under severe stress. Dr. Turner and Provost Schultz met at a think tank sponsored by the Assembly for Liberal Arts Colleges convened to specifically address the evolution of the traditional liberal arts model. Their long-standing commitment to international education and attracting international students, their willingness to experiment with new teaching technologies, and their reputation for academic excellence positioned the institution well to take the lead in the effort to find a new model.

Questions to Consider

- What networks could Peaceful Setting College tap to gather the expertise and resources necessary to undertake the task before them?

- What principles of the new science can the Provost employ to engender the cooperation and collaboration necessary for the planning process?
- How might the communication roles of hubs, gatekeepers, and pulse takers be used to advance the purposes of the Subcommittee on the Future of the Liberal Arts?
- How can the college, national associations, college stakeholders (e.g., alumni/ae), and others be brought together in ways that create the leadership necessary for the planning process?

Determining the Underlying Principles

The Subcommittee on the Future of the Liberal Arts met and outlined several underlying principles for their task. With the assistance of Dr. Turner and the skilled collaborative approach of the Dean of the College, the following principles were determined:

- The traditional liberal arts model of on-campus residence, small classes, limited majors and courses, and close student–faculty contact was too labor intensive and expensive to continue as the only model available to the college.
- The committee must suggest one or more new models while maintaining the core values of the institution: academic excellence, access to a diversity of students, global connectedness, and cutting edge leadership.
- The task was to suggest several more fiscally sustainable ways to achieve the goals of a liberal arts education.
- Any new model of delivering the liberal arts must achieve the related goals of increasing access and decreasing elitism.
- The new model should emerge from a collaborative process representing the best thinking of people internal and external to the college.
- Technology, a central feature of any new model, would be used in ways that fully utilized the potential of that powerful modern resource.
- The tension between allegiance to the familiar traditional model and promise of the new model should be balanced in a way that paved the way for innovation and creativity.

Questions to Consider

- What overlapping principles underlie the new science perspective and technologies such as the Internet, e-mail communication, and the World Wide Web?
- How is the principle of interconnectedness in the new science model expressed in the increasingly global nature of higher education?
- How can new science principles of trust and cooperation be used as a resource in a new model for liberal arts institutions?
- How can power be reconceived in a new model of liberal arts institutions?

Managing Uncertainty

Dr. Laurent took the opportunity of committee meetings to bring the members up to speed on national and international developments in higher education. She was most concerned about the development of "swirl," the enrollment pattern exhibited when students attend multiple institutions, often simultaneously. Although college students had always attended multiple institutions (Borden, 2004), distance and online learning made "swirl" more common. Dr. Laurent's specific interest in "swirl" was spurred by a conference she attended on the Bologna Process, a cooperative project within 47 European countries to form a European Higher Education Area (Gaston, 2010). With interinstitutional transfer and mobility as one of the primary goals of Bologna, Dr. Laurent felt that the days of attendance at one institution for 4 years (the so-called linear matriculation pattern) (Borden, 2004) were behind them. Peaceful Setting College would be in a precarious position if they did not respond to the growing interconnections between and among colleges and universities throughout the globe.

Dr. Laurent recognized the anxiety of many, particularly faculty and administrators, who feared the demise of the traditional liberal arts model. But, she was inspired by the prospect of building a new model for the liberal arts, one that took recent technological and learning-oriented developments into account. A product of a liberal arts education herself, Dr. Laurent was dedicated to the model, understood its strengths, and also believed that an updated model could make a liberal arts education more relevant and important in today's interconnected, complex world. Her thinking went beyond arguments for critical thinking that were often claimed when the traditional liberal arts model was challenged. She believed that any new model they created could combine the best of the old model with the best of new thinking.

Committee Recommendations

Although the committee's work was not complete, the group determined the following elements of a new model for the liberal arts. Dr. Laurent was pleased with their work so far but knew that additional hard work lay before them.

- Given the uncertainty of the future and well aware that planning can only identify a direction, not predict the future, administrators and faculty at Peaceful Setting College will build their future programs, majors, and initiatives on relationships between and among global partners.
- Partnerships with domestic and international institutions through consortia, articulation agreements, international branch campuses, and joint programs will be established to create a wide array of opportunities for students while containing the cost of faculty salaries, laboratory facilities, and other operating costs.
- The intense academic engagement and palatable sense of community long celebrated at traditional liberal arts colleges will be established through nonresidential facilities and programs. These efforts could include honors colleges, academic societies, a campus center, and other facilities programs.
- An academic advising center will be established to relieve the heavy advising load of faculty. The community built within the academic programs will be duplicated in the advising center so students feel a sense of home and connection.

The Future of the Liberal Arts Committee members realized that the college and liberal arts model generally will not survive without interrelationships, cooperation between and among universities, and international connections. They look forward to continued work on this new model.

DISCUSSION

The new science perspective, based on the assumptions of the quantum paradigm, holds significant promise as higher education reconceives its traditional missions. The assumptions of the paradigm and characteristics of the new science perspective create opportunities to establish new models, reimagine ways of operating, and determine different means to structure organizations. Using this perspective, challenging circumstances within higher education that are underscored with complexity, ambiguity, and uncertainty can be turned into strengths and new opportunities. Using the new science perspective, college and university administrators, faculty, policy makers, and others can view higher education holistically. By potentially breaking down the silos of faculty–administrators, faculty–students, and internal–external stakeholders, new possibilities can be established. Higher education, both domestically and internationally, has long employed models such as consortiums and partnerships. Rising costs and new technologies create an opportunity for increased cross registration, shared student bodies, and new models of operating. As Levine's (2000b) predictions about the increasing independence of faculty and students, growth of new models for the delivery of higher education, and growing capacity of students to set the agenda for learning are realized, the new science perspective provides insights for ways to manage the change.

NOTE

1. The phrase is borrowed from Kevin Kiley (2011, October 10). Starting to worry. *Inside Higher Education.*

14

FEMINIST

"Masculine" or "feminine" images embedded in the roles are inherent neither in the nature of the tasks themselves nor in the characteristics of men and women; instead, they are developed in response to the problems incumbents face in trying to live their organizational lives so as to maximize legitimacy or recognition or freedom. (Kanter, 1977, p. 5)

INTRODUCTION

In 1977, Rosabeth Moss Kanter wrote her classic text *Men and Women of the Corporation*, and expressed the nascent idea that men and women view the organization through gendered lenses. A sophisticated collection of feminist oriented organizational theory built on Kanter's work has since developed. The feminist perspective on organizational theory challenges "deeply entrenched assumptions and values" that drive structure, styles, planning, priorities, incentives, values, policies, and practices. Even the basic question, "what forms of activity count as work," is gender related (Meyerson & Kolb, 2000, p. 554).

This chapter introduces feminist perspectives and thinking about organizational theory, in particular, the work of Helgesen (1990, 1995, 2006), Calás and Smircich (1999), and Lipman-Blumen (1992). The web of inclusion highlighted to illustrate a feminist-oriented form is one possible way to organize higher education institutions. The web is fundamentally different from the hierarchical form long considered the norm in organizational life,

> Organizing human enterprise according to machine properties left people out of the equation—with the predictable result that they either became thoroughly wretched, or adapted and so lost their vitality and soul.... The subordination of people's skills and imaginations to the rigid architecture of the machine cut them

off from their original sources, and so has thrown the human world out of balance. (Helgesen, 1995, p. 17)

The feminist perspective is vastly different from other perspectives outlined in this book, many of which embrace "clear lines of authority, the accumulation of power and information, a win-lose decision process, and the value of sameness and homogeneity" (Rosener, 1997, p. 4). Female-style leadership, also called connective or relational (Lipman-Blumen, 1995), fits the interrelated and global environment of the 21st century. This interconnected world includes a higher education system in which single institutions span several locations, including countries, through branch campuses, articulation agreements, and scholarly exchanges.

FEMINIST THEORY AS A FOUNDATION FOR THE WEB OF INCLUSION

The web of inclusion is grounded in feminist theory, a postmodern approach. Assumptions that underscore this perspective include:

- Gender is socially constructed.
- All social processes including power relations are gendered.
- Transformation and social justice are goals for organizations, systems, and other forms of public life.
- Western culture has traditionally undervalued skills and qualities (e.g., sensitivity, nurturing, emotional expressiveness, intuition, nonverbal communication, and spirituality) culturally defined as female. Culturally defined male skills and qualities (e.g., competition, aggressiveness, decisiveness, ambition, progress) are often overvalued.
- Women, sexual minorities, people of color, and other underrepresented groups are inequitably treated in organizations. (Calás & Smircich, 1999; Kark, 2004; Meyerson & Kolb, 2000)

The strengths and weaknesses of feminist theory as a foundation for the web of inclusion are outlined in Table 14.1.

The social construction of gender and existence of gendered social relations means that all organizations reinforce and re-create gender dynamics within society. As such, organizational processes can be described as "gendering" (i.e., they create gender norms) and "gendered" (i.e., they reflect gender norms). The consideration of gender in colleges and universities is particularly important because gender roles are not simply expressed in these settings; they are created and re-created. Charged with the transmission of cultural knowledge, colleges and universities are collectively a major social institution that creates and sustains gender differences. Examples of "gendering" processes include topics covered in the curriculum, symbols and images portrayed on campus, and routine work practices where gender is explicit although often unexamined.

Although the word feminist is often attributed to women rather than men, one need not be female to adhere to the assumptions of the organizational and theoretical perspectives described in this chapter. The privileging of male characteristics means that men, regardless of a preferred style, are also pressured to express culturally defined

Table 14.1 Strengths and Weaknesses of Feminist Theoretical Foundation

Strengths	Weaknesses
Allows the manifestation of connection as well as independence and autonomy.	May feel too soft for many.
Enables women's voices to become included in organizational life.	May cause some to believe that the primary purpose of the organization is the care and tending of its members.
Provides an inclusive perspective where all genders are welcome.	Can alienate some organizational members who, due to personal style or worldview, prefer a more detached approach to institutional life.
Supplies a powerful analysis of how different styles of leadership and organizational functioning can engender trust, support, and nurturing.	May clash with traditional higher education assumptions based on the scientific method and assumptions of objectivity and detachment.
Facilitates a social justice perspective to be infused into traditional organizational life.	May be met with resistance from dominant culture members who see a new paradigm as a threat to their power and position within organizations.

masculine characteristics in leadership and organizational roles (Lipman-Blumen, 1992). The alienation created by the command and control leadership approach can be as debilitating to men as it is to women. This approach may also clash with the styles of people of color and sexual orientation minorities.

METAPHOR

The metaphor of the web is used in this chapter to describe feminist organizations. Coined by Helgesen (1990, 1995, 2006) after observing several women-led organizations, this image fits the woman-centered, feminist oriented organizations that she studied. In contrast to the organizational perspective metaphors of jungles, circles, or hierarchies discussed in this book, the web conveys pervasive connectedness. Like a spider web, touching one part of the organization causes systemic tremors to pass through all other parts. The web metaphor acknowledges that a change to one part of the organization will ripple through to all the other parts. Structural and procedural interconnectedness of communication, human interaction, and leadership underscore this approach.

STRUCTURE

Helgesen (1990, 1995, 2006) claimed that webs of inclusion are notable for their lack of a definitive and stable organizational structure. Helgesen described the web as

> roughly circular in shape, with the leader at the central point, and lines radiating outward to various points. The points formed loose concentric circles, which were bound together by an irregular interweaving of axial and radial lines that crisscrossed the structure in a kind of filigree … I added the term "inclusion" to the notion of the web because the women who led the organizations labored continually to bring everyone at every point closer to the center—to tighten ties, provide increased exposure, and encourage greater participation. (1995, p. 20)

Anyone accustomed to other organizational forms may find the web of inclusion's structure difficult to identify. In fact, to someone with a traditional bureaucratic approach in mind, an organization with a web structure may appear in need of fixing and tightening up. As such, the web of inclusion represents a transformed and transforming organizational structure. Organizations using this form are not simply tinkering around the edges of an otherwise bureaucratic structure. They are using new forms of communication, leadership, and power to change norms and ways of operating. These new forms are possible only when a completely different set of assumptions, in this case feminist theory, underscores organizational functioning.

MAJOR CHARACTERISTICS, CONCEPTS, AND PRINCIPLES

The web has been described as a pattern and a process. Webs are adaptable, open, and responsive; inclusive and collaborative processes mark these organizational forms; leadership is collaborative and connected; power is shared; and open communication processes are part of their functioning.

Adaptable, Open, and Responsive

Tangled in the daily operations and needs of the organization, the web of inclusion is intricately linked to the daily rhythms of an institution. These rhythms include how time is used, what roles people assume, how physical space is allotted, how people talk to one another, and how decisions are made (Helgesen, 1995). As both a pattern and process, the architecture of the web enables and is enabled by the arrangement of offices, the availability of organizational members (including the leader), and participation in decision making. The web enables connections and connections enable the web to function.

The specific organizational structure that is chosen or evolves is always closely related to the environment in which an institution operates. If the external environment is stable, a bureaucratic or collegial organization could meet the demands of that situation. But, very few, if any, higher education organizations exist in a stable environment. Volatile, rapidly changing environments are inevitable parts of today's higher education landscape. Because the medieval-inspired higher education bureaucratic structure is slow to change, the web of inclusion with its adaptability and flexibility may be a better fit for today's institutions. Organizational life is more uncertain, fragmented, and fast-paced, so the challenge for today's "organizations [is] to become less hierarchical, more flexible, team-oriented, and participative" (Kark, 2004, p. 161). In contrast to stable organizational forms, "webs serve as a vehicle for constant reorganization" (Helgesen, 1995, p. 29). Administrative roles, lines of authority, communication patterns, and other organizational features are not fixed but change according to the circumstance and task at hand. The web of inclusion contains several advantages that can help these institutions adapt to this ever-changing environment.

The web is notable in the way it shifts and adapts according to the rhythms and requirements of changing circumstances. Open office spaces allow the demands of projects to be addressed in highly adaptable ways. Flexible reporting lines allow people to shift among supervisors, work groups, and partners. Ubiquitous communication enables many to share their talents among the many parts of the organization. One can imagine college or university offices (e.g., career services, honors colleges, women's centers) where the adaptability and flexibility of the web structure would work well.

Other offices, particularly those with a need for confidentiality (e.g., student discipline services, human resources) would chafe against the openness of the web. The challenge of today's higher education environment is to imagine new ways of organizing that can assist faculty and administrators to address the needs of the organization in ways that were unimagined in the past. Could a university president's office be more effective with the accessibility and openness of the web structure? Can the participative decision making of the web be used during strategic planning processes?

Through its close connection to the environment, the web's edges remain open and responsive to its surroundings. This openness enables people, including stakeholders, to be continually pulled into decision making (Helgesen, 1995). Webs are "permeable at the edges ... [so] you don't necessarily know who is a member and who isn't" (Mahoney, 2002, pp. 2–5). Outsiders have access to the organization; insiders can get out. Inclusiveness is built through fluid membership, participative decision making, and omnidirectional communication. Through the permeable boundaries, innovation and responsiveness flows. Open communication, flexible roles, and adaptable structure enable talents and knowledge rather than position and protocol to shape organizational processes and practices. Titles are fluid; the structure shifts organically to redirect responsibility and information flow.

The interrelated, systemic (Allen & Cherrey, 2000; Lipman-Blumen, 1992) nature of the personal and professional lives of organizational members requires an adaptable, flexible, and dynamic structure like the web of inclusion. "There is a growing lack of fit [between] ... our increasingly large and complex institutions, and ... the demands of an interdependent world" (Lipman-Blumen, 1992, p. 191). The newer organizational structures (e.g., the web of inclusion, quantum organizations, spiritual perspective) better reflect organic forms; a structure with ways of operating that spontaneously adapts to complexity, dynamism, and interrelations. Newer connected and relational leadership styles help organizational members see "the world as a total system of interconnected, uniquely important parts, rather than as independent, competitive, isolated, and unequal entities" (Lipman-Blumen, 1992, p. 187). Older forms either cannot evolve or fail to evolve. Their structures were built for an environment that no longer exists. For example, a college that offers an outdated general education curriculum will find prospective students gravitating toward institutions with forms that are more responsive to today's demands. Residence hall staff who provide a bed to sleep in but have no connection with the academic program through living learning communities and service learning requirements will find themselves struggling to retain full occupancy. Institutions that neglect to incorporate a global perspective will see students transferring to colleges or universities with viable study abroad programs and a rich base of international students. The web's permeability is one of its most useful features for higher education institutions. Depending on the issue at hand, the edges of a college or university can more easily draw in, for example, community members (when the topic is town/gown), parents (when retention issues are foremost), alumni/ae (when fundraising is at issue), and state residents (when public funding is at stake).

Inclusive and Collaborative Process

Feminist approaches to organizations may appeal to anyone who feels outside of or alienated by the traditional bureaucratic approach. "People simply cannot *think* creatively and well if they do not feel valued, if they do not feel a sense of ownership of their work, if they do not have the freedom to give full scope to their talents" (Helgesen, 1995, p. 12). The full and equitable inclusion of all groups results in more effective organizational structures through decreased absenteeism, increased productivity, distributed leadership, and empowered employees (Meyerson & Kolb, 2000). People frustrated with the inequitable power structures and disillusionment born when talents are un- or underutilized (Helgesen, 1995, p. 11) argues for new organizational forms.

The web is notable for its assumption of inclusion, which leads to collaboration. The egalitarian use of space is one of the means by which inclusion in the web is communicated. Institutional privilege is symbolically expressed and practically exercised through the allocation of physical space within the organization. Although this characteristic may, at first blush, appear to have limited significance, reserved parking spaces, fortress-like office space, privacy in one's work space, assignment of corner offices, and office size and quality are signifiers for power and status within organizations. These symbols communicate who is valued, less valued, and not valued. In contrast, web organization office space is allocated by the requirements of the job and how the space serves organization purposes. Stephenson (2004) reflects these web and feminist principles when she argues for office space that is organized by communication patterns, not positional status.

Helgesen "found that the leaders of web-style organizations encouraged greater participation of everyone in the organization and created organizational cultures that focus on '*what* needs to be done rather than on *who* has the authority to do it'" (Mahoney, 2002, p. 1 of 5; emphasis in original). Rather than a decision maker, web leaders are collaborators, people who work with others to accomplish the organization's goals. The collaborative structure of the web with the leader in the center, at the locus of communication and resources, exists in marked contrast to structures where inaccessible leaders are shielded by numerous organizational layers. "Most American leaders, like others worldwide, achieve their success with the help of others. Nonetheless, our cultural achieving styles spectacles only permit a vision of the leader, not the collaborators, nor the ones who relinquished their own dreams to help the leader succeed" (Lipman-Blumen, 1992, p. 198).

The need for increased involvement and multiple opportunities to express talent within an organization is essential for higher education. These complex institutions with their multiple goals, diverse funding patterns, changing student populations, internal and external stakeholders, and simultaneous organizational forms require flexibility and adaptability. While a feminist perspective may not fit all higher education institutions, its use in some colleges and universities or incorporation in select offices or divisions may well serve the members and institutional purposes.

Collaborative, Connected Leadership

The leadership characteristics of webs are vastly different from other organizational choices for higher education institutions. The leadership in webs differs from the "first among equals" leadership in collegiums. The collegium's autonomy stands in stark contrast to the intense interconnection and interrelationships of the web. The web's deemphasis on conflict and competition is a vivid contrast from political organizations with those dynamics at their core. Web leadership is collaborative, consultative, and non-elitist.

Those who emerge in them [web structures] as leaders tend to be people who feel comfortable being in the center of things rather than at the top, who prefer building consensus to issuing orders, and who place a low value on the kind of symbolic perks and marks of distinction that define success in the hierarchy. (Helgesen, 1995, p. 20)

The accessibility and centrality of the leader has some unexpected benefits. In traditional organizations, managers are viewed as the thinkers (i.e., the head) while the workers are viewed as the doers (i.e., the hands). In webs of inclusion, distinctions between management and workers, leaders and followers are blurred because everyone is encouraged to accept responsibility for the conceptualization and execution of organizational practices; in other words, for leadership. Positional rank in webs of inclusion is disregarded (Helgesen, 1995). Trust, communication, and delegation are paramount as followers are empowered to exercise leadership throughout the entire organization. In webs, leadership is strongly exercised from the center but with the aim of having everyone included and active.

This active, engaged approach to leadership was depicted by Lipman-Blumen (1992) who teased out how leadership could be culturally defined by gender. She demarcated connective leadership as reflecting a traditional female style and direct achieving leadership as a traditional male leadership style. These two styles can be linked to leadership in web organizations. The differing leadership styles of connective and direct, achieving leadership have contrasting values and approaches to task and relationship (see Table 14.2).

The underlying assumptions of connectivity rather than isolation and individualism make connective leadership a congruent style for feminist organizations and webs of inclusion. Connective leadership, culturally attributed to women,

derives its label from its character of connecting individuals not only to their own tasks and ego drives, but also to those of the group and community that depend upon the accomplishment of mutual goals. It is leadership that connects individuals to others and *other's* goals. (Lipman-Blumen, 1992, p. 184)

Table 14.2 • Gendered Approaches to Leadership

Connective Leadership	Direct, Achieving Leadership
Communal	Individualistic
Collaborative	Competitive
Persuasive	Controlling
Networking	Isolated
Interconnected	Self-reliant
Power with	Power over
Works together	Works separately
Mutuality	Egocentric
Contributes to the goals of others	Takes credit for the goals of others

(Lipman-Blumen, 1992)

Connective leadership is grounded in the female predilection for relationship (Gilligan, 1982). Direct, achieving leadership, culturally attributed to men, "emphasizes individualism, self-reliance, and belief in one's own abilities, as well as power, competition, and creativity" (Lipman-Blumen, 1992, p. 185). Both men and women can practice either style, both of which are shaped by culture, tradition, and practice. Despite ongoing developments about the value of diverse perspectives concerning leadership, the presence of deep cultural beliefs about the value of male-oriented leadership prevails. Organizations, including higher education institutions (with the exception of women's colleges and other nonpaternalistic organizations) are dominated by the direct, achieving leadership style. When most think of leadership, they assume the decisive, command and control of directive, achieving leadership. The gendered nature of organizations means that voices with a feminine tone (including males with this style) are heard less than voices with a traditional male tenor.

> Leaders who dare step beyond the limits of their own followers to reach out to a broader, even a global constituency, risk the ire of their traditional constituents while simultaneously stirring fear and confusion in the hearts of outsiders.... They use their gifts of persuasion and negotiation, rather than aggression, power, and competition, to accomplish their goals. (Lipman-Blumen, 1992, p. 193)

Because male leadership styles are privileged in organizations, women often adopt male characteristics as a way to be successful. These women may adopt an assertive leadership style, competitive approach to job advancement, and commanding presence. If she uses a consultative style to make decisions or a quiet reserved manner during committee meetings or other public proceedings, the female leader could be viewed as weak. A competitive stance means that aggressive attacks, antagonistic challenges to ideas shared, and maneuvering for recognition are common behaviors in organizations; and they are behaviors that demoralize and discourage people who are exposed to them. The undervaluing of female defined talents and skills means that positions within institutions that utilize nurturing, relationship building, and listening have lower salaries than positions using traditionally defined male skills.

Although a positive aspect of feminist theory and approaches to organizations, the transformational assumptions and emphasis of the feminist perspective places an additional burden on women leaders. The weight placed on change means that women, people of color, and other underrepresented peoples devote an excess proportion of effort and time to activities to transform the organization (e.g., diversity work, recruiting a diverse workforce).

Shared Power

"Webs create lasting networks that redistribute power in the organizations" (Helgesen, 1995, p. 27): Flat organizational structures, open communication systems, and leaders who symbolically and physically sit in the center of an organization are practices that redistribute power within an organization. If everyone has access to the leader (e.g., has the "ear" of the university president), then that source of power evaporates. If lines of authority are diffuse and transient, power becomes equally so. If expertise is based on immediate need and available talent, then expert power is recognized as being possessed by all, depending on the context. Power, expert or otherwise, is more widely recognized and more equitably utilized throughout the organization. The web achieves a more equitable distribution of power than methods currently used in many colleges and universities. Higher education institutions often use task forces as mechanisms for collaboration and institution-wide participation. The use of these committees may give the impression that the power to make decisions, provide input, and express voice is being redistributed. The opposite is true. "Unlike a task force, which dissolves when the task is completed and doesn't redistribute power in the organization, a web recreates the way things are done" (Mahoney, 2002, p. 2 of 5).

Communication

Communication in webs of inclusion emanates from all directions and across all levels. The networks are open and dynamic through which information flow. Communication patterns in web organizations reflect the "dynamic connectedness" (Helgesen, 1995, p. 16) of these structures. Because the silos often constructed within higher education organizations (Manning, Kinzie, & Schuh, 2006) are forsaken in lieu of a flatter, circular form, communication flows freely among departments and organizational participants. The assumptions of vertical (e.g., up and down) communication in bureaucracies or informal, disruptive (e.g., rumor oriented) lateral patterns of political organizations are replaced with the assumption that all participants benefit from the open flow of communication. "Web-style organizations are built on free-flowing community across levels, addressing real subjects" (Mahoney, 2002, p. 2 of 5). Communication is often more direct and face to face.

In the web organizations studied, Helgesen (1995) found that spontaneous invitations by the leader to talk in "highly personal" ways were commonplace. At one of the web organizations Helgesen used as an example, *The Village Voice*, she noted that the publisher did not call staff meetings. Policy memos were not issued and there was no evident chain of command. One did not need an appointment to see the publisher and no secretary stood guard to control access. An open door and central, accessible location allowed communication to flow in organic, natural ways.

> I had never worked where communication was so constant, so built into the daily process. Information was exchanged via bulletin board (corkboard, in that pre-computer era) and took the form of both general and specific notices.... Debates and policy discussions raged on the corkboard. (Helgesen, 1995, pp. 4–5)

The result was constant communication built into the architecture including debates and deep discussion that were exchanged in public places. Decision-making expertise has shifted with the change in access to information.

Although not part of Helgesen's analysis, the presence of blogs, Twitter, and other social media now make this open exchange of information and ubiquitous flow of communication even more prevalent. Abundant access to information shifts earlier power structures built on the assumption that control over information was power. Old separations of leadership and task, thinking and doing, have disappeared with the new configurations of authority and access. A benefit of this approach is that these communication norms "made rumor and intrigue difficult to sustain and kept most traumas in the open and so under a measure of control" (Helgesen, 1995, p. 5). While this open, ever-present communication may appeal to some, others may find it chaotic and overwhelming. As with all organization styles, this model is not for everyone.

Table 14.3 Strengths and Weaknesses of the Feminist Perspective

Strengths	Weaknesses
The adaptability and flexibility of webs makes them more responsive to profound change.	The chaotic and blurry roles and structure can be a source of confusion concerning who is responsible for what.
The structure builds tolerance for mavericks and people at the margins.	More aggressive people may overpower the voices of less aggressive members.
The downplayed power and status within the structure makes webs less demoralizing and more humane places to work.	There is some question about whether the web of inclusion can work without a strong leader.
The open structure and access to leadership increases participation across the institution.	Change can be slow process as leaders solicit wide-ranging input and allow multiple voices to be heard.

(Helgesen, 1995; Mahoney, 2002)

STRENGTHS AND WEAKNESSES OF THE FEMINIST PERSPECTIVE

Each organizational perspective has its strengths and weaknesses. No one organizational structure can solve all problems, match the style of all organizational members, or seamlessly and adequately respond to the environment. As with other organizational perspectives, the feminist perspective on organizations has its strengths and weaknesses (see Table 14.3).

NEXT STEPS: BRINGING THE FEMINIST PERSPECTIVE INTO CURRENT USE

Leaders of the future will be progressively more cosmopolitan, innovative, diverse, and values-oriented. They will come from countries with enormous growth potential outside of North America and Europe ... places where leaders also must address daunting obstacles such as poverty or environment degradation, regardless of the sector or the focus of their enterprise. (Kanter, 2006, pp. 61–62)

The feminist perspective in research, organizational theory, and popular literature has embraced relationships as its core feature. Carol Gilligan's (1982) landmark work was an early articulation of the way that women value relationship over separation, connection over autonomy. Within this value on relationship the next steps of the feminist model take form in the sustainability movement within higher education: *"If we want the chance for a sustainable future, we must think relationally"* (Sterling, 2010, p. 77; emphasis in original). Growing from a coalition of environmentally conscious students, financial officers seeking cost savings and more sustainable practices, and practitioners seeking best practices for green buildings and facilities, the sustainability movement within higher education is quickly catching hold. This approach, embedded in systems thinking, paradigm shifts, and contextual learning, is offered here as the next steps for the feminist perspective.

Sustainability has many meanings. Senge, Smith, Kruschwitz, Laur, and Schley (2008) define it as "the need to live in the present in ways that do not jeopardize the future" (p. 9). Pappas (2012) stated that:

> A sustainable society possesses the ability to survive and prosper, not just with respect to environmental resources, but also with respect to quality of life as it pertains to social, economic, technical, and individual contexts, and especially the values and conditions that promote continued human prosperity and growth (e.g., opportunity, economy, privacy, community, the arts, education, and health). A sustainable society meets these needs simultaneously, and in the context of human respect and the ability to negotiate differences without violence. (p. 2; emphasis in original)

The underlying values within these definitions: nonviolence, connection, community, and human dignity, are ones that resonate closely with the feminist perspective. Values are not the only area of overlap with the feminist perspective. Similar to the web of inclusion, educating for sustainability can proceed in a networklike fashion with purchasing, required and elective courses, campus recycling efforts (particularly with student involvement), climate change awareness, composting, and other sustainability practices combining in ways that create a connected and synergistic approach to education.

Building sustainable campuses and, by extension, a sustainable world involves recognizing a new paradigm. Similar to the feminist perspective, this paradigm emphasizes relationships, connection, and care. Fritjof Capra (2005) outlined perceptual shifts necessary to work toward sustainability. These shifts include from parts to whole, from objects to relationships, from objective knowledge to contextual knowledge, from quantity to quality, from structure to process, and from contents to patterns. The shift from parts to whole recognizes the nonreductionist ways that all actions influence others. A feminist perspective, similar to liberation theology and other social justice oriented philosophies, reflects the desire to move from considering people and nature itself as an object. Rather, the interconnectedness of everything recognizes that relationships define the world as we know it. The move toward contextual knowledge is reminiscent of Gilligan's (1982) observations that those with a feminine approach must take the whole of the circumstance into account, not just the raw facts of the situation.

Senge and colleagues liken the paradigm shift toward sustainability to the Renaissance and the Industrial Revolution calling it "a collective awakening to new possibilities that changes *everything* over time—how people see the world, what they value, how society defines progress and organizes itself, and how institutions operate" (Senge et al., 2008, p. 5). Globalization with its accompanying interdependence both exacerbates the sustainability crisis as well as provides hope for easing its effects. If all peoples are connected to each other, then the water, weather, and food crises in some countries will become the concern of peoples in other, less affected ones. The sustainability movement warrants new organizational structures, institutional assumptions, and practices. The role of higher education institutions in the sustainability movement is central to its success. Higher education can work toward sustainability in two ways: through their campus practices and by educating for sustainability.

The sustainability movement has significant implications for how higher education institutions are organized and how they operate. Changes that will influence communication patterns and interactions among campus community members include the arrangement of office space, increase in telecommuting, and institutional resources dedicated to public transportation.

CONCLUSIONS

The web of inclusion provides a model that envisions organizations as inclusive, open, and collaborative. To some, the perspective may seem utopian and out of reach; to others, it may give hope that higher education organizations can achieve a more equitable and just state. Whether embraced in total or applied in pieces, a feminist perspective applied to organizations holds significant promise for higher education institutions.

Questions for Discussion

- How can feminist principles of organizing be used to effect change within higher education?
- What are sources of support for feminist ways of organizing? Sources of resistance?
- What aspects of an institution of higher education would have to change to incorporate feminist principles into the organization?
- How do feminist principles enable societal transformation? How do they constrain it?
- How do the principles of the feminist perspective and the sustainability movement overlap?

Recommended Readings for the Feminist Perspective

Casey, C. (2004). Contested rationalities, contested organizations: Feminist and postmodernist visions. *Journal of Organizational Change Management, 17*(3), 302–314.

Eddy, P. L., & Cox, E. (2008). Gendered leadership: An organizational perspective. In J. Lester (Ed.), *Gendered perspectives on community colleges* (New Directions in Community Colleges, pp. 69–80). San Francisco, CA: Jossey-Bass.

Eddy, P. L., & VanDerLinden, K. E. (2006). Emerging definitions of leadership in higher education: New visions of leadership or the same old "hero" leader. *Community College Review, 34*(5), 5–26.

Glazer-Raymo, J. (1999). *Shattering the myths: Women in academe.* Baltimore, MD: Johns Hopkins Press.

Hesselbein, F., & Goldsmith, M. (Eds.). (2009). *The leader of the future: Vol. 2. Visions, strategies, and practices for the new era.* San Francisco, CA: Jossey-Bass.

Iverson, S. (2011). Glass ceilings and sticky floors: Women and advancement in higher education. In J. L. Martin (Ed.), *Women as leaders in education: Succeeding despite inequity, discrimination* (pp. 79–105). Santa Barbara, CA: Praeger.

Temple, J. B., & Jari Ylitalo, J. (2009). Promoting inclusive (and dialogic) leadership in higher education institutions. *Tertiary Education and Management, 15*(3), 277–289.

15

CASE

A Clash of Collaborative and Competitive Leadership Styles

INTRODUCTION

Leadership is among the oldest and most complex set of social science theories. Scholars and laypersons alike have commented on and written about leadership for centuries. In this case chapter, the theories of collaborative leadership (Chrislip & Larson, 1994; Kezar, Carducci, & Contreras-McGavin, 2006; Komives, Lucas, & McMahon, 2007), connective leadership (Lipman-Blumen, 1992, 1998, 2002; Robinson & Lipman-Blumen 2003), and collaborative teamwork (Rawlings, 2000) will be discussed in the context of conflicting leadership styles within a large research institution.

COLLABORATIVE LEADERSHIP

In the 1990s, leadership theorists expounded on the differences between male and female leadership styles (Helgesen, 1990, 1995; Rosener, 1997). This literature focused attention on collaboration and nurturance as a culturally defined female leadership style versus power and control leadership as a traditional masculine style (Robinson & Lipman-Blumen, 2003). Although leadership, like any social phenomenon, is gendered (i.e., a social phenomenon), one's leadership style is not determined by one's sex (i.e., a biological phenomenon). The propensity to build and work in teams, shape an institutional culture that encourages cooperation, and invite participation in decision making is not based on gender but on preference. Both men and women are capable of collaborative leadership that is transformational and effective. Despite the popular culture and leadership literature tendency to describe leadership along the gender binary (i.e., male/female), continuing to view leadership styles as falling along these culturally determined predispositions will not result in the equity or goal attainment desired within institutions (Robinson & Lipman-Blumen, 2003).

Chrislip and Larson (1994) described the purposes of collaborative leadership as a process "to create a shared vision and joint strategies to address concerns that go beyond the purview of any particular party" (p. 5). Collaborative leadership is not about leadership from the top but a style that involves all in an inclusive, participative, and relational process. Kezar et al. (2006), in a review of leadership literature, described collaborative leadership as "interactive, inclusive, and addressing issues of the common good" (p. 76). Rather than depending on older forms of command and control leadership that focused on the leader, collaborative leadership involves all community members in shared action. Examples of strategies used in this type of leadership include group work, deemphasis on individual merit, new kinds of accountability, and reimagined mission, vision, and strategy to support collaborative work (Kezar et al., 2006). At a time when the conditions within higher education require new modes of collaborative thinking and acting, the challenges to achieving those ends could not be greater.

Traditional and Connective Leadership Styles

In a similar vein to collaborative leadership, Lipman-Blumen (1992, 1998, 2002; Robinson & Lipman-Blumen, 2003) elucidated the concept of connective leadership to challenge the overreliance on traditional command and control leadership styles. Lipman-Blumen used three sets of achieving styles (i.e., direct, instrumental, and relational) to outline a helpful contrast between the traditional leadership style ego ideal and the emerging connective ego ideal. While both men and women can embrace either ego ideal with its corresponding approach to leadership, Lipman-Blumen discussed the ways that men and women are socialized to assume different leadership roles within organizations. The traditional ego ideal represents a less optimal fit to those who have a more culturally consistent female leadership preference.

The ego ideal of the direct achiever is perhaps the most familiar leadership style. Based on the American ideal of rugged individualism and the self-reliant hero, leadership based on this approach entails individually based action, competition as a significant tactic, an orientation toward control, and emphasis on power (Lipman-Blumen, 1992). In contrast to this style, women are socialized to value communalism over individualism, cooperation over competition, and collaboration over control. Lipman-Blumen argued that the traditional rugged individualist style, often the basis of arguments for higher education institutions to operate like businesses, fits poorly for those institutions. Rather than borrow from the corporate world, Lipman-Blumen argued, "effective university leaders now may provide a better model for the new business world than such traditional, rugged individualists" (1998, p. 49). The long-standing traditions of shared governance, faculty as knowledge workers, emphasis on creativity and innovation, propensity for interdisciplinary efforts, and presence of diverse groups summons the talents of connective leadership, specifically the relational achieving style.

> Connective leaders [are] those with an eye for finding and then ethically exploiting the connections among diverse, often contentious groups. They recognize the groups' mutualities even while the parties themselves remain astigmatic. Connective leaders see the overlap between their own and others' visions and agendas. (Lipman-Blumen, 1998, p. 50)

In connective leadership, collaboration, teamwork, mentoring, and pride in others' achievements are ways to empower others and achieve organizational goals. Connective leaders possess a more multifaceted, flexible repertoire of behaviors and approaches (Lipman-Blumen, 1998). The relational achieving style requires an understanding of group process, willingness to rely on others, and ability to build relationships based on reciprocity and openness. The relational achieving style, more culturally consistent with women's leadership, is more fitting for the complex, globally connected, interdependent, and technologically integrated organizations of the 21st century. Such connective leadership is undervalued in organizations, which tend to reward direct achiever styles. For women or any other organizational members to resist command and control leadership styles and employ the connective style, like-minded others must be present: "For cooperation to take root, it is crucial to assemble a critical mass of individuals with cooperative, collaborative, and contributory skills" (Lipman-Blumen, 1992, p. 199).

Teamwork

Although teamwork is a stated value of modern organizations, effective teams are difficult to achieve.

> While leaders recognize the need for organizational collaboration, they often do not know how to build the capability for it. Harder still, they do not want to wrestle with the conflict that underlies their own team's lack of cross-functional collaboration. (Rawlings, 2000, p. 36)

Because individualism predominantly underscores the work of teams within organizations, teams struggle to find ways to work together (Lipman-Blumen, 1992). Rawlings suggests a different approach to teams than has traditionally been embraced in the past. Rather than seeing teams as being in effect only when a group is physically together, a re-visioned view of team and teamwork "means that members manage team and individual decision making in the context of team results and interdependencies among members" (Rawlings, 2000, pp. 38–39). It means sharing a vision, engaging in cross-functional collaborations, and undertaking collaborative initiatives. Too often, traditional teamwork has been limited to asking members "to share accountabilities, resources, and solutions to problems" (Rawlings, 2000, p. 37). Teamwork in a connective environment requires leaders to take their conceptions about leadership and teams to deeper levels.

> Leaders must question their own value systems as well as their beliefs about leadership, the company, and team members…. Ultimately, the work of a strategic leadership team is based on shared understanding, agreements, and mutual accountability. (Rawlings, 2000, p. 37)

The team leader has a particular obligation to imagine his or her work from the point of view of the team's overall goals. This view is in marked contrast to the traditional ego ideal discussed by Lipman-Blumen (1992); one in which leaders provide the vision and obtain rewards on the basis on their heroic achievements.

Rawlings (2000) suggests a move from the current thinking about leadership teams that emphasizes coordination, resolution of conflicts, increased communication, and coordination of individual contributions to the shared goals. Instead, a more updated style of leadership teams sees members working interdependently. Rather than being determined in a top-down manner, goals are shared with the idea of building organization-wide capabilities. Achievements are not limited to discrete divisions or functions but encompass the entire organization, at times transcending the organization. The team makes decisions together rather than simply consulting on individual team members' issues. They "challenge one another to think more deeply and creatively, learn from one another, and create integrated solutions that are built from everyone's ideas" (Rawlings, 2000, p. 41). This approach to collaborative teamwork means abandoning turf wars, parochial views, misalignments, and distrust. Team members must share the successes and setbacks in an open manner that builds a combined effort to lead effectively.

===================================== CASE =====================================

The following case describes attempts by a research extensive university president to use a collaborative leadership approach with faculty, the Board of Regents, and other members of the university community. The collaborative approach clashed with the system chancellor's view of leadership, which was more traditional and driven by political expediencies.

Context

Lone State University is the flagship university with approximately 22,000 students, 18,000 undergraduates, and 4,000 graduate students. A research extensive institution, Lone State University was established in 1868. With a proud history, the institution counts among its graduates several governors, two state attorneys general, and many prominent lawyers, doctors, and other professionals within the state. The university occupies a unique position as a public institution with extensive ties to state legislators and officials whose work directly relates to the university's budget allocation.

Questions to Consider

- What is the relationship between an institution, the state legislature, and business leaders?
- How do relationships with alumni influence campus leadership and decision-making styles?
- How do external constituents and stakeholders influence presidential leadership style?

Case Characters

Dr. Marla Wagner, President: President Wagner was appointed to office 18 months ago. The first woman appointed as president at Lone State University, Dr. Wagner was routinely and vigorously tested in her first 18 months in office. With extensive previous experience as a provost and 10 years as an academic administrator at a public college in the state, President Wagner assumed she would have some challenges adjusting to her new role but was confident that she could manage it. Her confidence was based on the fact that she had been remarkably successful as the provost in her previous institution. In fact, it was that success that brought her to the attention of System Chancellor Gardner who had recruited her to be president of Lone State.

Although Wagner had ambitions to advance to a president's position, she was ambivalent about assuming the position at Lone State. It was well known that the university had a well-established old boy network peopled with alumni and legislators who ran the institution from behind the scenes. This group had exerted profound influence on the university for years by managing appointments to the Board of Regents, exerting influence on the president to effect the decisions they felt were correct for the institution, and working with the governor to assure the success of the institution.

Mr. Knox Rendall, Alumnus and Former Board of Regents Chair: Mr. Rendall is a proud alumnus of Lone State University. A former chair of the Board of Regents for the university, Mr. Rendall had dedicated his life to the university. A personal friend of the previous president, Rendall was dubious about the appointment of Marla Wagner as president. He understood the need to appoint a woman as president but he was unsure of this particular woman. In his mind, no one could replace former President Loren Ward.

Dr. Loren Ward, Former Lone State President: After 8 years as president of Lone State, Dr. Loren Ward was happy to be back in the ranks of the faculty. This was the case despite the fact that as a political scientist, Ward had enjoyed the political machinations involved with being president of a major research institution. Because Knox Rendall and the alumni members of the Board of Regents who directed campus decision making had recruited him, Ward knew to whom he was beholden. There were times when Ward disagreed with Rendall and his colleagues but also knew when to pick his battles, a strategy that had worked well during his tenure as president.

Ward knew to stay out of the politics of campus governance after he no longer served as president. He could not help but watch with trepidation as the new president, a woman, assumed the reins. Ward immediately noticed a difference in style between him and Marla Wagner. Where he embraced a traditional leadership style of decisive action and skilled exercise of presidential power, it appeared to him that President Wagner had a "softer" style, one characterized by collaboration, discussion, and participation. He wished her luck and wondered if she would survive the rough and tumble politics at Lone State.

Dr. Brent Gardner, System Chancellor: Chancellor Gardner had been system head for 10 years. He had brought in the previous president of Lone State and was heavily invested in the success of the current president, Marla Wagner. The presidential search had been exhaustive but from the start he had supported this up and coming provost from an in-state institution. He had heard that her style was more collaborative than Loren Ward's but assumed that a few months in her new position would convince her of the need to take a more decisive stand on campus issues, manage her immediate staff with a more commanding presence, and direct the faculty on the curriculum changes deemed necessary by the Board of Regents. The issue of curricular change was particularly troubling for Gardner. Board of Regents members who were involved with the national, international, and local business communities were convinced that Lone State needed to complete the transformation from a regional state institution to a higher education institution with a global presence. The faculty at Lone State were resistant to the more business- and global-oriented approach to the curriculum. Wagner, as a former provost, was well aware of what it took to move a faculty along to a new way of viewing the curriculum.

Dr. Kristina Hayek, President of the Faculty Senate: Kristina Hayek was elected president of the Lone State faculty senate a year ago. One year into her 2-year term, Hayek was thrilled to be working with Marla Wagner. Hayek believed Wagner was in an enviable position because the faculty at Lone State University held her in high regard. Her collaborative style appealed to their sense of collegiality and community. She was one of them—an academic who understood faculty life.

Questions to Consider

- How do presidential and faculty governance leadership influence each other?
- What expectations might faculty have about president leadership?
- How might a president be influenced by the expectations concerning leadership by faculty?
- What relationships exist between a state campus, particularly the flagship, and the system office?

President's Style

Wagner felt that her appointment as president to Lone State University signaled a desire by the chancellor, Board of Regents, and university members as a whole for a more collaborative and participative style than had previously been exercised at the university. Although interested in collaborative approaches for years, she felt that, as the provost under a former president with a command and control approach, she had to emulate that approach. As chief executive officer, she could now set an institution-wide tone about the desired leadership style. Wagner planned to work closely with faculty who were responsible for the institution's curriculum. She continued her regular consultations with faculty governance and, importantly, built a highly functioning team of vice presidents. She understood that the vice presidents had been managed in ways that engendered competition between and among the divisions and units. She planned to use a collaborative style to minimize competition and generate support and cooperation within this group.

Questions to Consider

- What are some ways that a competitive leadership style can be inadvertently encouraged among team members?
- What are some advantages and disadvantages of a competitive leadership style?
- What are some advantages and disadvantages of a cooperative leadership style?
- How are leadership styles coordinated in a team of executive leaders?

The First Months as President

Dr. Wagner spent the first six months of her presidency assembling her team. Assessing the strengths she needed for her cabinet, Wagner built her team through a combination of existing executive members and new hires. Upon her arrival at Lone State, she employed the traditional practice of receiving resignations from the executive officers. She accepted some and refused others in an effort to build a collaborative, empowered team.

President Wagner would be the first to admit that she made some mistakes when assembling her executive team. She did not retain the vice president for administration and finance, a 25-year veteran of the institution with comprehensive knowledge of the budgeting system, trustee relationships, and capital improvements. She had received unsolicited advice from Knox Rendall about keeping the vice president but felt that the former chair of the regents' knowledge of the institution was dated. She required a vice president with up-to-date technical skills with budgeting software, bond acquisitions for facilities renovations, and human resources. These issues had been festering within the administration and finance division for years and had yet to be resolved. President Wagner remained hopeful that a new vice president in that area could bring about the needed change.

President Wagner's appointment of a new vice president for student affairs also raised controversy. She made the appointment without adequate consultation with the students. She quickly realized her mistake and pulled the students into interviews with candidates for the other vice presidential positions. She initiated biweekly meetings with the president of student government to indicate her interest in student issues. She trusted that the appointment of the vice president for student affairs would blow over once students saw the value in this person's impressive credentials. She felt that these missteps were minor and to be expected with a new president who was assembling her team.

Questions to Consider

- What team-related qualities should be considered when hiring vice presidents who serve on the presidential cabinet?
- In what ways might executive leaders with a traditional approach to leadership and team clash with team members with a more connective style?
- What campus groups are to be consulted when hiring vice presidents?
- What is the balance between consultation and presidential prerogative?

Old Boy's Club Monthly Meeting

Knox Rendall was at his monthly lunch with four colleagues. It was an impressive group, and Rendall was the unofficial chair who called meetings, set agendas, and facilitated discussion. Because their meetings always centered on the university and involved confidential information, they met in a private room at Rendall's club. Today's meeting focused on the president. The group agreed with Rendall that they had given the new president as much time as they could afford. After 18 months, they saw no evidence of significant leadership and believed that Wagner needed to be removed. They were meeting to work on a plan. Rendall had spoken to the governor and he agreed with their assessment. The problem was Chancellor Gardner. As head of the state's university system, Gardner was responsible for appointing President Wagner. Although he was dissatisfied with her performance, he wanted to work through the situation on his own.

Questions to Consider

- What role can be taken by stakeholders outside the formal institutional organization regarding the leadership and administration of a higher education institution?
- What means are available to a group of alumni to exert pressure on an institution?
- What means are available to a chancellor to discipline an institution president for poor performance?
- What procedures are available to a chancellor to assess an institutional president?

Vestiges of Traditional Leadership

Chancellor Gardner had always enjoyed an excellent relationship with the Old Boy's Group. He very carefully built this relationship over the years because he knew conferring with them on decisions was politically wise. In return, the group was generous in their donations to the university. Their advice and guidance had been invaluable. Gardner's faith in this group's value was one source of concern about President Wagner's performance. Knox Rendall had informed him that President Wagner had ignored his advice about retaining the vice president for administration and finance. Although Rendall had reached out to President Wagner on several occasions, she was slow to return his calls and had neglected to invite him to several campus events. Gardner was also concerned about Wagner's relationship to and with university faculty. It was evident that she viewed herself as a proponent of faculty issues. While constructive faculty relations were essential to presidential success, Gardner had the impression that Wagner felt that she worked for the faculty more than for the regents or chancellor.

An additional area of concern for Gardner was the way that Wagner led her executive team. Gardner's sources told him that Wagner often sat back during executive leadership meetings and let the vice presidents work out their differences. Rather than ask for reports on progress in the individual divisions, she continued to push them to work collaboratively and collectively on goals set by the group. Gardner viewed this as a waste of time. He had hired President Wagner to exert strong leadership. Her job was to determine the vision of the institution and then empower her executives to achieve that vision. All this talking and collaborating took up valuable time that needed to be spent on achieving goals and building a stronger university.

Questions to Consider

- In what ways does Gardner's perspective on leadership symbolize the traditional command and control approach?
- In what ways does Wagner's perspective on leadership embody a connective approach to leadership?
- What leadership behaviors are expected of university presidents? How do these expectations chafe against connective leadership?

A Negative Evaluation

Rendall and Gardner had recently met over lunch to discuss Wagner's performance. Rendall did not mince words in telling Gardner that Wagner needed to be dismissed. Although the chancellor believed that the president had not had enough time to test herself, he knew the political ramifications of ignoring Rendall and his group's advice. It was time for Wagner's 18-month review. Gardner would use the evaluation as an opportunity to communicate the dissatisfaction he felt about her leadership style and progress to date (see Figure 15.1).

Questions to Consider

- What leadership style does Chancellor Gardner's approach represent?
- What leadership style does President Wagner's approach represent?
- What actions could Wagner or Gardner take to work together?
- If you were President Wagner, how would you respond to Gardner's evaluation?

PRESIDENT EVALUATION

Chancellor's Office
Evaluation of President Marla Wagner

RATING SCALE
5 = OUTSTANDING. Consistently and significantly exceed expectations.
4 = EXCELLENT. Frequently meets and/or exceeds expectations.
3 = GOOD. Meets all expectations and minimum requirements, but has some inconsistencies.
2 = MARGINAL. Deficiencies in some areas but expectations are occasionally not met.
1 = UNSATISFACTORY. Does not meet the minimum expectations and requirements.

1. INSTITUTIONAL AGENDA   Rating: 2
How has the Lone State progressed during the president's tenure?
Comments:
Has yet to establish an agenda that advances the institution.

2. GENERAL MANAGEMENT AND PLANNING   Rating: 1
How effectively is the president overseeing the Lone State's leadership and organizational
structure?
Comments:
Does not understand how to be a decisive leader. Leaves decisions to others. Takes a minor role in leading groups.

3. FISCAL MANAGEMENT AND BUDGETING   Rating: 2
How effectively has the president influenced Lone State's budgeting and fiscal management
processes?
Comments:
Made strategic missteps in not retaining a pivotal leader in the institution's financial area. The current direction of the institution is in question. Does not show good judgment in this area.

4. INTERNAL RELATIONSHIPS   Rating: 3
How effective is the president in promoting an environment that enables student, faculty,
and staff success?
Comments:
Has excellent relations with faculty but appears to work for them rather than for the Regents or me, the chancellor.

5. EXTERNAL RELATIONSHIPS   Rating: 1
How effective has the president been in nurturing external relationships that benefit Lone State?
Comments:
Has alienated important external constituents who have exerted long-term influence on the institution. Has worked to bring new stakeholders into the mix but has done so by sacrificing important existing relationships.

6. DECISION MAKING AND PROBLEM SOLVING   Rating: 3
How well does the president delegate, make crucial decisions and facilitate problem solving?
Comments:
While President Wagner's ability to delegate may seem commendable, her style indicates weak leadership and inadequate management. Her team solves problems well but that seems to be despite rather than because of her.

Figure 15.1 President's Evaluation *(continued on next page)*

7. MODELING LONE STATE VALUES   Rating: 3

How well does the President keep Lone State's core values and guiding principles visible and integrated into the Lone State's everyday practices?

Comments:

President Wagner has a clear sense of institutional values and appears able to communicate those to the institution. But, those values were shaped by a prior administration so cannot be credited to Wagner's leadership.

8. INTERACTION WITH REGENTS   Rating: 1

How well is the president effectively engaging the potential of the Board of Regents?

Comments:

This is an area needing immediate remediation. Wagner does not seem to understand the role of the Regents or the fact that this group hired her. Although some regents believe her leadership skills are more "modern" than the last president, she needs to immediately adopt a strong leadership style that shows who is in charge.

9. STRATEGIC DIRECTION   Rating: 2

How well does the President manage Lone State's longer-term strategy?

Comments:

I am concerned about the future of the institution given Wagner's leadership. The institution seems rudderless and adrift.

10. AREAS OF EXCEPTIONAL ACHIEVEMENT

Comments:

There are none that I can identify.

11. AREAS REQUIRING ATTENTION

Comments:

My evaluative comments throughout this form indicate necessary areas of improvement.

12. ADVICE

What advice would you give the President regarding her leadership of Lone State?

Change your leadership style or risk losing your position.

Figure 15.1 President's Evaluation

Wagner's Response

President Wagner was completely blindsided by Chancellor Gardner's evaluation. She knew that they did not see eye to eye concerning leadership styles, but she was unaware of depth to which he disapproved of her leadership style. Obviously he did not respect her leadership style, which she had cultivated after learning about connective leadership. Wagner had surmised that some administrators at Lone State were not convinced that her leadership style could be effective. Others, most notably faculty, had expressed significant support for her.

Despite the support Wagner possessed within the institution, she tendered her resignation effective immediately. She could have stayed and worked to win over the chancellor and alumni like Knox Rendall. Rather than take that route, she pursued the presidency of a private institution in another state. She was highly sought after by presidential search firms and was confident that she could find an institution where her empowering leadership style would have more effect. Rather than participate in the meeting with Chancellor Gardner to discuss his evaluation of her, she sent her letter of resignation.

Questions to Consider

- What options were available to President Wagner?
- How might the president reconcile the differences in leadership style between her and Chancellor Gardner?
- In what circumstances does connective leadership excel?
- In what circumstances does a traditional approach to leadership excel?

DISCUSSION

Higher education leadership, indeed leadership as a whole, is on the cusp of a transformation. While some see traditional leadership as the only style of leading available, others, including administrators in the corporate world, are using collaborative methods to effect leadership in their organizations. Rather than separating these styles along gender lines, it is more helpful to think of leadership as a style that is chosen, rather than an approach determined by gender. The style of leadership required is determined by the context of the institution. A leadership style that fits the history, values, and traditions of the institution is essential if executive leaders are to be successful.

16

SPIRITUAL

Organizational theory is based on a culture's answers to questions about the self.
(Zohar, 1997, p. 96)

INTRODUCTION

Interest in religion and spirituality has seen a marked increase since the mid- to late 1990s (Briskin, 1996; Daloz, Keen, Keen, & Parks, 1996; Jablonski, 2001; Kessler, 2000; Peppers & Briskin, 2000). Higher education scholars and practitioners have pursued this interest through a variety of means but the majority of attention has gone to students and their development as spiritual beings (Astin, 2004; Astin, Astin, & Lindholm, 2010; Chickering, Dalton, & Stamm, 2005). A complementary interest in spirituality exists in the context of organizational theory, although the collection of scholarship is a modest one at the present time. This stream of scholarship is essential to understanding modern organizations because

> the spirituality in the workplace movement is the manifestation of a deep yearning for meaning and purpose in the work lives of individuals. People want to know that their work matters, that their efforts are in the service of something worthwhile, that their legacy is one of contributing to the betterment of humankind. (Rogers & Dantley, 2001, p. 601)

An exploration of organizations from a spiritual perspective is helpful because people within and outside of higher education institutions question the U.S. emphasis on materialism, deterioration of community, and search for something larger than the self. This chapter explores the spiritual perspective in organizations and organizational theory, including implications for the work lives of faculty, administrators, and staff. Focusing on the work of Danah Zohar and Alan Briskin, this chapter explores the implications of spirituality, interrelationships, leadership, power, and vision in the context of higher education institutions.

The differences between religion and spirituality, concepts often conflated but vastly different by definition, is helpful to explore prior to any discussion of spirituality. In this chapter, I borrow from Rogers (2003) who stated that "spirituality is an inner, private process while religion is an outward, public one" (p. 22). Chickering (2006) also teased out the differences between religion and spirituality.

> Being religious connotes belonging to and practicing a religious tradition. Being spiritual suggests a personal commitment to a process of inner development that engages us in our totality.... Spirituality is a way of life that affects and includes every moment of existence. It is at once a contemplative attitude, a disposition to a life of depth, and the search for ultimate meaning, direction and belonging. (Teasdale, 1999 as cited in Chickering, 2006, p. 2)

In this chapter, spirituality, not religion, is the focus of the discussion. Zohar (2010) clarified that there need not be a connection to religion to embrace the organizational spiritual perspective. Rogers and Dantley (2001, p. 591) note that: "Spirituality manifests in our search for wholeness, meaning, interconnectedness, and values." One of the places where that search occurs is in higher education organizations. Spirituality is a corporate and organizational concern, not one solely related to individual growth and development. Spirituality from this perspective has substantial implications for leadership, organizational vision, and interrelationships within organizations.

PSYCHOLOGY AS A FOUNDATION FOR THE SPIRITUAL PERSPECTIVE

Organizational theorists have a long history of approaching organizations from a psychological perspective. Motivation, job satisfaction, interpersonal relations, and leadership styles are underscored with concepts from psychology. Assumptions from this theoretical foundation include the following:

- An understanding of human nature and behavior can assist one's job performance and effectiveness.
- Organizations are sites where human agency can be acted and expressed.
- A place where humans can seek to become self-actualized is within organizations.
- One's psychological and emotional health (or lack thereof) will have an impact on organizational health.
- Psychological health and lack of psychological health can be expressed at both individual and organizational levels.

In addition to these assumptions, the spiritual perspective is particularly well suited to the assumptions of positive psychology, a recent arm of psychology that challenges the disease oriented approach of traditional psychology. "The positive psychology approach sought to bring a complementary focus to the psychology field's emphasis on remediating mental illness by attending to the study and practice of fostering human strengths and emotional well-being" (Mather, 2010, p. 158). This approach, a continuation of the work of Abraham Maslow, Carl Rogers, and other humanistic psychologists, is a particularly apt foundation for the spiritual perspective of organizational theory. Several aspects of positive psychology, as articulated by Mather (2010), include the following:

- Happiness is a goal of human living.
- Nurturing positive emotions can significantly affect individuals' sense of well-being.
- "Embracing the strengths of the heart" and telling one's healthy (as opposed to horror) story can lead to healing and growth. (p. 161)
- Seeking authentic goals such as intimacy, generativity, and spirituality promotes well-being.

Psychology as a theoretical foundation has strengths and weaknesses, similar to the foundations of all the organizational perspectives (see Table 16.1).

METAPHOR

Journey is the metaphor that best describes the spiritual perspective on organizations. Journey can be used as an image to describe organizational members' meaning-making processes as well as the journey an organization embarks upon to achieve its mission and purposes. The journey metaphor is a particularly apt one for this organizational perspective in the way it conveys enrichment, searching, and progression. As explained in the following sections, these characteristics underscore the spiritual perspective and the assumptions that form its structure and practices.

STRUCTURE

Different from other organizational perspectives described in this book, the spiritual perspective does not conform to one particular structural arrangement (e.g., web, hierarchy, circle). Rather, the principles and processes of this organizational perspective can be used with many organizational forms. Some configurations by their nature will be a better fit to this approach to organizational functioning and its underlying assumptions. For example, the web structure of the feminist perspective works well with the spiritual perspective's emphasis on interpersonal relationships. The rigid standard operating procedures of bureaucracies would be a difficult fit with the openness espoused in the spiritual perspective. The "first among equals" leadership of the collegial circle structure

Table 16.1 Strengths and Weaknesses of the Psychological Theoretical Foundation

Strengths	Weaknesses
Places the enduring human search for meaning into an organizational context.	May over-estimate the impact of one individual on the complex relationships within an organization.
Brings positive elements such as wholeness, beauty, and passion into the thinking about organizations.	The inclusion of psychological concepts and practices may feel intrusive to some organizational members.
Acknowledges that people bring the whole of themselves, including emotions, into the workplace.	An over-emphasis on the emotional and personal aspects of organizational functioning may distract members from other goals within the organization.
Can perpetuate individual and organizational well-being through the expression of positive emotions and a healthy work environment.	Can become a one-sided approach to examining organizational functioning.

would fit well with a spiritual perspective but the isolation and separation embodied in department structures potentially works against the connection and integration preferred in the spiritual approach. Depending on the organizational form, certain underlying assumptions would necessarily shift to accommodate the spiritual perspective.

ASSUMPTIONS

Danah Zohar (1997) was one of the first theorists to explore how spirituality impacts organizations and the theory that guides them. In her book, *ReWiring the Corporate Brain*, Zohar explored spirituality from the point of view of quantum theory. Using new science (i.e., postmodern) perspectives, Zohar discussed vision, interrelationships, cooperation, holism, context, and uncertainty. Because organizations are not value free, an understanding of organizational functioning at the paradigm level is essential.

> Higher education is not value free. Each policy and practice we adopt, each resource allocation judgment, staffing and personnel decision we make, expresses a value priority. The gap between our espoused values and the values actually in use is often large, unrecognized and unarticulated. (Chickering, 2006, p. 4)

The spiritual perspective makes organizational values explicit. Zohar's discussion of organizations and spirituality, in the context of new science perspectives, speaks to a different set of values than the Newtonian assumptions, particularly those used in the bureaucratic perspective and other orthodox theories.

MAJOR CONCEPTS, CHARACTERISTICS, AND PRINCIPLES

The spiritual perspective lends a unique understanding to organizations, including higher education institutions. Although people pursue higher education degrees for many reasons, including materially driven purposes (Pryor, Hurtado, DeAngelo, Palucki Blake, & Tran, 2010), students, faculty, and administrators are fundamentally and developmentally changed through their campus experiences. The purposes of higher education encompass the fulfillment of human potential, social justice, and social change. The underlying individual and societal principles and assumptions of these higher education institutions make the spiritual perspective (including discussions of spirit and soul, vision, leadership, interrelationships, and power) uniquely fitting to that environment.

Spiritual Capital and Intelligence

Human beings have spent eons in the search for meaning larger than the individual's experience. Zohar connected this search to organizational functioning through two concepts: spiritual capital and spiritual intelligence. Spiritual capital is defined as

> the wealth, the power, and the influence that we gain by acting from a deep sense of meaning, our deepest values, and a sense of higher purpose, and all of these are best expressed through a life devoted to service. (Zohar, 2010, p. 3)

Spiritual capital, much like cultural and social capital (Dowd, Sawatzky, & Korn, 2011; Lamont & Lareau, 1988), provides resources and capabilities to the person possessing it. This resource is linked to spiritual intelligence:

> It is by seeking meaning in our lives and acting in accordance with our deepest
> values that we can commit ourselves to lives of service based on the capacity
> that we are best suited to, whatever we choose to do personally or professionally.
> (Zohar, 2010, p. 3)

In linking service and meaning making to organizational functioning, Zohar raises
the purposes of these institutions to the level of vision, legacy, and commitment. "Exploration, cooperation, self- and situational-mastery, creativity, and service" replace the
motivators of fear, greed, and anger (Zohar, 2010, p. 3). Business becomes higher service;
jobs become callings; organizational values become linked to beneficial human purposes; and goals such as global understanding and environmental stewardship become
part of everyday organizational functioning. Given the historical developmental and
social change purposes of higher education, the spiritual perspective is a particularly
apt approach.

SOUL AND SPIRIT

Alan Briskin (1996; Peppers & Briskin, 2000), another author who explored organizational theory and spirituality, introduced the elements of uncertainty, interrelationship, and metaphor into his explanations of organizational theory. Briskin grounded his
discussion on organizations and spirituality in explanations of spirit and soul. Briskin,
portraying an historical view on soul, explained that the Hebrews viewed soul as vital-
ity; the Greeks saw this human aspect as underworld; others saw soul as containing a
spark of the divine (Briskin, 1996). "The challenge of finding soul in organizations, as in
life, is to embrace not only what we see, hear, and understand but also to attend to what
we don't know, what we cannot see at first glance or hear on first listening" (Briskin,
1996, p. 9). In particular, Briskin discussed the danger of neglecting soul in organizations. When the soul is ignored, both its positive and negative elements seep out in
unexpected ways.

Working from Jungian philosophy, Briskin (1996) discussed the ways that the underworld or shadow side of soul is as integral to life as the upper world aspects of soul.
When the upper world of soul is overemphasized and the underworld deemphasized,
organizations fail to account for these uniquely human aspects of organizational life.
Abandonment, rage, despair, and shame are as much a part of human living as wonder,
happiness, and joy (Manning, 2001). Shadow elements of organizations include power,
hierarchy, inequality, anger, impatience, and burnout.

> Modern business life arises from a love of the upperworld, of material products,
> of order and organization; it celebrates the material, light-filled portion of exis-
> tence. It is the world as we see it (or as we would like to see it) and as it most makes
> sense to us. But as many of us suspect in sensing the shock waves now traveling
> through our corporations and institutions, it is only half the story. (Manning,
> 2001, p. 29)

There is wisdom in the shadow side of soul, and without it the soul is incomplete.
With the full embrace of the positive and shadow sides of the soul, one can live with
the paradox that it is possible to be both generous and controlling, compassionate and

Table 16.2 Application of Soul to Higher Education

Upper World in Higher Education	Shadow Side in Higher Education
Patient	Impatient
Perfect	Overworked
Visionary	Burned out
Always correct	Bored
Optimistic	Unable to set limits
Collaborative	Controlling

cruel, efficient and ineffectual. Organizational members can use the creative polarity of the soul and apply this understanding to higher education administration and leadership (Briskin, 1996; Manning, 2001) (see Table 16.2). Briskin's account of the positive and negative aspects of soul and how this is expressed in organizations is a fascinating account of how these uniquely human groups reflect the best and worst part of human living. These elements should not be ignored but rather embraced as part of the sorrow and joy of working in organizations, including higher education institutions.

In addition to soul, Briskin explored the concept of spirit, which he defined as "wind of a divine inspiration. Different from soul, spirit comes from higher up and descends into the body.... Soul is in the middle, holding together spirit and body, lofty inspiration and physical limitation" (1996, p. 17). He discussed the fact that the spirit and physical worlds have been split off from one another. In the workplace, the remnants of spirit exist in "a thin and airy call for abstract workplace virtues such as teamwork, responsibility, accountability, and inspired leadership" (Briskin, 1996, p. 19). These thin concepts, particularly as discussed in the corporate and higher education leadership literature, fail to excavate the full depth possible when soul and spirit are incorporated into organizations. Materialism, profits, and inadequate relationships have become a poor substitute for matters of the soul and spirit.

Whether one embraces soul or spirit, both concepts lend aspects to organizational theory that have previously been ignored in the bureaucratic, political, collegial, and other traditional approaches. Briskin's work can assist higher education faculty and administrators to realize that human beings bring all of themselves to an organization. Rather than struggling to manage the Cartesian split of mind, spirit, and body or the feminist-challenged dichotomy of public versus private, the literature about spirituality and organizations provides a more holistic approach to management, leadership, and organizational theory.

Vision

Vision is inseparable from our spiritual intelligence.... Our striving, our drive toward perfection, our dedication, and our need to serve are bound up with our "spiritual intelligence." And these are the human qualities for which organizations must make room—indeed must nurture—if they want to unleash the full potential of human creativity and productivity. (Zohar, 1997, p. 14)

Briskin's work dovetails nicely with Zohar's theorizing on spirituality and organizations, which focuses on vision and interconnectedness. As meaning-making beings, humans long to endow their lives with meaning as well as connect our individual lives to a larger sense of purpose (Rogers & Dantley, 2001). One could propose that leadership is about building purpose into our lives and creating opportunities for others to do the same. One cannot have leadership without interdependence (there is no such thing as a leader of one) and interdependency links us to the purposes and desires of other people. True vision in organizations can only be enacted when the wisdom of the soul and the full impact of interrelationships are considered as legitimate aspects of organizational living. From Zohar's perspective, vision is only possible when the organization is viewed as a whole. This whole applies to the organization and the environment in which it exists. From this perspective, an organization that ignores the environment ignores the extraorganizational lives of its employees. When profits are emphasized above people, the organization will not be as productive or successful.

Interrelationships

Interrelationships are another aspect of organizations to which the spiritual perspective lends insights and understanding. Organizations are not mechanized, separate, and isolated entities, but connected organisms that affect one another across units, communal structures, and national borders. An organization, corporate, nonprofit, or otherwise, cannot act without having an impact on the political, social, and economic health of the surrounding communities. The economic crash of 2008 is an excellent example of the ways that everything is connected across borders and boundaries of organizational type. One industry, banking in this example, can have devastating effects on other companies in the same country and the global economic structure as a whole.

Organizational members operating from a spiritual perspective recognize the interconnectedness of organizations, their processes, and the people within them. Organizations from a spiritual perspective

> have infrastructures that encourage and build on relationships, relationships between leaders and employees, between employees and their colleagues, between divisions and functional groups, between structures themselves. It will also be aware of its environmental context, human, corporate, societal, and ecological, and will build infrastructures that encourage exchange and dialogue. (Zohar, 1997, pp. 123–124)

Interconnections through dialogue, associations, and networks create opportunities for creativity and innovation. Relationship forms a wholeness that can build toward the greater purpose required by organizations to succeed and by organizational members to feel fulfilled. Given the globalization and internationalization of higher education, the centrality of interrelationships and ability to transcend physical and conceptual boundaries is an essential dimension of organizational life.

Leadership

Rogers stated, "exceptional leadership incorporates the spiritual dimension"; in fact, "leadership is transformed when infused with the spiritual" (2003, p. 23). Infusing leadership with spirituality has resulted in a variety of forms: soul leader (Hagberg, 1994), servant leaders (Greenleaf, 2008), and stewardship (Block, 1993). This scholarship discusses the need for leadership to extend beyond the positional style where only those with a title deserve the designation of "leader."

Zohar determined the characteristics of what she called "quantum leadership." Leadership from this perspective has a subtler, more intuitive feel. It is "less goal oriented and more process-oriented" (Zohar, 1997, p. 89). Quantum, spiritual leadership is concerned with the creative process of the team, and less with the structure imposed in advance of the project, goal, or purpose being pursued. Spiritual leadership is more creative and trusting. The leaders' and followers' jobs from this perspective are to cultivate individual potential while drawing insight and inspiration from the group (Zohar, 1997). An understanding of the deeper spiritual meaning of leadership is essential, particularly in higher education, because "leaders have an unusual degree of power to create the climate in which people live. Leaders can create conditions that inspire the soul or cause despair. They can engender commitment to an emancipating vision or create a sense of isolation and fear" (Rogers, 2003, p. 20).

Leadership from a spiritual perspective contrasts sharply with orthodox varieties. Bureaucratic or traditional leadership is top-down, rule bound, fixed on the one best way, slow to change, and isolated from the environmental context. This traditional style of leadership is inadequate to today's organizations, including higher education. Zohar connected leadership to vision and stated that leaders, and this includes higher education administrators, must have the ability to "lead from that level of deep, revolutionary vision" (1997, p. 146). Spiritual intelligence gives leaders a way to envision the sense of self needed to relate to others, create meaning, and exist in community: "Spiritual intelligence, in essence, represents a dynamic wholeness of self in which the self is at one with itself and the whole of creation" (Zohar & Marshall, 2000, p. 124). The ability to attain the vision essential to leadership in higher education is not a solitary activity but one rising from "a deep sense of the interconnectedness of life and all its enterprises"; leaders "must have a sense of engagement and responsibility, a sense of 'I *have* to'"; and they "must be aware that all human endeavor … is part of the larger and richer fabric of the whole universe" (Zohar, 1997, p. 153; emphasis in original). With leadership and vision, engagement and responsibility connect to form a whole that is larger than the sum of its parts.

As a concept related closely to leadership, Zohar (1997) postulated that genuine empowerment occurs when the organization (including leadership) is viewed holistically and the dichotomy between leader and follower is dismantled. The notion that everyone can exercise leadership, given their particular take on the organization and sphere of influence, supplants the disempowering leader–follower dichotomy: "Leadership, not only 'at the top' but throughout the organization, is critical" (Chickering, 2006, p. 5).

Similar to the interconnectedness of Zohar, Briskin, and organizational theorists embracing a spiritual perspective, Allen and Cherrey (2000) discussed the systemic leadership of relational organizations. These organizations embody networked forms that acknowledge the interconnectedness of all organizational elements. Allen and Cherrey (2000), by envisioning leadership in an organic, networked system, used a combination of orthodox organizational theorizing and new perspectives, to enable meaning making, energy flow, renewal, and organizational learning. Although Allen and Cherrey did not use the language or principles of the spiritual perspective, their conceptualization of leadership echoes Zohar's and Briskin's ideas.

Allen and Cherrey (2000) encouraged new ways of leading and relating that result in deeper understandings about the self, leadership, and the organization. In a traditional view of leadership and organizations, goals are optimal; from a relational leadership standpoint, core values are given priority. Rather than rigidly linking performance reviews to standard operating procedures and static job descriptions, organic and dynamic systems are nurtured by encouraging employees to innovatively flirt with organizational boundaries. Noticing patterns and responding to their occurrences allows the organization to remain dynamic. Either-or thinking is abandoned in favor of an approach that embraces both ends of a paradox. Tension between opposites is optimized as a way to encourage innovation and organizational and individual growth. Planned change is seen as an oxymoron. Instead, fluctuations are noticed as opportunities (Allen & Cherry, 2000). Organizations become more nimble and adaptable to minor and major changes in the internal and external environment.

Allen and Cherrey (2000), Briskin (1996; Peppers & Briskin, 2000), Zohar (1997; Zohar & Marshall, 2000), and other proponents of systemic, servant, and spiritual leadership are united in their call to transform the traditional command and control style of leadership. This approach, long embraced and overdue for change, has left members of organizations tired and disempowered and leaders desperate and helpless. The traditional hero or heroine style of leadership has not worked for anyone. The spiritual organizational theorists urge us to choose a different path. "Work is an expression of the Spirit at work in the world through us. Work is that which puts us in touch with others, not so much at the level of personal interaction, but at the level of service in the community" (Briskin, 1996, p. 143). Rather than seeing organizational life as drudgery, these authors suggest that people use spirit as a way to find joy and balance within their employment.

Power

Power is a topic of organizational functioning to which the spiritual organizational theorists lend significant insight and inventiveness. Regardless of whether one views power as a limited or unlimited resource, power is an element of organizational theory that must always be considered. The spiritual perspective lends a unique point of view on power and defines it as the

> capacity to express one's inner self, one's talent, passion, skill. The soul loves power because without it we cannot effectively negotiate the interaction between inside and outside. Soulfulness requires both inner work—finding meaning and purpose—and outer work—seeking avenues for expression. (Briskin, 1996, p. 208)

When power and spirituality are linked, it becomes a force for the achievement of external purposes and goals as well as an internal resource for meaning, fulfillment, and joy. Rather than a competitive approach to power (i.e., power as a finite resource), the spiritual perspective considers the ways that power can be a potent source of energy for the people working in the organization and those served by institutions such as colleges and universities. Power from a spiritual perspective is given away, not hoarded or

Table 16.3 Strengths and Weaknesses of the Spiritual Perspective

Strengths	Weaknesses
Provides hope in situations including those previously dominated by competition and control.	May be off-putting to people who see spirituality as religion or those who do not believe in a spiritual presence.
Can bring diverse perspectives into the organizations.	May seem overly optimistic, bordering on naïve.
Provides concrete means to use collaboration and cooperation within organizations.	May not express a sufficiently sophisticated analysis of followership.
Provides an alternative to bureaucracies.	Can convey a romanticized approach to leadership.
Can be empowering.	May appear too "new age" for many.
Marginalized and/or disenfranchised organizational members can voice dissimilar points of view.	May seem impractical in many organizations focused on profits or conventional measures of success.

manipulated. This perspective offers an optimistic and idealistic view of organizational life.

STRENGTHS AND WEAKNESSES OF THE SPIRITUAL PERSPECTIVE

The spiritual perspective lends several helpful points of view on organizational theory. Organizational theories that separate the mind and spirit operate in mechanical ways, as if human beings lack the ability to make meaning of their lives, including their lives in organizations. When meaning making is taken into account, the full potential of human productivity, sense of accomplishment, and satisfaction is unleashed. Similar to other organizational perspectives, the spiritual approach has strengths and weaknesses (see Table 16.3).

NEXT STEPS: BRINGING THE SPIRITUAL PERSPECTIVE INTO CURRENT USE

Of the various organizational perspectives offered in this book, the spiritual perspective is among the most contemporary. Despite its popularity among some corporate organizational theorists, particularly in Europe, the perspective is rarely used in U.S. higher education settings. The detached scholarly demeanor in higher education organizations makes it particularly difficult for many to embrace a spiritual approach to their practice. Both in and out of the classroom, higher education administrators and faculty are dedicated to divorcing the public and private, the intellectual and the spiritual, the mind and spirit. Perhaps nowhere is the Cartesian split more evident than on college campuses. Faculty are distinctly divided into disciplines, administrators are accustomed to a bureaucratic way of operating, and students, rightfully begrudgingly, know their "place" within the higher education structure. The presence of these traditional approaches to organizational life makes higher education an important location for theorists and practitioners to consider the spiritual perspective. "We who are in the positions to do so have to bridge the polarity that exists in the academy. We have to welcome mind, body, heart, and soul into the learning process" (Rogers, 2003, p. 26).

The idea of incorporating the ways of understanding and operating beyond cognitive intelligence, the form most highly valued in higher education, has expanded in the last several years. Howard Gardner (1993) is the most prominent theorist in this area. His elucidation of multiple intelligences includes information on linguistic, logical, mathematical, musical, spatial, bodily kinesthetic, interpersonal, and intrapersonal intelligences. Most relevant to the organizational perspectives offered in this book, Gardner (1995) applies his multiple intelligence theory to leadership to describe the ways that exceptional organizational members apply more than simply their brains to the task of leadership.

Tirri and Nokelainen (2008) and Tirri, Nokelainen, and Ubani (2006) adapted Gardner's theory and added an additional intelligence, spiritual intelligence, to his collection. The researchers' four dimensions of spiritual intelligence are awareness sensing, mystery sensing, value sensing, and community sensing. In addition to an extension of Gardner's theory, their work relates to that of Daniel Goleman on emotional intelligence and Zohar and Marshall's work on spiritual intelligence. The latter theorists claim that spiritual intelligence is our ultimate intelligence, necessary to use and integrate the multiple intelligences and emotional intelligence (Zohar & Marshall, 2000). Strange (2001) applies Zohar and Marshall's (2000) conception of spiritual intelligence to higher education by stating that the two authors

> suggest that those most capable of addressing such concerns [of self-definition and understanding] are distinguished by advanced levels of "spiritual intelligence" (p. 15), a dimension they describe in terms of certain capacities and qualities (being flexible and self-aware, having the capacity to face and use suffering, being inspired by vision and values, being reluctant to cause unnecessary harm, and tending to see connection between diverse things and to ask Why? or What if?—while seeking fundamental answers). (p. 59)

Further exploration of spiritual intelligence aptly fits higher education's mission of self, intellectual, and personal development.

Although space does not allow for a full explanation of multiple, spiritual, and emotional intelligences, research in this area holds significant promise for higher education. These ideas can be used to explore the personal and professional fulfillment of higher education leaders and faculty, staff, students, and administrators. The spiritual perspective provides a foundation upon which faculty, administrators, staff, and students can create meaning, build community, explore the mysteries of life, and determine their deepest values. The current popularity of student learning communities, faculty-led study aboard programs, service learning, and other effective educational practices (Kuh, 2008) advances higher education's commitment to transform lives, empower through education, and create viable communities. If through using spiritual intelligence we can "address and solve problems of meaning and value" (Tirri, Nokelainen, & Ubani, 2006, p. 39), this approach can assist higher education faculty, students, administrators, and staff as they confront the challenges that exist within these institutions. This approach could assist all who seek to fulfill the long-standing purposes of higher education regarding societal change, equity, quality of life, and social justice.

Higher education organizations are unique among modern organizations in their emphasis on individual and societal development, growth, and improvement. The products of higher education are not tangible, material objects but intangible qualities developed in individuals. The intangible nature of this "product" means that one must often take its achievement on faith; that is, faith grounded in a belief in the power of education, a force larger than oneself.

CONCLUSIONS

A powerful aspect of the spiritual perspective is its critique on the nearly normative use of bureaucracy in organizations, including higher education. The spiritual perspective theorists, particularly Briskin (1996), criticized the rational, logical, and impersonal bureaucratic perspective on organizations. Bureaucracies with dehumanizing and soulless approaches to management and administration do not take all aspects of human living into account. "Organizations are (ideally) a place to express one's intellect, and perhaps one's physical skills depending on the job, but one's emotional and spiritual dimensions are typically not welcomed or nurtured" (Rogers & Dantley, 2001, p. 592). Similar to a critique offered by Ferguson (1985), Briskin (1996) offered the following observations on bureaucracies:

> They dehumanize the people who work and live in them by reducing their actions to a routinized set of standardized procedures.

> At a certain point, humans become dispensable in the name of efficiency.

> When problems arise, the individual, not the system or structure, is seen as flawed and in need of re-training or replacement.

> Upper management in bureaucracies is seen as the brain while laborers are viewed as hands that know nothing about how organizations could be structured and managed.

> Progress and growth are major goals, regardless of the size, or sustainability of the advancement.

> Standard operating procedures and policies are intended to limit thinking, creativity, and ingenuity.

Bureaucracies are the antithesis of the spiritual perspective. Where bureaucracies limit thought and initiative, spiritual organizations seek to humanize and include all. In bureaucracies, people are urged to separate professional from private; spiritual organizations seek to consider the whole person. "People cannot simply become mechanisms of production without losing connection with their own experience: fragility, wonder, passion, and mystery. These qualities are critical to health, creativity, and compassion for others" (Briskin, 1996, p. 134). These organizational theorists support the idea that the efficiencies of bureaucracy are offset by the losses to community, beauty, and meaning.

Questions for Discussion

- How does the spiritual perspective differ from other perspectives of organizational functioning?
- What advantages are gained from employing a spiritual perspective? What disadvantages ensue?
- How is vision used in higher education organizations?
- How can all organizational members within higher education be involved in the vision-setting processes at the institution?
- What conceptions of power would have to change to embrace a spiritual perspective on this concept?
- How is leadership different in the spiritual perspective in contrast to other perspectives offered in this book?
- What are the ramifications of ignoring the underworld of soul within higher education institutions?

Recommended Readings for the Spiritual Perspective

Briskin, A., Erickson, S., Ott, J., & Callanan, T. (2009). *The power of collective wisdom: And the trap of collective folly*. San Francisco, CA: Berrett Koehler.

Daloz, L .A. P., Kenn, C. H., Kenn, J. P., & Parks, S. D. (1996). *Common fire: Lives of commitment in a complex world*. Boston, MA: Beacon Press.

Jablonski, M. A. (2001). *The implications of student spirituality for student affairs practice* (New Directions for Student Services, No. 95). San Francisco, CA: Jossey-Bass.

Kessler, R. (2000). *The soul of education: Helping students find connection, compassion, and character at school*. Alexandria, VA: Association for Supervision and Curriculum Development.

Leider, R. J. (2004). *The power of purpose: Find meaning, live longer, better* (2nd ed.). San Francisco, CA: Berrett Koehler.

17

CASE

Considering the Whole Person, Establishing a Family Leave Policy

INTRODUCTION

In a book hailed at the time as a landmark publication, Douglas McGregor (1957/1976) proposed two approaches to working in organizations: Theory X and Theory Y. In Theory X, directing employees was the task of management who based their authoritative behavior on a set of beliefs about employees. Principles for Theory X included the following:

1. Management is responsible for organizing the elements of productive enterprise— money, materials, equipment, people—in the interest of economic ends.
2. With respect to people, this is a process of directing their efforts, motivating them, controlling their actions, modifying their behavior to fit the needs of the organization.
3. Without this active intervention by management, people would be passive—even resistant—to organizational needs. They must therefore be persuaded, rewarded, punished, controlled—their activities must be directed. (McGregor, 1957/1976, p. 57)

According to the prevailing beliefs of Theory X, employees were lazy people who managed their work lives so they could work as little as possible. Corresponding with the lazy demeanor, employees, according to Theory X, preferred to be led, were unconcerned about organizational needs, resisted change, and were not very bright.

The Theory X approach was contrasted by McGregor with what was, at the time, an alternative way of viewing management and employees, Theory Y. He sought to change the assumptions about human nature by proposing the following:

1. Management is responsible for organizing the elements of productive enterprise— money, materials, equipment, people—in the interest of economic ends.

2. People are *not* by nature passive or resistant to organizational needs. They have become so as a result of experience in organizations.

3. The motivation, the potential for development, the capacity for assuming responsibility, the readiness to direct behavior toward organizational goals are all present in people....

4. The essential task of management is to arrange organizational conditions and methods of operation so that people can achieve their own goals *best* by directing *their own* efforts toward organizational objectives. (McGregor, 1957/1976, pp. 61–62; emphasis in original)

Theory X and Y are diametrically opposed. While the former is based on lack of trust and faith in people, the latter theory holds that people could be trusted to manage themselves and be productive in organizations. At the time, Theory Y was a revolutionary approach to working with people. The refashioned beliefs, combined with theories such as Abraham Maslow's and Frederick Herzberg's approaches to motivation, became the foundation of the human resources approach to organizational functioning.

Elton Mayo and the Hawthorne Experiments

In the context of Theory X and Y beliefs about management and employees, Elton Mayo conducted experiments at the Hawthorne Works of the Western Electric Company in Chicago. These experiments were the first of their kind to explore the issue that people working in organizations were affected by their emotions, personal lives, and work environments. Work features such as motivation, personality, human behavior, and the informal aspects of work life were embraced as topics of consideration in organizational functioning.

Human relations work usually shares two general propositions which shape an understanding of the relation between people and their organizations. The first is that "informal" patterns of interaction set up expectations and constraints that cannot be explained simply by reference to an organization chart or a desire for monetary reward. The second is that an employee's beliefs, attitudes and values are brought with them from non-work contexts and impinge upon the way they think about themselves and their organization. (Parker, 2000, p. 32)

The process of considering humans and their behavior as part of the organizational equation resulted in the ideas that people's work improves when they have control over their environment; are more satisfied at work when they are involved in decision making; and have increased motivation when personal and professional goals are congruent.

McGregor, Mayo, and other human resources organizational theorists introduced concepts that brought the human element into organizational functioning. Because employees were considered as a whole, this approach can be viewed as a precursor to the spiritual perspective. Both perspectives embodied the belief that people bring all of themselves to the work environment. While the human resources approach does not delve into the meaning making and self-discovery of the spiritual perspective, both approaches consider the connections between the personal and professional; mind, body, and spirit; and the in-work and nonwork environments. In this book, the spiritual perspective provides a helpful way to consider the whole person within an organizational context. The Cartesian split of mind/body/spirit is rejected in the spiritual perspective where people are thought to bring their personal and private, including spiritual, lives to an organization.

Considering the Mind, Body, and Spirit

When people bring their whole selves to the organization, they also bring their views and feelings about family to that setting. Organizational policies (including family leave policies) and federal laws reinforce the notion that employees work best when the whole of their selves are taken into account. The topic of this case chapter, family leave policies and creating family friendly campus environments, regardless of societal progress toward women's equality, are connected to lingering sexist notions that exist within higher education. Some of these remaining points of view entail the following: (a) the private sphere as the purview of women; (b) the public sphere as that of men; (c) the primary caretaker role is the responsibility of women; and (d) the primary wage earner role is assumed by men.

Questions to Consider

- What are several justifications for the separation of personal and private lives within higher education organizations?
- What are several current trends that lead to an erosion of the separation of the personal and professional spheres?
- In what ways might consideration of the whole person be related to employee job satisfaction and productivity?
- How can a consideration of the whole person be used as a way to improve organizational functioning?

=================== CASE ===================

Institutional Context

Private Urban University is located on 25 acres in a city of 5 million people. Founded in 1920, the institution has seen the city grow up around its campus. Once on the outskirts of the city, high rise condominiums and office buildings now surround the institution. The campus maintains a separate identity from the city environments by the existence of nearly century old high walls and buildings that face the internal university green. Because of the prevalence of dual career couples and urban professionals who worked at the Private Urban University, the issue of balancing professional and personal lives has been a long-standing issue. The cost of living in the city means that many faculty and administrators live in dual salaried households as the only way to afford housing and the high cost of living. Private Urban University's location gave employees and their partners the opportunity to find well-paying career oriented jobs, a situation that also led to the high number of dual career couples and multiple wage earners within families. The institution embraces an urban mission by providing adult education, executive business classes, and extensive services for commuting students. Commuters, particularly students over 25 years of age, comprise the majority of their student body. Partnerships with community nonprofits and businesses are extremely important to the college. These organizations are the sites of numerous student internships and faculty research projects. In return, the local businesses have been generous with donations to the university.

Characters

Ms. Noami Parkerson, Director of Human Resources: Although she is a 20-year veteran of human resources work in higher education, Ms. Parkerson has only been at the Private Urban University for 3 years. Because she raised four children with her partner, she is well aware of the challenges facing university employees who are raising families while building a career. Because of her knowledge and personal experience, Parkerson is dedicated to creating family friendly environments in the institutions in which she works.

Dr. Hillary Ryburn, President: During her interviews for the presidency at Private Urban University, Dr. Ryburn recognized that the institution lacked intact family leave policies and procedures to encourage a family friendly environment. During her interviews and the information gathering after her appointment, Dr. Ryburn learned that the relatively new director of human resources had particular expertise in family leave policies and creating family friendly environments. The new president was interested in instituting these policies and practices as soon as possible. In fact, during her interview, the Committee on Women's Success members voiced the need for leadership in this area and she made a commitment to take on this agenda if she were appointed as president. Within a week of arriving on campus, Ryburn directed Kurt Tetrault, vice president for administration, to work with the director of human resources to institute policies and practices in this area.

Mr. Kurt Tetrault, Vice President for Administration and Finance: Vice President Tetrault understood that the current generation of faculty, staff, and administrators were different from when he was first hired at Private Urban University 35 years ago. A veteran of the institution and nearing retirement, Tetrault and his wife raised four children while Tetrault was employed at Private Urban. They were fortunate to have the level of salary to exercise the option of having his wife stay at home and raise the children until all had left for college. Although this meant financial sacrifices on their part, the Tetraults felt that this situation would be most advantageous for their children. While Vice President Tetrault understood that the work environment and family situation had changed, this had not translated into a sense of urgency about establishing family leave policies. In his mind, there was a separation between the personal and professional, the public and private. The university provided generous benefits packages. He was not convinced that providing family leave policies beyond what the federal government mandated was necessary.

Dr. Saundra Eberhart, Co-Chair, Committee on Women's Success: Dr. Eberhart, a professor of English for 22 years at Private Urban University, was pleased to be asked to cochair the Committee on Women's Success. A long-time advocate for women's issues, Dr. Eberhart saw this appointment as an opportunity to institute the long overdue family leave policy. But she and other colleagues did not see the family leave policy and establishment of a family friendly environment as solely a women's issue. Over the years, many female and male colleagues had pushed for the policy to no avail. Dr. Eberhart was optimistic that the combination of a new president and relatively new director of human resources would result in what she saw as a long overdue policy.

New Leadership, New Agenda

President Ryburn arrived at Private Urban University and quickly assessed the reasons for the delay in establishing a family leave policy. Although sympathetic to the plight of young parents, Vice President Tetrault seemed disinterested in moving forward on the initiative. While his intentions were good and promises had been made, the years stretched out with no policy in sight. While there was willingness by the director of human resources to establish a policy, her short tenure at the institution was occupied with priorities set by Tetrault. There simply had not been time in the last 3 years for Ms. Parkerson to establish the policy.

Immediately upon her arrival on campus, President Ryburn directed Tetrault to work with the director of human resources to establish a family leave policy. The president felt that the absence of such a policy and accompanying family friendly campus practices threatened the hiring of the best candidates for faculty and administration positions. They were competing in a national and international market for employees; their policies had to be progressive, comprehensive, and employee-centered.

Questions to Consider

- How can Zohar's principles related to a spiritual perspective be applied to this case?
- In what ways is President Ryburn exercising spiritual capital or spiritual intelligence in her efforts to create a more family friendly campus environment?
- What are some challenges within higher education to balance priorities such as cost effectiveness versus employee fulfillment?
- What is the relationship between meaning making, service, and productivity among organizational members?

The Family Leave Policy So Far

Over the past 10 years, various groups had made some progress on the family leave policy. Research was conducted, policy drafts were written, and several campus committees and groups implemented components of the policy. The Committee on Women's Success researched policies at competitor and aspirant institutions. They drafted a policy that had worked its way through their committee and several other groups on campus. The work completed was the result of a wide coalition of people within the university. Academic department chairs felt strongly that the lack of a family leave policy interfered with their efforts to help young professors who were starting both careers and families. Without a policy, it was difficult to recruit young faculty and mentor them successfully through reappointment, promotion, and tenure.

Although the human resources office knew of the Committee on Women's Success and the work completed by that group, there had been little collaboration between them or other groups on campus for that matter. The academic assistant deans, responsible for budget and personnel issues within the colleges and schools, were interested and involved in family policies. They met monthly to share ideas and solutions to jointly faced issues. As a group, they were acutely aware of the dilemmas faced by female and male faculty, staff, and administrators who were struggling to juggle careers and family lives.

Questions to Consider

- How can family leave and similar employee centered policies build spiritual capital and intelligence within a university workforce?
- What components of a family leave policy would enhance an employee's commitment and connection to the institution?
- What are some relationships among spirit, motivation, and fulfillment?
- What emotions from the underside of the soul are expressed when personal desires become sidelined by professional ambitions?

Human Resource Involvement

Ms. Parkerson was pleased that the Vice President Tetrault had shuffled some deadlines and projects so she could finally work on the family leave policy. These changes made it possible for her to work on the project, which had been a goal of hers since arriving at Private Urban University. She was aware that the university was behind in establishing a policy that enabled their employees to live the emotionally and spiritually fulfilling lives she knew were necessary for job satisfaction and productivity. At her most recent institution she had established family policies for new parents, parents of children requiring special care, and employees needing time to care for aging parents. There she had converted several restroom lounge spaces into private breast-feeding rooms, instituted ways for employees to use technology and work from home, established a "take your child to work" day, and introduced compressed work weeks to build flexible scheduling. She instituted a policy where job sharing, elder care referral services, and other adaptable ways of working were part of the ways the university operated.

Parkerson was an avid proponent of the connections among mind, body, and spirit and the relationship of this connection to success in the workplace. A leading expert in this area, she had developed substantial expertise on crafting environments that took the connections between and among different elements of the human experience into account. Using the writings of Danah Zohar as they related to the connection of vision and interrelatedness and Alan Briskin's ideas of spirit and soul, she was convinced that the infusion of spiritual elements into the workplace would increase job satisfaction. At her last institution, she nearly single handedly increased employee satisfaction as measured by institutional surveys distributed through the Office of Institutional Research. She achieved these impressive results by expanding faculty, staff, and administrators' wellness class offerings (e.g., yoga classes, stress reduction, personal–professional balance workshop) and urging employees to take their allotted vacation time.

She oversaw the expansion of the small university childcare center and introduced innovative ways to create a campus environment that was open to different ways of operating. Her plans at Private Urban University included expanding the university's definitions of what constituted family. Although the state in which Private Urban University was located did not recognize same sex marriages, Parkerson believed that the campus could take steps to create a more inclusive environment. In fact, she believed that, as a leader in the city's business community, the university had an obligation to lead the way on these matters. The institutional mission and affirmative action statements provided room for her planning regarding the refashioned definition of family. Both mentioned the inclusion of all persons, regardless of sexual orientation or gender expression, in the university community.

Questions to Consider

- How can the inclusion of inclusive campus policies engender the optimism, patience, and collaboration characteristics of the upper world of the soul?
- How can inclusive policies encourage employees to appropriately express all of themselves within their work environment?
- How is the public/private dichotomy eased through the use of family friendly policies and practices?
- How does the vision expressed in the spiritual perspective relate to this campus's efforts to establish more open and inclusive environments?

Expanding the Definition

Although the Committee on Women's Success under the previous president had drafted a family leave policy and provisions for making the campus more family friendly, they felt that their involvement kept the issue situated as a women's concern. Many felt strongly that these were issues that had an impact on all employees. If one took a more expansive view of family, then all people, including those who were not parents, would encounter a situation where family needed to take precedence. In addition, they felt that the schedule flexibility and other provisions within the family friendly practices could benefit all employees. Family leave policies and family friendly practices applied to all genders, sexes, and sexual orientations.

Contention among the members of the Committee on the Success of Women had bogged down the policy work of the committee. One group within the committee felt that the final policy should be more women-centric. This was based on the belief that, despite the progress over the last 30 years, women continued to shoulder the majority of childcare responsibilities in families. Some members felt this was obviously the case for female same-sex partners where two women assumed the responsibilities for child rearing. Other committee members were insistent that the policy be more inclusive. The argument from this contingent of the committee was based on the idea that societal ideas about child rearing would not change until everyone assumed responsibility for raising children. Others in the group felt that the family leave policy, as currently conceived by the Committee of Women's Success, focused too much on child rearing and not enough on other issues of family leave, for example, aging parents and disabled siblings. To reconcile these two approaches, cochair Eberhart tasked two subcommittees to write one woman-centric and one inclusive family leave policies, which they would send to the president via Vice President Tetrault and Human Resources Director Parkerson.

Questions to Consider

- How can an individual's personal struggles be expressed in the shadow side of organizations?
- How can taking the shadow side into account help individuals express the positive and negative sides of their human experiences?

- How can the upper and lower worlds of the soul be balanced in an organization to help people appropriately express the joys and challenges of personal and professional lives?
- What happens in an organization when the expression of the shadow side is discouraged or forbidden? When only the upper world of the soul is allowed to be expressed?

The Committee on Women's Success members were very aware of the unique challenges facing women faculty and professional women on campus. Family exigencies shaped the need for priority on class scheduling and a tenure and promotion timeline that took pregnancy and child rearing into account. The women faculty on the committee were concerned that there was inadequate understanding that women faculty often did not ask for accommodations relating to family issues. They did not want to be seen as less able or professional than their male colleagues, with more need to take advantage of the available options. Others on the Committee on Women's Success felt that family leave policies were important but not as important as the blatant sexism expressed on campus. Gender equity studies on campus provided evidence that sexism was particularly evident during tenure and promotion and the promotion of administrators and staff.

Faculty Issues and the Family Friendly Campus

As directed by Vice President Tetrault at the instruction of President Ryburn, Parkerson was to assemble a task force of people from the Committee on the Success of Women, the human resources office, and the assistant deans' group to finish the family leave policy. The finished policy was to be delivered to the vice president within the month. Because so much work had been completed, Parkerson was optimistic that she could fast track the policy, so she assigned the associate director of human resources to take the lead as chair of the task force.

Questions to Consider

- What structural aspects of higher education could mitigate the completion of the policy?
- How might assumptions about women as the primary caregivers of children and elderly parents interfere with the crafting of a more inclusive family policy?
- How can assumptions about the private and public spheres enhance or interfere with a holistic, spiritual perspective?
- How are interrelationships between and among people enhanced through a spiritual approach to organizational functioning?

As the task force explored the family leave policies and family friendly practices, they realized that their work was connected to human resources issues that were erupting on campus. Family issues created tremendous stress on employees; stress that affected their performance. A survey conducted by the Office of Institutional Research on family issues asked, do you feel that you can discuss family issues with your supervisor or department chair? Ninety-three percent of respondents said that they did not feel that they could discuss family issues in the work environment. The prevailing attitude within the institution was that these issues should be dealt with privately rather than being brought into the university environment.

Members of the task force, who desired a more holistic approach, believed that the public–private separation, with its underlying division of mind/body/spirit, negatively affected the work performance of employees. This paralleled the exclusion of any expression of personal, religious, or spiritual beliefs on the part of the employee. Task force members believed that the vice president of administration promulgated this attitude when he ruled that time away from one's desk for wellness activities was an inappropriate use of work time. He believed that such activities were in the purview of employees' private lives. The task force concluded that the current situation of low morale of faculty, staff, and administrators at the institution came from the stark separation of the spiritual, physical, and private lives of the employees.

Working off the assumption that different solutions emerge when situations are viewed creatively, the task force crafted a set of expectations grounded in the assumptions of the spiritual perspective on organizational functioning. The result was a family leave policy and family friendly practices model that became a model for other higher education institutions. Outcomes included improved employee morale and the belief that the human resources department understood the connection between the personal and professional lives of employees.

DISCUSSION

The spiritual perspective provides a progressive way to address the complex issues of professional-personal, public-private, and self-other. As higher education institutions and the lives of those who work in them become increasingly more complicated, this unique perspective could provide insights into ways to solve long-standing institutional issues.

18

CONCLUSION

INTRODUCTION

Higher education faculty, staff, and administrators perform their life's work in extremely ambiguous, complex, and politically charged settings. By understanding the theories and perspectives offered in this book, effective programs can be built, stimulating curriculum shaped, and meaningful policy and planning created. Comprehensive understanding of the ever-changing world of higher education necessitates that faculty, administrators, and staff use multiple models and theories in their work. When one model becomes the explanation for all situations and context, that understanding fails to provide a broad or deep perspective concerning higher education functioning. Different models allow diverse insights and assessments. The use of multiple perspectives with which to view higher education is more important now than ever before. Technology and the introduction of social media have amplified the degree to which the lives of those in and outside of higher education are interconnected. Relationships have always been important in higher education but never as essential as they are today. Internationalization and globalization have expanded the reach of individual institutions and the systems in which they exist.

PARTING THOUGHTS

In addition to the knowledge and cases presented in this book, the following thoughts are offered as we reconceive higher education for the future.

- The trend toward a chief executive officer model should be abandoned in lieu of a relationship-oriented leadership model.
- Open learning and engagement could be embraced in lieu of traditional approaches to teaching.
- The teaching, research, and service model of faculty work is no longer sustainable. Rather than pursuing these three aspects of faculty work simultaneously, models

that build in an ebb and flow across these three areas could better fit the generative nature of faculty work.

- The administrative bloat built over the last 20 years could be decreased to achieve flatter organizations and less expenditure. This goal could be accompanied with refocused attention on the fundamental priorities of higher education institutions.
- The comprehensive model of colleges and universities is no longer possible given the proliferation of disciplines and areas of expertise.
- Distance and online learning combined with consortia and interinstitutional partnerships could save valuable resources and provide better education for students.
- The competition established between and among higher education institutions has built an arms race where all lose. The race to build the best amenities and facilities has distracted the attention of students, faculty, and administrators alike from the fundamental purposes of higher education: the achievement of a high quality education.
- The 4-year model of progress to graduation is a myth worth abandoning. Reimagined academic calendars, less rigid course delivery approaches, and improved ways to organize class times can help faculty consider how students learn over time in ways unencumbered by the restrictions of a 4-year graduation expectation.
- The push toward interdisciplinary learning requires that faculty look beyond their home disciplines to discover the ways that disciplines inform and enrich one another.
- All involved in higher education can shape an expectation that the wisdom of higher education comes from all who are involved in the enterprise: faculty, students, administrators, and stakeholders,.

These recommendations require shifts in thinking from competition to collaboration, teaching to learning, passivity to engagement, elitism to inclusion, bureaucracy to inclusion, and scarcity to abundance.

The purpose of this book was to expand the number of models used to consider higher education organizational structures. The traditional models of collegial, political, cultural, and anarchic (Birnbaum, 1991) were expanded to include contemporary models as well as those infrequently discussed in the higher education literature. Both the traditional and contemporary perspectives have much to offer higher education. As our institutions increase in complexity, particularly in complexity by function, we will need extensive available knowledge to meet the challenges before us.

REFERENCES

Aguirre, A., & Martinez, R. (2006). *Diversity leadership in higher education* (ASHE Higher Education Report, 3). San Francisco, CA: Jossey-Bass.

Allen, K. E., & Cherrey, C. (2000). *Systemic leadership: Enriching the meaning of our work*. Lanham, MD: University Press of America.

Alpert, D. (1985). Performance and paralysis: The organizational context of the American research university. *Journal of Higher Education, 56*(3), 241–281.

Amaral, L. A. N., & Uzzi, B. (2007). Complex systems—A new paradigm for the integrative study of management, physical, and technological systems. *Management Science, 53*(7), 1033–1035

American Association of University Professors. (1968). *Statement on faculty workload with interpretive comments*. Washington, DC: Author.

American Association of University Professors. (1990). *Statement of principles on academic freedom and tenure with 1970 interpretive comments*. Washington, DC: Author. (Original work published 1940)

American Association of University Professors. (2007). Trends in faculty status, 1975–2007 all degree-granting institutions; national totals. Retrieved from http://www.aaup.org/AAUP/pubsres/research/

American Council on Education. (2007). *The American college president*. Washington, DC: Author.

Andrews, J. G. (May–June 2006). How we can resist corporatization? *Academe Online*. Retrieved from http://www.aaup.org/AAUP/pubsres/academe/2006/MJ/feat/

Aronowitz, S. (2000). *The knowledge factory: Dismantling the corporate university and creating true higher learning*. Boston, MA: Beacon Press.

Aronowitz, S., & Giroux, H. (2000). The corporate university and the politics of education. *The Educational Forum, 64*(4), 332–339.

Astin, A. (2004). Why spirituality deserves a central place in higher education. *Spirituality in Higher Education Newsletter, 1*(1), 1–12.

Astin, A. W., Astin, H. S., & Lindholm, J. A. (2010). *Cultivating the spirit: How college can enhance students' inner lives*. San Francisco, CA: Jossey-Bass.

Baden-Fuller, C., & Stopford, J. M. (1994). *Rejuvenating the mature business: The competitive challenge*. Boston, MA: Harvard Business School Press.

Baldridge, J. V. (1971a). *Academic governance: Research on institutional politics and decision making*. Berkeley, CA: McCutchan.

Baldridge, J. V. (1971b). Introduction: Models of university governance—Bureaucratic, collegial, and political. In J. V. Baldridge (Ed.), *Academic governance: Research on institutional politics and decision making* (pp. 1–19). Berkeley, CA: McCutchan.

Baldridge, J. V. (1971c). *Power and conflict in the university*. New York: Wiley.

Baldridge, J. V., Curtis, D. V., Ecker, G., & Riley, G. L. (1974). *Alternative models of governance in higher education* (Research and Development Memorandum, No. 129). Stanford, CA: School of Education, Stanford University.

Baldridge, J. V., Curtis, D. V., Ecker, G., & Riley, G. L. (1978). *Policy making and effective leadership.* San Francisco, CA: Jossey-Bass.

Beatty, R. W., & Ulrich, D. O. (1991). Re-energizing the mature organization. *Organizational Dynamics, 20*(1), 16–30.

Bell, D. (1992). *Faces at the bottom of the well: The permanence of racism.* New York: Basic Books,

Bergquist, W. H., & Pawlak, K. (2008). *Engaging the six cultures of the academy.* (2nd ed.). San Francisco, CA: Jossey-Bass.

Bess, J. L., & Dee, J. R. (2008). *Understanding college and university organization: Theories for effective policy and practice.* Sterling, VA: Stylus.

Birnbaum, R. (1991). *How colleges work: The cybernetics of academic organization and leadership.* San Francisco, CA: Jossey-Bass.

Birnbaum, R. (1992). *How academic leadership works: Understanding success and failure in the college presidency.* San Francisco, CA: Jossey-Bass.

Block, P. (1993). *Stewardship: Choosing service over self-interest.* San Francisco, CA: Jossey-Bass.

Bok, D. (2003). *Universities in the marketplace: The commercialization of higher education.* Princeton, NJ: Princeton University Press.

Bordas, J. (2007). *Salsa, soul, and spirit: Leadership for a multicultural age.* San Francisco, CA: Berrett Koehler.

Borden, V. M. H. (2004). Student swirl: When traditional students are no longer the tradition. *Change, 36*(2), 10–17.

Briskin, A. (1996). *The stirring of soul in the workplace.* San Francisco, CA: Jossey-Bass.

Brubacher, J. S. (1990). *On the philosophy of higher education.* San Francisco, CA: Jossey-Bass.

Burns, J. M. (1978). *Leadership.* New York: Harper & Row.

Calás, M. B., & Smircich, L. (1999). Past postmodernism? Reflections and tentative discussions. *Academy of Management Review, 24*(4), 649–671.

Capra, F. (2005). Speaking nature's language: Principles for sustainability. In M. K. Stone & Z. Barlow (Eds.), *Ecological literacy: Educating our children for a sustainable world* (pp. 18–29). San Francisco, CA: Sierra Club Books.

Carnegie Foundation. (2010). Classification description. Retrieved from http://classifications.carnegiefoundation.org/descriptions/basic.php

Carneiro, R. L. (1981). Herbert Spencer as an anthropologist. *The Journal of Libertarian Studies, 5*(2), 153–210.

Chait, R. P. (Ed.). (2002). *The questions of tenure.* Cambridge, MA: Harvard University Press.

Chait, R. P., Holland, T. P., & Taylor, B. E. (1996). *Improving the performance of governing boards.* Phoenix, AZ: Oryx Press.

Chickering, A. W. (2006). Authenticity and spirituality in higher education: My orientation. *Journal of College & Character, 7*(1), 1–5.

Chickering, A. W., Dalton, J. C., & Stamm, L. (2005). *Encouraging authenticity and spirituality in higher education.* San Francisco, CA: Jossey-Bass.

Childers, M. E. (1981). What is political about bureaucratic-collegial decision making? *The Review of Higher Education, 5*(1), 25–45.

Chrislip, D. D., & Larson, C. E. (1994). *Collaborative leadership: How citizens and civic leaders can make a difference.* San Francisco, CA: Jossey-Bass.

The Chronicle of Higher Education. (2011). President, University of Utah. Retrieved from http://chronicle.com/jobs/0000690251-01

Clark, B. R. (1963). Faculty culture. In T. Lunsford (Ed.), *The study of campus cultures* (pp. 39–54). Boulder, CO: Western Interstate Commission for Higher Education.

Clark, B. R. (1980). *Academic culture.* New Haven, CT: Institute for Social and Policy Studies.

Clark, B. R. (1986). *The higher education system: Academic organization in cross-national perspective.* Berkeley, CA: University of California Press.

Clark, B. R. (2007). Development of the sociology of higher education. In P. Gumport (Ed.), *Sociology of higher education: Contributions and their contexts* (pp. 3–16). Baltimore, MD: Johns Hopkins University Press.

Clark, B. R., & Trow, M. (1966). The organizational context. In T. M. Newcomb & E. K. Wilson (Eds.), *College peer groups: Problems and prospects for research* (pp. 17–70). Chicago, IL: Aldine.

Clark, D. L. (1985). Emerging paradigms in organizational theory and research. In Y. Lincoln (Ed.), *Organizational theory and inquiry: The paradigm revolution* (pp. 43–78). Beverly Hills, CA: Sage.

Cohen, M. D., & March, J. G. (1986). *Leadership and ambiguity* (2nd ed.). Boston, MA: Harvard Business School Press.

Cohen, M. D., March, J. G., & Olsen, J. P. (1972). A garbage can model of organizational choice. *Administrative Science Quarterly, 17*(1), 1–25.

Cooper, H., Braye, S., & Geyer, R. (2004). Complexity and interprofessional education. *Learning in Health and Social Care, 3*(4), 179–189.

Cyert, R. M., & March, J. G. (2005). A behavioral theory of organizational objectives. In J. M. Shafritz, J. S. Ott, & Y. S. Jang, *Classics of organization theory* (6th ed., pp. 135–144). Belmont, CA: Thomson Wadsworth. (Original work published 1959)

Daloz, L. A. P., Keen, C. H., Keen, J. P., & Parks, S. D. (1996). *Common fire: Lives of commitment in a complex world*. Boston, MA: Beacon Press.

Deal, T. E., & Kennedy, A. A. (1982). *Corporate cultures: The rites and rituals of corporate life*. Reading, MA: Addison-Wesley.

DeCuir, J. T., & Dixson, A. D. (2004). "So when it comes out, they aren't that surprised that it is there": Using critical race theory as a tool of analysis of race and racism in education. *Educational Researcher, 33*(5), 26–31.

DeGeorge, R. T. (2003). Ethics, academic freedom and academic tenure. *Journal of Academic Ethics, 1*(1), 11–25.

DiMaggio, P. J., & Powell, W. W. (1991). Introduction. In W. W. Powell & P. J. DiMaggio (Eds.), *The new institutionalism in organizational analysis* (pp. 1–38). Chicago, IL: University of Chicago Press

Dixson, A. D., & Rousseau, C. K. (2005). And we are still not saved: Critical race theory in education ten years later. *Race Ethnicity and Education, 8*(1), 7–27.

Doeringer, P. B. (1987). Make way for mature industries. *Labor Law Journal, 38*(8), 453–457.

Dowd, A. C., Sawatzky, M., & Korn, R. (2011). Theoretical foundations and a research agenda to validate measures of intercultural effort. *The Review of Higher Education, 35*(1), 17–44.

Duncan, J. C. (1999). The indentured servants of academia: The adjunct faculty dilemma and their limited legal remedies. *Indiana Law Journal, 74*(2), 514–526.

Eckel, P. D. (2000). The role of shared governance in institutional hard decisions: Enabler or antagonist? *The Review of Higher Education, 24*(1), 15–39.

Fayol, H. (2005). General principles of management. In J. M. Shafritz, J. S. Ott, & Y. S. Jang (Eds.), *Classics of organizational theory* (6th ed., pp. 48–60). Belmont, CA: Thomson Wadsworth. (Original work published 1916)

Ferguson, K. (1985). *The feminist case against bureaucracy*. Philadelphia, PA: Temple University Press.

Fraser, S. W., & Greenhalgh, T. (2001). Coping with complexity: Educating for capability. *British Medical Journal, 323*, 799–803.

Freire, P. (1997). *Pedagogy of the oppressed*. New York: Basic Books. (Original work published 1970)

Gardner, H. (1993). *Multiple intelligences: The theory in practice*. New York: Basic Books.

Gardner, H. (1995). *Leading minds: An anatomy of leadership*. New York: Basic Books.

Gaston, P. L. (2010). *The challenge of Bologna: What United States higher education has to learn from Europe, and why it matters that we learn it*. Sterling, VA: Stylus.

Geertz, C. (1973). *The interpretation of cultures*. New York: Basic Books.

Giddens, A. (1979). *Central problems in social theory: Action, structure, and contradictions in social analysis*. Berkeley, CA: University of California Press.

Giddens, A. (1984). *The constitution of society: Outline of the theory of structuration*. Berkeley, CA: University of California Press.

Gilligan, C. (1982). *In a different voice: Psychological theory and women's development*. Cambridge, MA: Harvard University Press.

Giroux, H. (2002). Neoliberalism, corporate culture, and the promise of higher education: The university as a democratic public sphere. *Harvard Educational Review, 72*(4), 425–463.

Gladwell, M. (2000, December 11). Designs for working: Why your bosses want to turn your new office into Greenwich Village. *The New Yorker*, 60–70.

Gleick, J. (1987). *Chaos: Making a new science*. New York: Viking.

Goldman, E. (1910). *Anarchism and other essays*. New York: Mother Earth.

Goodman, P. (1962). *The community of scholars*. New York: Random House.

Gouldner, A. (1957). Cosmopolitans and locals: Toward an analysis of latent social roles—I. *Administrative Science Quarterly, 2*(3), 281–306.

Gouldner, A. (1958). Cosmopolitans and locals: Toward an analysis of latent social roles—II. *Administrative Science Quarterly, 2*(4), 444–480.

Greenfield, T. B. (1986). Leaders and schools: Willfulness and nonnatural order in organizations. In T. J. Sergiovanni & J. E. Corbally (Eds.), *Leadership and organizational culture: New perspectives on administrative theory and practice* (pp. 142–169). Chicago, IL: University of Illinois Press.

Greenleaf, R. (2008). *The servant as leader*. Newton Center, MA: Greenleaf Center.

Greenwood, R., Oliver, C., Shalin, K., & Suddaby, R. (2008). Introduction. In R. Greenwood, C. Oliver, R. Suddaby, & K. Sahlin (Eds.), *The SAGE handbook of organizational institutionalism* (pp. 3–45). Los Angeles, CA: Sage.

Gruenewald, D. A. (2003). Foundations of place: A multidisciplinary framework for place-conscious education. *American Educational Research Journal, 40*(3), 619–654.

Guetzkow, H. (1965). Communications and organizations. In J. G. March (Ed.), *Handbook of organizations* (pp. 534–573). Chicago, IL: Rand McNally & Company.

Gulick, L. (2005). Notes on the theory of organization. In J. M. Shafritz, J. S. Ott, & Y. S. Jang (Eds.), *Classics of Organizational Theory* (6th ed.) (pp. 79–87). Belmont, CA: Thomson Wadsworth. (Original work published 1937)

Hagberg, J. (1994). *Real power.* Salem, WI: Sheffield.

Hedlund, G. (1986). The hypermodern MNC—A heterarchy? *Human Resource Management, 25*(1), 9–35.

Helgesen, S. (1990). *The female advantage: Women's ways of leadership.* New York: Doubleday Currency.

Helgesen, S. (1995). *The web of inclusion: A new architecture for building great organizations.* New York: Doubleday.

Helgesen, S. (2006). Challenges for leaders in the years ahead. In F. Hesselbein & M. Goldsmith (Eds.), *The leader of the future: Vol. 2. Visions, strategies, and practices for the new era* (pp. 183–190). San Francisco, CA: Jossey-Bass.

Institute of Educational Sciences. (2010). *Digest of educational statistics.* Retrieved from http://nces.ed.gov. ezproxy.uvm.edu/programs/digest/d10/tables/dt10_259.asp

Institute of International Education. (2011). *Open doors: Fast facts.* New York: Author.

Jablonski, M. A. (2001). *The implications of student spirituality for student affairs practice* (New Directions for Student Services, 95). San Francisco, CA: Jossey-Bass.

Johnson, A. B. (2008). Privilege as paradox. In P. Rothenberg (Ed.), *White privilege: Essential readings on the other side of racism* (pp. 117–121). New York: Worth.

Kanter, R. M. (1977). *Men and women of the corporation.* New York: Basic Books.

Kanter, R. M. (2006). How cosmopolitan leaders inspire confidence: A profile of the future. In F. Hesselbein & M. Goldsmith (Eds.), *The leader of the future: Vol. 2. Visions, strategies, and practices for the new era* (pp. 61–70). San Francisco, CA: Jossey-Bass.

Kark, R. (2004). The transformational leader: Who is (s)he? A feminist perspective. *Journal of Organizational Change Management, 17*(2), 160–176.

Kerr, C. (2001). *The uses of the university.* Cambridge, MA: Harvard University Press.

Keller, G. (1983). *Academic strategy: The management revolution in American higher education.* Baltimore, MD: Johns Hopkins University Press.

Kessler, R. (2000). *The soul of education: Helping students find connection, compassion, and character at school.* Alexandria, VA: Association for Supervision and Curriculum Development.

Kezar, A. (2006). Rethinking public higher education governing boards performance: Results of a national study of governing boards in the United States. *The Journal of Higher Education, 77*(6), 968–1008

Kezar, A., Carducci, R., & Contreras-McGavin, M. (2006). *Rethinking the "L" word in higher education: The revolution in research on leadership* (ASHE Higher Education Research Report, 31[6]). Hoboken, NJ: Wiley.

Kezar, A., Lester, J., & Anderson, G. (Fall 2006). Challenging stereotypes that interfere with effective governance. *Thought and Action, 22*(2), 121–134.

Kiley, K. (2011, October 10). Starting to worry. *Inside Higher Education.*

Kimberly, J. R. (1980). Initiation, innovation, and institutionalization in the creation process. In J. R. Kimberly, R. H. Miles, & Associates (Eds.), *The organizational life cycle: Issues in the creation, transformation, and decline of organizations* (pp. 18–43). San Francisco, CA: Jossey-Bass.

Kincheloe, J. L. (2006, Fall/Winter). A critical complex epistemology of practice. *Taboo, 10*(2), 85–98.

Kleiner, A. (2003). Karen Stephenson's quantum theory of trust. *Strategy + Business, 29,* 1–14.

Kolodny, A. (2008, September–October,). Tenure, academic freedom, and the career I once loved: We're being underfunded out of existence. *Academe, 94*(5). Retrieved from http://www.aaup.org/AAUP/pubsres/academe/2008/SO/

Komives, S. R., Lucas, N., & McMahon, T. R. (2007). *Exploring leadership: For college students who want to make a difference* (2nd ed.). San Francisco, CA: Jossey-Bass.

Kuh, G. D. (2008). *High impact educational practices: What they are, who has access to them, and why they matter.* Washington, DC: Association of American Colleges and Universities.

Kuh, G. D., Kinzie, J., Schuh, J. H., Whitt, E. J., & Associates. (2005). *Student success in college: Creating conditions that matter.* San Francisco, CA: Jossey-Bass.

Kuh, G. D., Schuh, J., Whitt, E., & Associates. (1991). *Involving colleges: Successful approaches to fostering student learning and development outside the classroom.* San Francisco, CA: Jossey-Bass.

Kuh, G. D., & Whitt, E. J. (1988). *The invisible tapestry: Culture in American colleges and universities* (ASHE-ERIC Higher Education, No. 1). Washington, DC: ERIC Clearinghouse on Higher Education.

Kuhn, T. S. (1962). *The structure of scientific revolutions.* (2nd ed.). Chicago, IL: University of Chicago Press.

Ladson-Billings, G. J. (1998). Just what is critical race theory and what's it doing in a nice field like education? *International Journal of Qualitative Studies in Education, 11*(1), 7–24.

Lamont, M., & Lareau, A. (1988). Cultural capital: Allusions, gaps and glissandos in recent theoretical developments. *Sociological Theory, 6*(2), 153–168.

Leiser, B. M. (1994). Threats to academic freedom and tenure. *Pace Law Review, 15*(1), 15–53.

Levine, A. (2000a, March 13). The soul of a new university. *New York Times.* Retrieved from http://www.nytimes.com/2000/03/13/opinion/the-soul-of-a-new-university.html?pagewanted=all&src=pm

Levine, A. (2000b, October 27). The future of colleges: 9 inevitable changes. *The Chronicle of Higher Education,* B10–B11.

Levine, A. (2001). Higher education as a mature industry. In P. G. Altbach, P. J. Gumport, & D. B. Johnstone (Eds.), *In defense of American higher education* (pp. 38–58). Baltimore, MD: Johns Hopkins University Press.

Lincoln, Y. S. (Ed.). (1985). *Organizational theory and inquiry: The paradigm revolution.* Thousand Oaks, CA: Sage.

Lipman-Blumen, J. (1992). Connective leadership: Female leadership styles in the 21st century workplace. *Sociological Perspectives, 35*(1), 183–203.

Lipman-Blumen, J. (1998). Connective leadership: What business needs to learn from academe. *Change, 30*(1), 49–53.

Lipman-Blumen, J. (2002). The age of connective leadership. In F. Hesselbein & R. Johnson (Eds.), *On leading change: A leader to leader guide* (pp. 89–101). San Francisco, CA: Jossey-Bass.

Mahoney, A. I. (2002, October). Recalibrating for the customer. *Association Management Magazine.* Retrieved from www.asaecenter.org/PublicationsResources

Manning, K. (1997, April). *Student affairs in the mature industry of higher education.* Speech given at the National Association of Student Personnel Administrators Region V, Pullman, WA, Washington State University.

Manning, K. (2000). *Rituals, ceremonies, and cultural meaning in higher education.* Westport, CT: Bergin & Garvey.

Manning, K. (2001). Infusing soul into student affairs. In M. A. Jablonski (Ed.), *The implications of student spirituality for student affairs practice* (New Directions for Student Services, No. 95, pp. 27–35). San Francisco, CA: Jossey-Bass.

Manning, K., Kinzie, J., & Schuh, J. (2006). *One size does not fit all: Traditional and innovative models of student affairs practice.* New York: Routledge.

March, J. G. (1981). Footnotes to organizational change. *Administrative Science Quarterly, 26*(4), 563–577.

Marcus, G. E., & Fischer, M. M. (1986). *Anthropology as cultural critique: An experimental moment in the human sciences.* Chicago, IL: University of Chicago Press.

Martin, R., Manning, K., & Ramaley, J. (2001). The self-study as a chariot for strategic change. In J. Ratcliffe, E. S. Lubinescu, & M. A. Gaffney (Eds.), *How accreditation influences assessment* (New Directions in Higher Education, No. 113, pp. 95–115). San Francisco, CA: Jossey-Bass.

Mather, P. C. (2010). Positive psychology and student affairs practice: A framework of possibility. *Journal of Student Affairs Research and Practice, 47*(2), 157–173.

Matsuda, M. J., Lawrence, C. R., Delgado, R., & Crenshaw, K. W. (1993). *Words that wound: Critical race theory, assaultive speech, and the First Amendment.* Boulder, CO: Westview Press.

McGregor, D. (1976). The human side of enterprise. In W. R. Nord (Ed.), *Concepts and controversy in organizational behavior* (2nd ed., pp. 56–64). Santa Monica, CA: Goodyear. (Original work published 1957)

Merton, R. K. (2005). Bureaucratic structure and personality. In O. J. S. Shafritz, M. Jay, & Y. S. Jang (Eds.), *Classics of organizational theory* (pp. 103–111). Belmont, CA: Thomson Wadsworth. (Original work published 1957)

Meyer, J. W., Ramirez, F. O., Frank, D. J., & Schofer, E. (2007). Higher education as an institution. In P. Gumport (Ed.), *Sociology of higher education: Contributions and their contexts* (pp. 187–221). Baltimore, MD: Johns Hopkins University Press.

Meyerson, D. E., & Kobl, D. M. (2000). Moving out of the "armchair": Developing a framework to bridge the gap between feminist theory and practice. *Organization, 7*(4), 553–570.

Michigan State University. (2010). *Faculty handbook.* Retrieved from http://www.hr.msu.edu/documents/facacadhandbooks/facultyhandbook/incompetence.htm

Miser, K. M. (1988). *Student affairs and campus dissent: Reflection of the past and challenge for the future.* Washington, DC: National Association of Student Personnel Administrators.

Morgan, G. (2006). *Images of organization* (3rd ed.). Thousand Oaks, CA: Sage.

Museus, S. D. (2007). Using qualitative methods to assess diverse institutional cultures. In S. R. Harper & S. D. Museus (Eds.), *Using qualitative methods in institutional assessment* (New Directions for Institutional Research, No. 136, pp. 29–40). Hoboken, NJ: Wiley.

Newman, F., Couturier, L., & Scurry, J. (2004). *The future of higher education: Rhetoric, reality, and the risks of the market.* San Francisco, CA: Jossey-Bass.

Nikias, C. L. M., & Tierney, W. G. (October 30, 2011). Commentary: Now more than ever, a need for bold ambition. *The Chronicle of Higher Education.* Retrieved from www.chronicle.com

The Observatory on Borderless Higher Education. (2011). Borderless 2011. Retrieved from www.obhe.org

Ogilvy, J. (1977). *Many dimensional man: Decentralizing self, society, and the sacred.* London: Oxford University Press.

Olsen, J. P. (2001). Garbage cans, new institutionalism, and the study of politics. *American Political Science Review, 95*(1), 191–198.

Orton, J. D., & Weick, K. E. (1990). Loosely coupled systems: A reconceptualization. *The Academy of Management Review, 15*(2), 203–223.

Pappas, E. (2012). A new systems approach to sustainability: University responsibility for teaching sustainability in contexts. *Journal of Sustainability Education, 3*, n.p.

Parker, M. (2000). *Organizational culture and identity.* Thousand Oaks, CA: Sage.

Pasque, P. A. (2007). Seeing more of the educational inequalities around us: Visions strengthening relationships between higher education and society. In E. P. St. John (Ed.), *Confronting educational inequality: Reframing, building understanding, and making change* (Vol. 22, pp. 37–84). New York: AMS Press.

Patton, L. D., McEwen, M., Rendon, L., & Howard-Hamilton, M. (2007). Critical race perspectives on theory in student affairs. In S. R. Harper & L. D. Patton (Eds.), *Responding to the realities of race on campus* (New Directions for Student Services, No. 120, pp. 39–54). San Francisco, CA: Jossey-Bass.

Peppers, C., & Briskin, A. (2000). *Bringing your soul to work: An everyday practice.* San Francisco, CA: Berrett-Koehler.

Pfeffer, J. (2005). Understanding the role of power in decision making. In O. J. S. Shafritz, M. Jay, & Y. S. Jang (Eds.), *Classics of organizational theory* (pp. 289–303). Belmont, CA: Thomson Wadsworth. (Original work published 1991)

Pryor, J. H., Hurtado, S., DeAngelo, L., Palucki Blake, L., & Tran, S. (2010). *The American freshman: National norms fall 2010.* Los Angeles, CA: Higher Education Research Institute, UCLA.

Rawlings, D. (2000). Collaborative leadership teams: Oxymoron or new paradigm? *Consulting Psychology Journal: Practice and Research, 52*(1), 36–48.

Rhoades, G., & Slaughter, S. (2004). Academic capitalism in the new economy: Challenges and choices. *American Academic, 1*(1), 37–60.

Robinson, J. L., & Lipman-Blumen, J. (2003). Leadership behavior of male and female managers, 1984–2002. *Journal of Education for Business, 79*(1), 28–33.

Roethlisberger, F. J. (2005). The Hawthorne experiments. In J. M. Shafritz, J. S. Ott, & Y. S. Jang (Eds.), *Classics of organizational theory* (pp. 158–166). Belmont, CA, Thomson Wadsworth. (Original published in 1941)

Rogers, J. (2003). Preparing spiritual leaders. *About Campus, 8*(5), 19–26.

Rogers, J., & Dantley, M. (2001). Invoking the spiritual in campus life and leadership. *Journal of College Student Development, 42*(6), 589–603.

Rosener, J. B. (1997). *America's competitive secret: Women managers.* New York: Oxford University Press.

Rosser, V. J. (2003). Historical overview of faculty governance in higher education. In M. Miller & J. Caplow (Eds.), *Policy and university faculty governance* (pp. 3–18). Charlotte, NC: Information Age.

Rost, J. (1993). *Leadership for the twenty-first century.* Westport, CT: Praeger.

Rudolph, F. (1990). *The American college and university: A history.* Athens, GA: The University of Georgia Press.

Saltzman, G. M. (2008). Dismissals, layoffs, and tenure denials in colleges and universities. *The NEA 2008 Almanac of Higher Education* (pp. 51–65). Retrieved from http://www.nea.org/home/32972.htm

Schein, E. H. (2010). *Organizational culture and leadership.* (4th ed.). San Francisco, CA: Jossey-Bass.

Selznick, P. (1996). Institutionalism "old" and "new." *Administrative Science Quarterly, 41*(2), 270–277.

Selznick, P. (2005). Foundations of the theory of organization. In J. M. Shafritz, J. S. Ott, & Y-S. Jang (Eds.), *Classics of organizational theory* (6th ed., pp. 125–134). Belmont, CA: Thomson Wadsworth. (Original work published 1948)

Senge, P., Smith, B., Kruschwitz, N., Laur, J., & Schley, S. (2008). *The necessary revolution: How individuals and organizations are working together to create a sustainable world.* New York: Doubleday.

Simon, H. A. (1955). A behavioral model of rational choice. *The Quarterly Journal of Economics, 69*(1), 99–118

Simon, H. A. (1956). Rational choice and the structure of the environment. *Psychological Review, 63*(2), 129–138.

Simon, H. A. (1957). *Models of man: Social and rational.* Oxford, England: Wiley.

Simon, H. A. (1979). Rational decision making in business organizations. *American Economic Review, 69*(4), 493–513.

Solórzano, D., Ceja, M., & Yosso, T. (2000). Critical race theory, racial microaggressions, and campus racial climate: The experiences of African American college students. *Journal of Negro Education, 69*(1), 60–73.

Stephenson, K. (2001). What knowledge tears apart, networks make whole. *Internal Communication Focus, 36*, 1–6.

Stephenson, K. (2004, Winter). Space: A dialectic frontier. *Reveal,* 20–21.

Stephenson, K. (2005). Trafficking in trust: The art and science of human knowledge networks. In L. Coughlin, E. Wingard, & K. Hollihan (Eds.). *Enlightened power: How women are transforming the practice of leadership* (pp. 242–265). San Francisco, CA: Jossey-Bass.

Stephenson, K. (2010). Neither hierarchy nor network: An argument for heterarchy. *Perspectives.* Retrieved from http://www.rossdawsonblog.com/HRPS_Heterarchy.pdf

Sterling, S. (2010). Ecological intelligence. In S. Arran (Ed.), *The handbooks of sustainability literacy* (pp. 77–83). Devon, England: Green Books.

Strange, C. C. (2001). Spiritual dimensions of graduate preparation in student affairs. In M. A. Jablonski (Ed.), *Implications of student spirituality for student affairs* (New Directions for Student Services, No. 95, pp. 57–67). San Francisco, CA: Jossey-Bass.

Taylor, F. W. (1947). *Scientific management.* New York: Harper and Row.

Thomas, K. W. (1976). Conflict and conflict management. In M. D. Dunnette (Ed.), *Handbook of industrial and organizational psychology* (pp. 889–935). Chicago, IL: Rand McNally.

Thomas, K. W. (1977). Toward multidimensional values in teaching: The example of conflict behavior. *Academy of Management Review, 2,* 484–490.

Thornton, P. H., & Ocasio, W. (2008). Institutional logics. In R. Greenwood, C. Oliver, & K. Sahlin-Andersson (Eds.), *The Sage handbook of organizational institutionalism* (pp. 99–129). Thousand Oaks, CA: Sage.

Tierney, W. (1998). Tenure is dead. Long live tenure. In W. Tierney (Ed.), *The responsive university: Restructuring for high performance* (pp. 38–61). Baltimore, MD: Johns Hopkins University Press.

Tierney, W. (2004). *Competing conceptions of academic governance: Negotiating the perfect storm.* Baltimore, MD: Johns Hopkins University Press.

Tierney, W. (2006). *Trust and the public good: Examining the cultural conditions of academic work.* New York: Peter Lang.

Tirri, K., & Nokelainen, P., (2008). Identification of multiple intelligences with the Multiple Intelligence Profiling Questionnaire III. *Psychology Science Quarterly, 50*(2), 206–221.

Tirri, K., Nokelainen, P., & Ubani, M. (2006). Conceptual definition and empirical validation of the spiritual sensitivity scale. *Journal of Empirical Theology, 19*(1), 37–62.

Toma, J. D. (2010). *Building organizational capacity: Strategic management in higher education.* Baltimore, MD: Johns Hopkins University Press.

Toma, J. D. (2012). Institutional strategy, positioning for prestige. In M. N. Bastedo (Ed.), *The organization of higher education: Managing colleges for a new era* (pp. 118–159). Baltimore, MD: Johns Hopkins University Press.

Turner, V. W., & Bruner, E. M. (Eds.). (1986). *The anthropology of experience.* Chicago, IL: University of Illinois Press.

U.S. Department of Education. (2006). *A test of leadership: Charting the future of U.S. Higher education.* Washington, DC: The Secretary of Education's Commission on the Future of Higher Education.

Walsh, M. (1992). *Authentic anarchy and the transformation of the residence hall.* Higher Education and Student Affairs, University of Vermont, Burlington, VT. Unpublished manuscript.

Weber, M. (1947). *The theory of social and economic organization* (Trans. A. M. Henderson & T. Parsons). London: W. Hodge.

Weber, M. (2005). Bureaucracy. In J. M. Shafritz, J. S. Ott, & Y. S. Jang (Eds.), *Classics of organizational theory* (6th ed., pp. 73–78). Belmont, CA: Thomson Wadsworth. (Originally published in 1946)

Weick, K. E. (1976). Educational organizations as loosely coupled systems. *Administrative Science Quarterly, 21*(1), 1–19.

Weick, K. E. (1989). Loose coupling: Beyond the metaphor. *Current Contents, 20*(12), 14.

Wheatley, M. J. (2007). *Finding our way: Leadership for an uncertain time.* San Francisco, CA: Berrett-Koehler.

Wheatley, M. J. (2010). *Leadership in the new science: Discovering order in a chaotic world* (3rd ed.). San Francisco, CA: Berrett-Koehler.

Whitt, E. J. (1993a). "Hit the Ground Running": Experiences of new faculty in a school of education. In C. Conrad, A. Neumann, J. G. Haworth, & P. Scott (Eds.), *Qualitative research in higher education: Experiencing alternative perspectives and approaches* (pp. 599–611). Needham Heights, MA: Ginn Press.

Whitt, E. J. (1993b). "Making the familiar strange": Discovering culture. In G. D. Kuh (Ed.), *Cultural perspectives in student affairs work* (pp. 81–94). Lanham, MD: American College Personnel Association.

Zohar, D. (1997). *ReWiring the corporate brain: Using the new science to rethink how we structure and lead organizations.* San Francisco, CA: Berrett-Koehler.

Zohar, D. (2010). Exploring spiritual capital: An interview with Danah Zohar. *Spirituality in Higher Education Newsletter, 5*(5), 1–8.

Zohar, D., & Marshall, I. (2000). *SQ: Connecting with your spiritual intelligence.* New York: Bloomsbury.

INDEX